THE EXECUTIVE JUNGLE

THE EXECUTIVE JUNGLE

IRWIN L. RODMAN

Nash Publishing · Los Angeles

Library of Congress Catalog Card Number: 79-143015
Standard Book Number: 8402-1181-3

Published simultaneously in the United States and Canada
by Nash Publishing Corporation, 9255 Sunset Boulevard,
Los Angeles, California 90069.

Printed in the United States of America.

Second Printing

To my wife Dorothy and her side of the apple,
To Jennifer, Catherine and Douglas,
our children and claim to immortality,
And to Harold and what he stands for

Acknowledgment

No man is an island. For whatever he contributes during his lifetime he must, of necessity, pay homage to at least a select few. So it is in the writing of this book that I must, not only out of necessity but out of deep respect and gratitude, recognize the very real and meaningful contribution of Ted Thackrey, Jr. While the experiences and philosophy of this book are mine, to be evaluated for their intrinsic worth as the reader might best judge for himself, the freshness, much of the style and what I believe to be a very capable interpretation belong to Ted. To Ted Thackrey, Jr., then, my very sincere thanks for his contribution to our association.

Preface

My name is Irwin Rodman.

For more than two decades, I have been in practice as an industrial psychologist. My specialty is executive evaluation —and I wrote the book you now hold in your hand as a method of sharing some of the discoveries I have made.

In it, I have drawn upon my personal evaluations of more than 5,000 executives.

Corporation politics, the basic differences between individuals, and the tremendous pressures of modern business can, as you might imagine, produce some pretty unusual personalities in the executive suite. But the purpose of this book is neither to titillate nor to amuse. And I had no thought of writing a textbook.

My purpose, hopefully, was to present certain information —useful, I think, to any person presently performing an executive function or considering such a career—regarding various types of individuals and a number of situational problems which I have observed, with recommendations for various courses of action in each case.

I hope you'll find the book enjoyable. I hope you'll find it useful. And I hope it will add to your own store of the only factor which keeps the Executive Jungle from becoming a true jungle of vines and underbrush and predators:

I hope it will add to your store of knowledge.

IRWIN RODMAN

Contents

Part
1
Safari

1
Fitting Out

No sane man goes unarmed into a jungle.

Dangers abound; jungle denizens may or may not be friendly—and there is always the chance of becoming lost.

The logical approach, therefore, is to carry armament appropriate to the area—and to hire a knowledgeable guide.

Such precautions are a necessary prelude to safari.

They spell survival and success, or *increasing one's chances* for survival and success.

And the Executive Jungle is no exception to the rule....

True, the dangers here are of a somewhat different nature; inimical denizens are somewhat more difficult to identify, and the jungle trails are much differently marked.

But the penalties for miscalculation and/or poor equipage are no different. Precautionary armament is still a necessity.

It is still a matter of survival and success.

So we begin with the armament. That is the first order of business because we must be careful to take neither too much nor too little. You do not defend yourself against elephants with peashooters; you do not combat mosquitoes with artillery. Fortunately, the proper armament for the Executive Jungle is of a type which adds little to the load.

In fact, it can be reduced to a single word:

Knowledge.

Grouped under that heading, however, are several sub-headings or sub-species of armament.

1. First and foremost, there is knowledge of *self.*

To insure survival and success, each individual must possess sufficient understanding of his own basic abilities, aptitudes, interests and goals to be able to select first the path he is to follow, the pace at which he intends to travel and the point at which he will stop.

He must be able to assay the cost, too; nothing is free. A hunting trip to the Adirondacks is one thing. A hunting trip to Victoria Falls or the headwaters of the Amazon quite another. And a man who really would *like* an African safari may settle for a trip to Yosemite—quite satisfactorily—if he knows the African adventure would be at a price he is not prepared to pay.

Similarly, a man who would like a trip to the headwaters of the Executive Suite (or an expedition into stock-option highlands where the winds blow cold and fellow climbers are few) may forgo the trek if he decides the cost in terms of family life, personal effort, risk-acceptance* or personal security is too great.

---

*Deceptive, that. A real gambler is one who risks that which has value in his own eyes. In that sense, almost every man who takes a job, drives a car or has a family is a far greater gambler than the late Nick The Greek. Nick never valued money for itself; he never risked anything of value . . . at the tables, or anywhere else.

The only way he can decide these things, however, is to know himself.

2. The next step down on the list of sub-types of armament is knowledge of the field in which one will seek to operate.

A man who knows himself possesses good primary armament, but it will be of no use to him without a knowledge of the area of technical expertise in which he is expected to function. He must be able to do the job he says he can do.

And this, too, will have only a limited utility unless he also knows the size and kind of company in which he intends to work—and the differences between the various firms of that size. A man who can function quite happily in firm A may be unable to do so in firm B, despite the fact that both deal in the same kind of product and are of comparable size.

3. And finally, there is knowledge of the Executive Jungle denizens with whom one will have to interact.

Nobody does his work in a vacuum; not even the occasional Lone Wolf in the business world. Interaction between human beings is as necessary as breathing in any business situation, and every single human being is unique.

In Part II of this book, we'll have a close look at some of the denizens of the Executive Jungle. For purposes of examination, we'll even group them into species and breeds; assign general family attributes, and discuss possible ways of dealing with them.*

But these are generalizations.

And generalizations are for the sake of convenience. Even when we discuss a specific case, the conclusions we draw will be general. And generalizations are tricky; no *other* individual fits precisely into the pattern of any specific person, and no

---

*If, indeed, they can *be* dealt with. Some situations, like some people, are the kind you can fight only with your hat. Grab it, and run!

individual fits precisely into any generalized pattern. Indeed, the examples selected for examination were selected *because* they are *extreme* (to make my point)—not because they are representative of any general norm.

So it's still a matter of individuals.

And it's still a matter of knowledge.

And it's still a matter of survival and success.

And now, if you're ready . . . perhaps we'd better join the hunting party. The safari into the Executive Jungle is about to begin. . . .

2
The
Hunting
Party

Executive Jungle safaris are conducted by two kinds of hunting parties:

There are companies hunting executives.

And there are executives hunting jobs.

If either is to succeed—if the company is to find the *right* executive, if the executive is to find the *right* position—it seems obvious that the hunter must be able to recognize the quarry.

Unhappily, the Jungle is full of parties who seem unaware of this basic fact.

Can you imagine going to Africa after an "elephant" without, at the very least, having obtained a picture of the animal and perhaps a few statistics as well (size, weight, color, feeding habits, etc.)? Neither can I.

And the executive who doesn't know quite where he wants

to go, or what he can do best, is an all too common hunter in the Executive Jungle. And the company that is seeking an executive whose exact abilities and background it cannot exactly describe can be found thrashing around in the tall grass, too.

Both have gone hunting unarmed.

Both lack the basic weapon of knowledge.

Sometimes, of course, the result is still a happy one. Blind men have been known to shoot lions, and blind hunters have been known to return from the Executive Jungle wilds with the exact quarry they sought—even when they didn't know the shape of the beast.

But these cases are rare. They involve the kind of pure luck which can't be predicted or expected. And there is little chance that a subsequent foray will be as successful.

How does a company know its quarry?

Everyone has a different approach, needless to say. But the one I would call most workable is for the man directly responsible for recruiting to sit down together with the man responsible for selection and list all the specfic jobs the executive will have to perform—all the hats he must wear in order to function properly—and all the people with whom he will have to interface.

Now, with this information in hand, it should be possible with very little effort to list the requirements, the *specifications*, if you will, for the executive positions to be filled.

Is there government work to be handled? Well, then, it's likely the man will need a security clearance; no sense even considering a person who for one reason or another would be unable to qualify.

Is there a specific bit of technical expertise involved? If so, the best-qualified manager in the world would be no use unless he had the proper technical background.

Will he have to handle a particularly difficult employee

relations problem? Then you'd better have a man with some knowledge, training, experience and/or natural talent for this kind of work.

Must this executive deal with the public? Then a man with the personality, interest and background in such an area must be specified.

On the other hand, it is ruinous to ask too much.

A position requiring a Secret clearance does not equate with one requiring a Q clearance; a position requiring a man who *knows* engineering or *knows* the technical aspects of a given situation does not *necessarily* imply the need for a man with a formal, academic *degree* in that field.

Specifications, therefore, should be kept as flexible as possible—should be the *minimum*, not the *maximum* for the position to be filled. Otherwise, you run the risk of specifying an executive who simply does not exist, or who at the very least is such a *rara avis* that the hunt for him may take more time than you've got.

Suppose, then, that a properly flexible set of specifications has been drawn up, with trade-offs (permissible substitutions of, say, experience for formal training, of latent ability for demonstrated capacity) outlined, and the whole thing turned over to the company's personnel recruiter (or whoever holds the comparable position).

Chances are he'll come up with several possible candidates.

But there's just *one* job.

How do you pick the man who best fits the position?

The first thing, of course, is to do a little checking on the man and the statements he has made in applying for the job.*
He says he was assistant vice-president of company A for six years and left to accept a better position with company B? Well . . . maybe you'd better touch base with company A and

---

*Some people stretch the truth—and conveniently omit it. Sad.

company B if you have that liberty; maybe he hasn't told the *whole* story. Maybe, in fact, all his past history and references need a check. They *do*, in fact. And if you do the work properly, you'll check it all out—right back, if the circumstances suggest it, to his academic qualifications and the kind of grade he made in which subjects when he was in school, and the kind of military record he made (if any).

Even after all this back-checking, however, a great deal remains to be done. A job candidate who looks good on paper may, in fact, be just what the doctor ordered . . . for some other employer, but not for you.

Why?

There can be a lot of reasons. But two of the most common are personal interface problems and what I might call "lack of equity." Let's talk about the former first.

Interface problems don't have to do, primarily, with the question of whether you do or do not like a man. You can have an extremely negative reaction to his personality and still, objectively, know he's the right man for your job opening because he supplies a need.

And not just his expertise or past experience, either; the man himself, his individual weaknesses and/or strengths—the very things which cause you to dislike him, perhaps—may be just what you need.

Are you (or the man with whom he'll work, anyway) the type who hates to say "no" or the type who has trouble pushing his subordinates toward some selected goal?* Then, chances are, you won't really have much personal use for the kind of man who *can* do these things. And the chances are, that's exactly the kind of man you need in your organization.

---

*I'm talking about the Man in the White Hat (Chapter 12). Things like that can be a real problem. You'll see.

Are you, conversely, a hard-nosed and hard-driving type who is in a little trouble through a basic lack of sensitivity to your subordinates' difficulties? Then you'll probably have little personal use for the kind of executive whose personality always seems to act as a balm on the feelings of others, who becomes in short order a kind of father-confessor to one and all. And, once again, chances are this is precisely the kind of man you need.

The trick is to have a close look at your own problem, your own organization—yes, and at yourself as well—and come to some realistic conclusions about what you really need in the way of an executive . . . as opposed to what or who would be easiest to find and most personally compatible with you.

Stress that word: *realistic*.

It goes back to the original dictum about the basic armament of the executive. His job is to know himself and his organization. That knowledge can only be based on reality, on an objective appraisal of himself and his company. Without realism and objectivity—he's guessing, and the rather unreliable element of luck again enters the picture.

Now about the matter of "equity."

Did you ever see a successful marriage where either the man or his wife did all the work, while the other just seemed to be along for the ride? Inequitable, wasn't it? Also—in the long run—it will probably cease to be a successful marriage (if it ever *was* one) because sooner or later the one active partner will get tired of carrying the whole load.

Well, the placement of an executive in a specific position within a company is something very close to marriage. It has, I might say, most of the advantages (except one) and most of the disadvantages—because the two have pretty well united their fortunes for the time being.

If the executive can't or won't pull his share of the load, the company suffers and is likely to become dissatisfied with the arrangement before long.

And the reverse also applies: a company which does not supply the needs of the newly hired (or long-employed) executive is in short order going to have a dissatisfied individual on its hands. And dissatisfied people are a very bad bargain. Strange how few employers understand that.

Somewhere along the line they have gotten hold of the idea that every person in their employ should, somehow, be grateful just to be there—regardless of the circumstances. They appear to think that the weekly paycheck is the whole show.

And it's not.

Because, while salary is a highly valid and necessary goal of any job-seeker (if nothing else, it's a fairly accurate score-keeping method; a way for a man to know how well or ill he's progressing) it is *never*, at least in my experience, the only factor that interests him.

Don't forget . . . the hunting party on which the company has embarked in seeking an executive is not the only one in the forest.

The individual job-seeking executive is leading a hunting party himself. And a dollar sign is only one of the attributes of the game he seeks.

How does the job-seeker know its quarry?

Again, we have the question of self-knowledge. All too many men are all too eager to settle for the quickest answers they can spout when asked a question like this.

Standard answers are "a company where I can grow and realize my potential; some place where I feel I am doing a good job; some place where I feel there is real appreciation and chance for advancement. . . ."

Good words. Significant words. But *not* if they come

rushing off the very top of the mind. Because they are nonspecific; they communicate a seeking for nirvana rather than any given job or any individual company.

They can only have real meaning when the job-seeker has real self-knowledge.

He needs, for instance, to analyze—objectively and realistically—his own abilities (basic intelligence, special aptitudes, special interests, personality traits and quirks) and legitimate goals and ambitions.

He needs to know whether he would be happier in the milieu of a small company, a medium-sized company, or a big company; whether he is best fitted—and happiest—in a line or staff (direct-command or advisory) position; whether he is capable of the loneliness of the presidency or happier in a directorship or sub-manager spot.

In a way, of course, his quest is really no different from that of the company that is looking for a man to fill a specific position. Both need a set of *minimal* specifications.

And each must understand that *equity* is an *essential* if any industrial marriage is to survive.

That is: if a company's needs are to be adequately supplied by a candidate's capability, then the company must offer that candidate something that he wants. And vice versa.

Simple?

Well . . . it sounds that way, doesn't it?

But if the problem were all that easy, how would you explain the vast number of executives who mentally (and sometimes vocally) chafe at the jobs in which they find themselves; the company managers who grit their teeth every time they assign a task to one or the other of their subordinates?

These industrial marriages are unsatisfactory; perhaps—even probably—doomed to early divorce.

But it need not be so.

Time was when couples considering divorce were the only ones who approached a marriage counselor seeking professional help. More recently, however, couples considering marriage—no matter how deeply they believe themselves to be in love, no matter how sure of their own chances for happiness—are visiting a marriage counselor *before* the vows are exchanged.

Sometimes this visit turns up deep-seated problems of which neither was aware; problems which appear to foredoom such a union. More often, the visit merely discloses possible areas of conflict with which—knowledge, as always, being the best armament—they are better prepared to deal on a reality basis.

And at the risk of stretching an analogy, in this sense prospective parties to an industrial marriage might well take a page from the bride's book. Indeed, many of the biggest—and smallest—firms in the nation have already begun to do so.

The industrial marriage counselor is not a recruiter, not a reference-checker (though, in a limited number of cases, he may do a bit of this as a favor or in order to complete his own data—and not a mere professional snoop.

His job is specific: to determine the chances of success in the prospective industrial marriage.

He is called an industrial psychologist.

And he is hired as trail guide for *both* hunting parties. . . .

3
The Guide

"Psychologist" is a word with as many different meanings as there are people in the world.

Webster defines it as: "A student of or specialist in the science of the human mind in any of its aspects, operations, powers or functions."

But dictionary definitions seldom have anything to do with the reactions of individual human beings to the word. It can inspire anything from mild interest to scorn to open hostility and/or fear. (Odd, isn't it, the way people react to labels?)

But when the label becomes a compound such as "clinical psychologist" or "experimental psychologist" or "educational psychologist" some of the reaction-producing magic seems to get lost, perhaps because few people can define the precise nature of these fields of specialty.

And when you say "industrial psychologist" the usual reaction is something like a complete blank.

Actually, industrial psychologists come in a lot of different forms. There are, for instance:

—The "human factors" specialists, who concern themselves with hardware and the fact that a human being interrelates with hardware, must use it, in which case the human being's reaction time, learning capability, etc. become important in the design or redesign of that hardware.

—Some deal with market research, public opinion, or opinion polling . . . no need to elaborate, I think.

—Others deal with such items as advertising techniques, packaging, etc. from the standpoint of increasing sales of a consumer item.

—And heaven only knows how many other types and specialties. Far too many, I'm sure, to enumerate here. New applications (and applications of applications) are popping up all the time.

In my own case, I'm what's called a psychological evaluator.

I've been at it for more than 20 years.

And, in a way, the path I took in entering this field illustrates a couple of important points about the field itself. You see, I didn't intend to do anything of the sort. My original notion—while I was growing up—was to become a veterinarian.*

That's what I had in mind when I enrolled in a premedical course, back in 1942. But there was a war on, so I enlisted in the Navy . . . and wound up in the motor machinist's mate school. (No complaint on that score; I picked the school.

---

*There will be a brief pause while we all try to think up some devastatingly funny remark. All done? Good.

Always did want to work with engines, and the Navy was fresh out of animals at the time.) But I never became a motor machinist's mate. Instead, while I was in boot camp, I came down with what turned out to be a whole series of illnesses, physical ones mind you.

And a curious thing happened while I was in the hospital. I saw, and was impressed by, the kind of supportive help some of the hospital pharmacist's mates gave the patients—including me. They were a hell of a bunch. Really. So when I got back to Great Lakes, I asked for and obtained permission to switch over to hospital corps school. I was ultimately trained for independent operation (without supervision of a physician) and spent the war practicing this specialty.

I enjoyed it and, returning to school when the shooting stopped, discovered I was much more open-minded about considering various fields.

Part of the pre-med curriculum was an introductory course in psychology—which all but turned me off for good. I found it dull, in fact, and might have skipped the whole thing but for the title of a certain advanced course which came to my attention. It was called "Psychology of the Normal Personality."

It traced the psychological, physical, neurological development of the human being from birth to death, and the material was fascinating—to me, anyway. I was hooked, for good. But one of the things I recognized about myself from the beginning was that while I could be a supportive person—could assist others in making judgments meaningful to them—I just couldn't be a "therapist." Clinical psychology was out.

Sympathy? Sure. *Rapport*? Fine. So long as it was for the purpose of obtaining information which would help me make recommendations. But work through the problems of those with gross maladjustments to life . . . well, it just took too much time so far as I was concerned. I'm not that patient.

One by one, I checked off the various specialties.

And finally narrowed the field to one which would allow the kind of one-to-one interface with people that I enjoy, without the long-term involvement required for clinical practice.

The field was called psychological evaluation.

Why the personal anecdote?

Because, for one thing, it illustrates a point worth remembering for any person intent on selecting a career: it's always a good idea to have a few alternatives in mind since you never know what circumstances will mitigate against your original choice. (If I'd stuck to the vet medicine idea I might *still* be waiting for an opening; only eleven schools in that field when I started applying, and almost none of them would accept anyone from out of state!)

For another thing, it underlines a principle which is basic to the field of evaluation and career selection. *Interest* in any field is virtually meaningless unless it is solidly backed by *ability* to perform in it. And *ability* alone won't make much difference to a man who really isn't *motivated* in a given field.

That's one of the biggest jobs of the psychological evaluator:

He tries—through psychological testing, through a careful check of job and academic history, and through personal interviewing—to determine (a) the basic interests of the individual, (b) how these interests match up with ability strengths and/or weaknesses, (c) how both of these fit into the subject's job and educational background, and (d) how the personality strengths and/or weaknesses fit into the particular executive milieu for which he is being evaluated.*

One thing for sure: the "perfect" man for any given position, if he exists at all, is pretty unlikely to turn up at the moment he's needed. That's for fairy tales and textbooks, I think. You just don't run into it in actual practice.

In actual practice, you have a set of (hopefully) *minimum* specifications for a particular position, plus (if you've had a chance to become acquainted with the company for whom you're performing the evaluation) a fair idea of the kind of executive group into which a successful candidate must fit. A word about this latter requirement before we go on:

Evaluators are of two types, in-house and independent.

I've functioned in both capacities and—aside from my purely personal preferences—I think there's a lot to be said for both sides.

An in-house evaluator, one who works for a specific firm to the exclusion of all others and who is in fact an employee of that organization, has an absolutely unparalleled opportunity to know the kind of men with whom the job candidate must interface—and, therefore, to estimate with optimum accuracy the chances of such an interface being productive and workable.

On the other hand, an independent evaluator, one who works on an as-needed or on-call basis for a number of firms, may have a somewhat freer hand in his evaluation plus a

---

*He may try to get a close look at the candidate's family situation. Has he got problems with a wife, his kids, or aged parents which might mitigate against travel? Has he a marital situation which may detract from or add to his ability to be effective? The hell of it is, that sort of information's not always too easy to come by. People lie a lot in these areas, too.

chance to meet and become closely acquainted with a number of different companies, situations and candidates.

Free hand? Well, yes . . . not that the in-house man's hand isn't free. But, since the small and middle-sized firm seldom has the need (or financial capacity) for a full-time evaluator, the in-house man usually works for a much larger organization; one of the giants, perhaps. And this means (a) a constant and pressing need for personnel to fill open positions and (b) more than a little pressure to get *someone* for the job.

And pressure can be bad. Because the evaluator, independent or in-house, really *wants* to be able to tell his client or firm they've got a winner. After all, their problem is finding the right person; they want to say yes. And when an evaluator is forced to express considerable doubt, while he may have saved a lot of future headaches for the people who hired him, he has left their basic problem unsolved—and left the candidate's job-seeking problem unsolved as well.

Given all these data-inputs, then, sometimes the evaluator is still in no position to give a specific "yes" or "no" answer either to the company or the client. What he does instead, is express the probability of successful placement of *this* individual in *that* job in terms of percentage.

Actually, there are two figures the evaluator must consider, however. It works this way: say the candidate would have an 85% (very high) chance of functioning well and meeting the specifications of the job that's open; that is, of satisfying management's desires. But remember—there are *two* parties to this industrial marriage. And suppose the company's probability of satisfying this individual's needs and goals is only 40%.

In a case like that, you've got to settle for the lower percentage. The chance of that marriage working out is only

40%. You explain this to *both* parties, and you tell both why, if possible. Maybe steps can be taken to improve the odds. . . .

Of course, evaluation can be awfully useful in other ways than mere* specific-job placement.

Sometimes a firm wants a complete psychological evaluation of its top and middle management executives. This can be helpful in making decisions about who works with whom, in deciding what can be done to improve the efficiency of a specific individual or department, or perhaps it's a matter of management wanting to be sure every party to their little group marriage is getting enough out of the relationship to encourage him to put forth his best effort.

The same kind of over-all evaluation might also be undertaken in cases where a sale or merger of one firm with another is contemplated. An audit of financial, production and equipment facilities is all very well. But the indispensable part of any successful company is its human resources—the people who work there. Without them, it's just real estate and machinery and dollars; it has no life and may even be a liability.

Then, too, there's the executive who comes to the evaluator on an independent basis, seeking knowledge of self.

I need hardly add that cases of this sort are of particular satisfaction to most people in my field. Because the name of the game, brother, is knowledge. And here's a man who can be truly receptive. Sometimes the results can be pretty startling to all concerned.

In a great many cases, of course, the evaluator's findings are merely supportive to what the man thought about himself

---

*"Mere"? Well . . . I guess not, at that. In fact, I've always thought it was pretty important. What's more, I bet you do, too. . . .

in the first place. But nobody—*nobody*—in this world is exempt from a slight bolstering of confidence when he hears his beliefs and opinions confirmed.

In other cases, you get a sparkle-eyed *uh-huh! yes! yes!* reaction of delight when you come up with something the man has had in the back of his mind (but possibly never dared express openly) and bring it out in the open where he can examine it as his own.

And then at times you get the real wide-eye. Here you may have a man who has been bashing his head in against a stone wall for years—never quite understanding why—and you get the chance to tell him: "Well, you should have been in so-and-so all along. But it's never too late . . . you can *still* go in that direction, and it ought to be pretty clear sailing to a man with your ability."

Never let them tell you a psychological evaluator's rewards are entirely monetary . . . !

And while we're on the subject of money (i.e., fees):

In most cases, the fees for my evaluation are paid by the *client firm*—the company that's trying to find the right man to fill its job.

But that *doesn't* mean the company is the sole beneficiary, or that I consider the company my *only* client.

I formed the policy, years ago, of taking each evaluation on a flat-fee basis. That's because I want to be able to put financial considerations entirely aside and address myself to the case at hand. And both sides obtain maximum benefit when time expended is not at issue; a candidate or a company is entitled to check back with me *at any time* on my evaluation. I'll discuss and/or suggest with regard to that specific case just as long as there are additional benefits to be derived.

What I'm getting at is that, while the company pays the fee

and is solely entitled to see the written report I make of the evaluation (it's poor practice to give a copy to the candidate; such a thing *could* be misused) I play back my findings verbally to the candidate, and stand ready to discuss any point he finds either interesting or debatable.

My duty to the candidate is no fraction of a percentage point less important than the duty to the company, and that is an implicit understanding when I accept any case for evaluation.

I'm there to furnish both parties with knowledge* and, to the limit of my ability, to assist both in making best use of it.

I'm an industrial marriage-broker.

I'm trying to arrange a union that will satisfy *both* parties. The hatchet-man role is not one I fit . . . or would accept.

Sad to say, however, there can be—and there is—a great deal of misunderstanding on this point. "Privacy" is a word that gets bandied about a good deal these days. You invade a man's privacy to a certain degree if you ask his name. To a slightly greater degree when you want to know his address, his age, his marital status, etc.

But, while most job candidates will accept *this* kind of privacy invasion,† there is a limited class of applicants who *will not* accept the kind labeled "psychological evaluation." And a larger class who, while they will accept it, do so under duress (i.e., "Well, here I am. Guess I got to hold still for this skull probing, huh?").

Sessions of this type are likely to be less productive than they should be; my major effort in every case—whatever the

---

* That is still the name of the game, baby!

†Invasion of privacy is really not the concern of most people—really. Their real concern is the *abuse* of their privacy—and here I would agree with them.

attitude of the candidate—is to put the man at ease and somehow get across to him that I am not equipped with fangs, and in fact put my pants on one leg at a time just like everyone else. But the individual who feels threatened and/or fearful of psychological evaluation is going to be harder than most to handle accurately. (And of course, no evaluation is possible—except for the obvious negative one—in the case where such an evaluation is flatly refused.)

What a pity.

And what a loss to all concerned!

Hunting party-safaris are difficult and risky enough even when you have the services of a guide.

Without one . . . !

Fortunately, this attitude is not the usual one. And even an ambivalent candidate can usually be made to see the advantages to him as well as to the company of such knowledge as may be forthcoming from evaluation.

But obtaining it is not always easy. . . .

4
The
Hunt

The candidate who comes to a psychological evaluator for the first time, whether actively seeking self-knowledge or merely as a part of an executive selection process, usually brings with him a certain amount of conscious or unconscious anxiety.

This anxiety may or may not have a basis in reality—usually the latter.

And the few cases where the candidate really does have at least *some* cause for trepidation are usually confined to situations where there is a necessity to find a job *right now* as a matter of putting food on the table. (Which is one reason why I prefer to deal with individuals who are not under extreme pressure to find a position; fear or any other acute emotional discomfort gnawing at the back of a man's mind can have a decidedly negative effect.)

At any rate, my first job is to put him at ease.

Which is one of the reasons my office is in my home; most of the evaluation session and its playback are conducted there in as easy and unstructured an atmosphere as I can manage.

We begin with plain talk.

If the candidate has been referred to me by a client company, I explain, I am in general not particularly interested in the impression of him formed in advance by anyone in the firm; I try to enter into the evaluation with a completely unbiased and open mind—as I hope he may be able to do—and, too, I try to stress the fact that evaluation is in no sense a popularity contest.

Our strictly personal reaction to each other, whether we have a potential to become friends if you please, is simply not at issue. We are seeking knowledge. Both of us. Personal liking or disliking is simply not an issue.

I try, too, to acquaint him with the nature of psychological evaluation—that it contributes to the terms of a marriage contract between company and executive, and the chances that contract has for fulfillment.

From the general, then, we go to the specific: this meeting with me and what it will be like.

In most cases, it requires the better part of a day. Sometimes more; occasionally (very *damn* occasionally) a little less. That's why I prefer to take individual evaluations on a flat-fee basis; it's better for all concerned if we're not tied to any specific number of hours.

The evaluation day, I further explain, is divided (for convenience of description; in fact there are no hard and firm dividing lines) into three parts:

1. A battery of standard tests and profiles aimed at developing specific input data regarding the candidate's basic intel-

lectual capacity, his special talents or abilities, areas of interest/disinterest, personality traits, etc.

2. A discussion of his many histories: academic, employment, family, medical, etc. In essence, a *depth* interview.

3. Playback; an opportunity to discuss results of the evaluation in as open and candid (and constructive) a manner as we two are capable of achieving.

With regard to phase three: I tell the candidate I will discuss those results with him, and I do that; I make it clear he is in no way obligated to accept anything I say as being valid—that's entirely his own affair—but I feel it is my responsibility to him as a person and a client to provide the data for his consideration, since it possibly may indicate some positive action on his part.

This third step of testing, by the way, can really be broken down into two distinct parts: the playback itself, which is mostly Rodman talking—telling the candidate what he believes he has discovered about him in the course of testing and depth interviewing, followed by the discussion in which I will elaborate on anything I haven't made clear and/or consider anything the candidate has to say about any specific point of data which the candidate considers either unfair or incorrect.

One little reservation, however: I will tell the candidate what I've uncovered and will even make recommendations to him for further professional aid if I think it's indicated—but I try to be very careful to give my listener the information in as tactful and constructive a way as possible, and I will deliberately *withhold* anything I do not believe he possesses the ego-strength to hear.

(In this regard, let me illustrate with a story:* a woman

---

*One that has haunted me, a bit, ever since I first heard it.

had been under treatment by one doctor for asthmatic allergy, but he was out of town when she had an attack and needed her prescription refilled. Another doctor was called, but he refused to issue such a prescription without examining her. And when he did examine the patient, he refused the prescription saying she didn't need it because her trouble was psychosomatic, not purely physical. Fine! The woman's asthma attacks ceased at once. Never had another. *But* within a very short time she was having *cardiac* attacks—simulated ones, but triggered by the same anxieties and frustrations as the asthma—which were far more debilitating. You don't take a man's crutch until he's ready to walk. . . .)

And a final point I'd like to mention, while we're on the subject of the interview: three subjects are deliberately omitted from the evaluation session. I don't try to find out anything about a candidate's political persuasions, religious beliefs or sexual practices. They're really none of my damn business. And, unless one of these areas has in some way brought the candidate into public disrepute—a fact which would have been discovered in the course of most careful background checks by his prospective employer—they're not of the client-company's business, either.

Now, then—does all this mean I'm in a position at the end of an evaluation session to tell a client "yes, you will" or "no, you won't" be hired? And do I, in fact, tell him so?

Absolutely *not*!

The decision's not mine; remember, I said I express the probability of a successful industrial marriage in percentage terms when reporting to the client-company. This input of mine is not an absolute; not a hiring decision in itself. It is just another independent input, the sole purpose of which is to increase the accuracy of management's *own* determination of the probability for success.

How important a part does it play in this determination?

Well—that can depend on several factors. First, what's my track-record with this particular outfit? Am I new to the company? Have I been doing this kind of thing for them for a long time? Does management have reason to trust my evaluations, and have they proved accurate in terms of the company's needs in the past? All these factors tend to weight the influence my work may have on the final decision.

In short, what I'm trying to say to the candidate all through the evaluation session—and what I honestly mean—is "trust me."

And, in almost every imaginable situation, he can.

Of course, conflicts *do* arise.

It's inevitable, I suppose, since you have *two* clients involved, despite the fact that only one is paying my fee. And in this situation, I have to make my own decision about who gets protected—and how much.

A case in point: One man, sent to me for evaluation as a candidate for upgrading within the executive ranks of a client company, admitted to me that there were certain periods in his job history for which he could not account—and which had, somehow, been missed by the company's personnel department.

He had spent the time in prison. And, while there, he had even taken part in an attempted prison break.

When he was finally released, he had experienced a long period of rejection; more prospective employers than he could number had turned him down because of that prison record. So, finally, he had simply stopped admitting it or mentioning it on job applications.

Well . . . *hell!**

---

*To put it mildly.

This guy gave me real evidence of having made a very good job of rehabilitating himself; more, he had been with the client-firm for better than a year and was performing in an outstanding manner (as witness the very fact that he was now a candidate for upgrading.) He said he would, ultimately, like to confess and discuss his prison record with his employer—but he also felt that the time now was simply not the right one to do so. (On weighing the facts, I certainly had to concur in this.)

The conflict was obvious, as far as I was concerned: who do you protect? And to what degree?

In this particular case, I agreed to hold the information in confidence. It remains so to this day. Yes—he lied. Sure. I suspect that a finger-wagging moralist would make a big thing of that. But moralizing isn't my field. And he did it only after being turned away from a number of jobs when he told the truth. There were no security considerations involved; the company wasn't in defense work, or the FBI would have done a background check that would have turned up the guy's record pronto.

So I shut my mouth.* I kept the matter out of the evaluation report. He got the promotion . . . and performed well in the new position.

Who would have been the loser if I'd included this bit of information in the evaluation summary I sent to the company? Both, I believe.

It's not *always* that way, of course. Sometimes other factors give me good reason to suspect that in protecting the confidence of the candidate I'd really be letting the company in for a really bad time. And sometimes, I feel there's something of less-than-general knowledge that the candidate

---

*And held my breath. Believe me, brother—psychological evaluation is *not* for the faint of heart!

ought to know, too; something I'd be out of line in with-holding from him.

Each case is individual.

But the chance of a candidate actually shocking or offending me with any bit of information is just about nil. In more than 20 years, brother, I've evaluated male homo-sexuals, lesbians, drug addicts, alcoholics, people who've spent time in psycho wards, uncaught thieves, psychopathic liars, people involved in incest . . . you name it. Believe me, I'm shockproof.

And I'm not God. . . .

So what's it all about, in the end? What's the purpose of the testing, the interviewing, the playback?

We said it in the beginning:

Knowledge, and the use that knowledge can play in making meaningful decisions—the ones that maximize your chances for success (and survival.)

In subsequent sections of this book, I'll introduce you to several denizens of the Executive Jungle whom I've found especially interesting. Chances are you'll never find any specific individual—yourself or anyone you know—who fits exactly into the mold of any one of these. The cases were selected because they are extreme, after all, not because they were the average. But there's a little bit of some of them in each of us. And a clear perception of this "little bit" can be a helpful bit of understanding.

We'll also examine a few of the pitfalls and other dangers which lurk in the depths of the Executive Jungle.

And I'll make some suggestions I think are pertinent. . . .

Read it.

Think about it.

Dismiss it if you will—accept it if you can. And above all,

keep in mind its purpose. If it amuses you, fine. If it interests you, well and good. But the purpose is neither; the purpose is to add to your own individual store of knowledge and perception, to add to the effectiveness and satisfaction of your life.

For in the final analysis, the fundamental imperative for any human being—the single command he disobeys at his mortal peril—may be summed up in a single word:

Know!

Part 2
Denizens of the Jungle

The Stranglers[1]

Remember the Boston Strangler?

Here was a guy with a severe kink in the psyche, wandering around the city strangling women who could be lured into answering a doorbell. The whole city—indeed, before he was caught it was almost the whole country—was scared witless. It's a line of conduct which seldom carries with it much real hope of general public approval.

Still, it's a thing that happens in even the most civilized of societies; a far more common occurrence than you might imagine.

Not all Stranglers confine their activities to the city of Boston.

And defenseless women are not their only—or even their most common—victims.

Stranglers abound, in fact, in the Executive Jungle; their

victims are defenseless business establishments ... some of which they themselves have founded and nurtured in infancy and now, like the overprotective and smother-loving parent, are proceeding to destroy.

Stranglers of the Executive Jungle come in various shapes and sizes. Now a few, like their better-known counterpart in Boston, pose a problem of detection and identification.

Some I call "Smart" Stranglers.

Some I call "Dumb" Stranglers.

Some are "Lucky" Stranglers.

Some are honest.

Some are not.

It's easy enough to identify such Jungle denizens after the fact; bankruptcy calendars are clogged with the mangled affairs of their hapless victims. But by then the whole thing's academic. To be useful, identification of the Strangler must come before matters have reached such a pass.

Let us consider a few representative cases; beginning with that of a man I will always remember as

John, the Smart Strangler

I met John in New Mexico, where he was known as an ideal Self-Made Man; an example of what a poor farm boy can do if he puts his mind and back into it. On the surface, he seemed to be just that.

Growing up in a rural environment, John had early discovered in himself a considerable mechanical aptitude. He was in demand for such work as repairing family cars, trucks and the kind of mechanical equipment found around farms. His finances and personal inclination both mitigated against college training, but the high school he attended offered fairly detailed and varied vocational training courses, and apparently he took most of them.

Moreover, he was a hard worker in school. By the time he

graduated, he could run any machine in any of the shops; was proficient in drafting and similar skills and had a true craftsman's approach to such work.

The fact that he was concurrently earning a considerable amount of money by applying the skills he learned to regular jobs outside brought him a sense of pride, of being wanted and needed, of the kind of self respect and independence most men find gratifying.

He assumed a great deal of financial responsibility both for himself and other members of his family (John was the eldest of six children born to parents who had married late in life) while still in his teens. His responsibilities were further increased when he married while still quite young and sired two children.

Employment was scarce when John finally graduated from high school.

But he found a job. It was just the kind of thing his entire life to that point might have fitted and aimed him for, in the factory of a large company that produced precision machine parts.

John ate it up. His supervisors at the plant quickly noted his ability to produce and his eagerness to learn. They gave him ever-increasing opportunities—both in learning and in doing—and within a few years he was placed in a supervisory position, directing a small group of craftsmen who were considered especially able in their trade.

There were a few problems, however,

While John's progress on the job had been well above average, his financial requirements had more than kept pace.*

---

*Parkinson's Law: Living expenses expand to fit income. If you don't believe it, examine your bankbook. If you still don't believe it, examine your honesty. If you *still* don't believe it, examine your sanity. And if you *still* don't believe it . . . how'd you like a job as my financial advisor?

He needed money for his own family and for helping his parents, his brothers and his sisters.

His response to such a need was typical for a man of his type.

John had started machining parts for small companies and individuals in his home garage at night, "moonlighting" with surplus equipment he had bought from his employer. This sideline, by the way, did not conflict with the employer's business; the kind of small orders John was handling simply would not have been profitable to the larger firm.

And that's how things went for a while. John was making enough money with the little garage-machine shop, which he later enlarged to provide space for increased orders. It might have gone on that way forever.

But it didn't. Through no fault of his own (John's employer had lost a big contract and there were the inevitable cutbacks) he had to take a cut in salary.

That left him with a brand-new problem.

John thought it over and finally, with the encouragement of his family and his few customers, took the Big Leap. He quit the factory job and went into business for himself as a machine parts specialist.

For a time, his financial position worsened.

He had foreseen this possibility, however, and took the obvious corrective action of going hammer-and-tongs after new customers. There were two facts in his favor: John's overhead factor was favorable, so he could be quite competitive in the matter of price—and the parts he turned out were first-rate. Business picked up rapidly, and John was smart enough to know it was the quality of his workmanship that was chiefly responsible.

When he had to increase his work-force, he would have

nothing but the most skilled artisans in his shop. And when the time came to do so, he was at considerable pains to improve the quality of the equipment of his little plant and to move it as soon as possible to more suitable quarters.

He plowed most of his ever-increasing profits right back into the business, seeking always to improve both capacity and quality. He was a perfectionist in all things, and the result was clearly evidenced by the high regard in which he and his products were held by his customers.

No raw material, no outside service entered John's plant unless it met every one of the customer's specifications. No sequence of operations was overlooked. No item left the premises before it was thoroughly checked and re-checked. His dedication to quality was almost fanatical.

He was, in fact, almost the ideal supplier from the customer's point of view.

And it was this very perfectionism which finally created a near-fatal crisis for his fledgling firm . . . and exposed him for the Strangler he truly was.

Amoebas, we are told, are capable of splitting themselves in half; this process is called fission and it results in two separate animals which are exact duplicates of the original. It's a good trick, and if John could have accomplished it in his own case he would have had no problem.

However, John was no amoeba.

He was a human being and he could only be in one place at a time, though a good many of his employees would probably have been willing to question that. He seemed to be everywhere.

As chief executive of his firm, John made *all* the customer contacts. He purchased *all* the materials, dealt with *all* the outside suppliers, supervised *all* the machinists in his plant (he frequently made machine setups himself, while the men he had hired because of their expertise in such work stood by, sighing inwardly).

Being a stickler for detail, John also carried with him a little black book (it became a kind of trademark) which he was forever whipping out to note some item to be checked or remembered.

And when the plant was small, this system worked.

But, just as there is a point in nuclear physics called "critical mass" where things really begin to happen, there is a similar point which is reached in the history of any growing business.

John's firm reached that point.

Suddenly, there weren't enough hours in John's day. There were simply too many customers, too many outside suppliers, too many machines, too many problems to deal with personally. He knew he should be able to handle it—after all, far larger companies than his had accomplished the feat—and it must be said for him that he tried.

But when twenty-hour days still weren't long enough, when the little black notebook seemed to fill up overnight, it finally became obvious to him that he had to make one of two decisions.

He could reduce the size of the business.

Or he could delegate some of his authority.

Unhappily, the first alternative was out of the question. The firm was committed, legally and morally, to a size and output at least the equal of its present capacity; if anything, it was going to have to expand even more.

And letting someone else do any of the jobs which might influence the quality of his product amounted in his mind to disaster. He was "certain" it would swiftly reduce the plant's output to mediocrity, destroying his valued reputation for excellence. He simply couldn't trust anyone to do anything with the same care as himself.

Which is why I call John a "Smart" Strangler.

He was smart enough to know he had a problem he couldn't solve; smart enough to see that either alternative was unacceptable to him. Of course, being smart enough to identify a problem is no guarantee of ability to surmount it. John—and his strangling, infant firm—might well have gone down the tube.

But John was a lucky Strangler as well as a smart one.

His firm had reached this critical point at a time when the mini-conglomerate firms had just begun to grow and stretch their tentacles. And one such, which had a number of customers in John's area, was at that moment rather anxious to impress the financial community with its apparent growth in sales and profits.

The mini-conglomerate made an offer.

There was a period of negotiation.

And John sold out—at a very handsome profit.

That's why I call him smart—he had sense enough to get out of the business at a time when he could obtain maximum profit. He had sense enough to know that waiting could be suicide; could leave him with no more cash than the plant equipment would bring on the auction block; could even cost him the reputation he had so painstakingly constructed.

Unhappily, Smart Stranglers are not the sole representative of the Strangler species extant in the Executive Jungle.

Just as numerous are their cousins, a species I think best exemplified by a gentleman whom we will call

Frank, the Dumb Strangler

In a way, it seems almost unfair to use Frank as an example of this breed. Calling him "dumb" goes somehow against the grain for he did, in fact, possess a brilliant mind and an excellent academic background as well as a considerable record of apparent achievement in the field of industry. He had two engineering degrees. In logic and decision making he was swift, almost intuitive—but not intuitive about people. In an argument, he was a true genius when it came to getting his own way. He had an almost insidious ability to flip any dispute up on its end and turn it around in such a way as to make any opponent wind up feeling both dull and inadequate.

In short, he was on the surface an ideal managerial type.

Which is just what his boss considered him at the time I was first introduced to Frank.

His recent record of advancement was impressive. He had been employed by a small firm (a marginal operator, as it later developed) as Chief Engineer.

That was the credential which had prompted a much larger industrial concern to take him on as division manager—a considerable step upward—to head one of the firm's newest acquisitions.

And that's when push really came to shove.

This new division Frank was to control was a dog. It had been sold to Frank's new employer in a kind of classic misrepresentation. The company had, in the years before its sale, limped along from year to year with little or no hope of amounting to anything. Finally, the company's chief executive and major stockholder had decided to get out from under . . . and had been something less than ethical about how he did it.

Somehow, the man had managed to talk another firm into giving him a multimillion-dollar contract, for a quantity and quality of products the head of the supplier firm knew full well he could not possibly deliver.

That, in itself, was dishonest.

But it was only step one in the plan; armed with this huge "backlog" of orders, the proprietor was able to peddle the company outright—orders and all—to the larger corporation that had hired Frank. That was step two, and when it was completed the old owner was home free. Let the new owner worry about how to fill that impossible supply schedule. He wept sympathetic tears all the way to the bank.

So Frank was on the spot.

In all honesty, I don't know if anyone on earth could have pulled this one out of the fire. The situation was as near impossible as could be imagined. But certainly any hope of success lay in the new division manager having sufficient ability to see the whole picture, plan what had to be done, and make sure the program was followed even if it meant running at a loss for an acceptable period.

Frank did nothing of the kind. Impulsive, energetic and intuitive as always, he rushed directly into the thick of things, treating symptoms instead of the disease and slapping on a quick "patch" every time the hot air balloon developed another leak.

Result: one weird patchwork balloon.

He gave the impression—quite impressive to his new employers—of a dynamic, energetic executive working 14 hours a day and more to get a faltering enterprise back on its feet. And in the beginning, his approach actually got some results.

For one thing, a few of the true inadequates in the organization went over the side. Frank's energy and decision-making ability made them feel as foolish as they actually were. This was a plus, since their very presence had been a source of dissatisfaction to those who really were effective.

But not all the deadwood departed. Quite a few, glib and adept at political intrigue, not only maintained their tenure with the company by playing up to Frank but actually increased their stature in the new order of things. Not that

Frank played favorites. Far from it. He was quite capable of firing a man on the spot if he decided he just couldn't hack the job, personal friendship notwithstanding.

On the other hand, Frank would back any subordinate to the hilt if he thought he was effective—and it was an easy impression to give, if the man played his cards right, because men like Frank are not difficult to manipulate. Their own drive and relative insensitivity works against them in this respect; they tend to support men who are able to give at least the surface impression of being as driving, determined and generally gung-ho as themselves.

Trouble is, an attitude like this frequently tends to fill the employee ranks with talented mimics rather than truly effective personnel.

The perfectly legitimate insecurity felt by such lackeys took the form, in Frank's new division, of a self-protective modus operandi intended to preserve them in their jobs even if their somewhat unpredictable boss should change his mind about their abilities at last.

In short, they held back bits of highly strategic information.

Most of these people had been around the division in its days as an independent entity, and had considerable experience with its product line, customers and general operations.

They held these bits of expertise, in effect, for ransom. In their heads and in little private notebooks they were careful not to flaunt, they retained stores of knowledge simply unavailable elsewhere, information which appeared to make their retention not only desirable but mandatory.

Amazingly, Frank did not seem to object. Indeed, he was quick to pay such robbers compliments on their abilities, to credit them with whatever progress actually seemed to be made.

Still, he actually was successful in attracting some relatively competent personnel. Somehow he found, or made, time to interview a goodly number of jobseekers—and he had the trick of convincing the people he wanted that not accepting an offer from him was like admitting feeble-mindedness.

For Frank was, above all, a salesman. None of his other many qualifications in the field ever counted as much in his favor as the fact that he really was able to *believe* every single thing he heard himself saying to others. And this sincerity got through to whatever audience he happened to select.

It was a quality which made him a highly competent recruiter; some reasonably able men even took pay cuts to join Frank's team.

And everybody was just happy as a clam* . . . for a while.

Frank worked closely with the key men he retained and those he recruited. Indeed, he worked closely with everyone. Of course, the fact that he was calling every single shot himself was "only natural" in the beginning. Just getting the boys off to a good start; giving them the benefit of his interest and counsel to make sure they were firmly grounded before giving them their head. Sure. Of course.

It seemed natural. Anyone entering a new industrial environment would need a little initial aid and direction.

But as the weeks—and finally the months—went by without any notable change in their new boss's attitude, some few of these recruits (the most competent and aggressive of the lot) began to entertain a few well-founded suspicions.

When was this guy going to get off their backs?

---

*What a silly expression! Did you ever see a happy clam? For that matter did you ever see an *unhappy* clam? How could you tell the difference? What difference would it make, anyway—unless you're another clam?

It seemed he was forever breaking ranks to handle the most trivial of decisions; second-guessing and countermanding to a point where no one—not even Frank—had more than the vaguest idea of exactly what was going on.

That old balloon was acquiring more and more patches. But, because some of Frank's eternal meddling was now done on the basis of incomplete information or a mistaken appreciation of the true situation as assessed by some member of his "team," more often than not the patches had a negative value, and more and more of the able people in the division began to notice it.

A few finally began to speak their minds—to Frank.

And Frank explained. He took their complaints without apparent emotion, made whatever explanation he thought necessary, and went right on doing it the same old way. When they were subjected to the well-known Frank-style statesmanship, they found themselves mentally admitting that perhaps they just didn't know all they needed to know about the "special circumstances" surrounding the matter at issue. They nodded, shut up, and watched Frank slap on his latest patch.

Had they been stupid, incompetent, or basically unsure of their own abilities such "explanations" and "patchwork" might have served to keep them bemused and responsive to Frank and his methods forever. Or at least until the roof really fell in.

But in the end, the best of them gradually came to recognize the truth of the situation; that Frank meant to run the whole show himself from beginning to end, and that he was utterly incapable of change.

A few tossed in the sponge—openly and with a clear statement of their motives—right then. They quit and went jobhunting.

Others, less confident or at least more cautious, quietly

revamped the old résumés which had attracted Frank's notice not so long ago, and enlisted friends or executive-placement agencies outside the firm to help them relocate as quickly as possible.

One by one, they drifted away.

This, at last, was a reaction Frank could appreciate.

So could the company's president.

But the initial alarm Frank might have felt at such numerous defections lasted, apparently, only for a moment. He convinced himself he had simply been "mistaken" about these people; they had seemed to have proper qualifications for the posts he had entrusted to them, but they "couldn't stand the gaff" when the going got really rough.

He convinced the president that this was the case (the old Frank-style salesmanship was still in top form) and the game went on, and on, and on with changes only in the names of the players. Frequent changes.

The hell of it was, Frank's methods *did* seem to be successful.

Somehow, by hook or crook, his shipments managed more or less to meet the projected dates and quantities specified in that impossible contract which had been the former president's bloody bequest to the firm he was cutting adrift.

Shipments mean invoicing. And invoicing means dollars coming in—and that counted heavily with Frank's boss.*

As long as invoicing remained high, so did Frank's star with the company. What the president apparently failed to note, however, was that each shipment seemed to require an almost fanatic bit of desperation-effort; that returns of

---

*It counts with most bosses, I have noticed. There are exceptions to this rule, of course. But most of them, in my experience, seem to become ex-bosses in a very short time. If that seems peculiar to you, perhaps you're due for a refresher course in Economics.

substandard goods were running ever-higher, and that the confusion created by Frank's methods could by no stretch of the imagination be interpreted as leading to establishment of any system by which his subordinates could work together in a harmonious business relationship.

Instead, things simply drifted slowly but very surely from bad, to worse, to still worse, to awful. . . .

Which is why I call Frank the Dumb Strangler.

His basic defect was no different, really, from the one besetting John the Smart Strangler. But John—while possibly possessing less basic intelligence and certainly far lesser educational qualification than Frank—would never have let the thing get so far out of hand as to endanger his reputation for quality. John at least had sense enough to know (a) that he couldn't change, and (b) some positive action had to be taken before the whole thing blew up in his face.

Not Frank!

God alone knows where it would all have ended, had it not been for what I can only characterize as Pure Dumb Luck.

While Frank had been running himself ragged (and driving his subordinates nuts) patch-patching away at his creaky division, other divisions of the parent company had grown and prospered. In a reorganization, whether by design or by chance (just possibly that easily conned president wasn't so dense after all) Frank was shifted from his post as division manager to a new job as Vice-President for Corporate Marketing.

Green light!

Here was a job uniquely suited to Frank's basic talents and personality. Bright, energetic, a self starter fully devoted to the company, he was in short order able to bring in all sorts of business.

Uncontrolled, this go-gettism might have been equally as

disastrous as his stint as division manager. But as marketing chief—which translate as supersalesman—he was *not* uncontrolled. In the beginning, he had about a 50-50 record on the kind of business he attracted; some was profitable, some was not.

But instead of having to make all his own decisions about what business to bid and accept, Frank's judgment was tempered, now, by that of all the individual division managers. They had the power to veto his recommendations, and the practical realism not to be carried away by his enthusiasm.

Result: a dramatic increase in Frank's batting average, a satisfied and competent marketing executive . . . and a company prosperous as never before.

Did I say Frank was a Dumb Strangler?

Well, that's true. Slap him back in a job where a steady and dependable production job depends on Frank being able and willing to delegate authority to competent and informed subordinates, and he will be one again. But, having said that about him—say this, too: Frank was a Lucky Strangler.

In the end, it is sometimes possible for the one quality to make up for the other . . . and that's all to the good. Still, it's not what you could call an inevitable combination. And woe to him who possesses the one quality without the redeeming influence of the other!

If John was a Smart Strangler and Frank a Dumb Strangler, however, it can at least be said for them that they were honest. John was doing his best to turn out a quality product; Frank was right in there, really *trying* to get that ailing division of his off the dime. Whatever their other qualities, they were at least doing their best.

But there is a third kind of Strangler, and the same, alas, cannot be said for him. As a final, horrible, example of the breed I cite the case of a man we will identify as

Mort, the Crooked Strangler

The chief thing I remember about Mort was that he was not what you'd call a candid talker.*

Like the inadequate personnel of Frank's firm, Mort had formed the habit of keeping to himself a vast store of unique knowledge—information regarding his company's customers, the present status of their relations with the company and their probable future needs, etc.—which should, legitimately, have been on record for the benefit of the firm's management.

What would have happened to that company if Mort had been suddenly stricken deaf and dumb, run over by a truck, kidnapped by SMERSH or otherwise removed or incapacitated, I hate to imagine.

Which, of course, was exactly why Mort wasn't talking.

I first encountered Mort after having been a consultant to his employers for perhaps eighteen months. I was brought in to evaluate applicants for key positions. Mort was such a candidate—for promotion from within—and we went through the usual process of testing and interview.

He was forty-seven years old, married for twenty-six years, and had several children whose problems probably contributed to his own.

His own childhood had not been pleasant. His parents had divorced when he was young and his mother did not remarry until he was grown and gone from the household, thus depriving him of much chance to identify with a male figure. Also, they were poor. His mother had been a low-wage production worker and Mort had been forced to work at various odd jobs to supplement the family coffers at a far younger age than was common in his peer group.

---

*Compared to Mort, the Sphinx was a regular chatterbox.

He saw himself, at that time, I think, as a mature person; the "man of the family"—and this attitude contributed to certain behavior problems in his late teens. He simply could not be controlled. He was just short of high school graduation when he dropped out to join the army.

A poor beginning, indeed. But Mort had apparently made a nice compensation through what I think can be interpreted as sheer determination on his part. After army service he managed to overcome a number of difficulties and roadblocks to finish college with a bachelor's degree—and moved almost at once into a relatively low-level job in the marketing support field, but left that company (opportunity for promotion seemed sharply limited) to join a similar firm, in a similar capacity, which he also abandoned in short order.

That, in fact, became an important facet of Mort's job history; he simply would not stick with any job or any organization which did not continue to provide above-average opportunity for his own professional—and financial—growth.

Fortunately, his third job was with a fast-growing firm where he was able to make considerable progress. He stayed several years, learning in depth support functions in the general field of marketing, until a small-scale reorganization of the company placed him under a supervisor with whom he simply could not establish a working relationship.

He quit forthwith, joined a large aerospace firm (a mistake; in short order he became so frustrated that he quit again) and then moved to my client's company where he quickly became Vice-President for Marketing, the position he held at the time of our first meeting.

The testing revealed that Mort had a superior IQ, extremely good command of language and an ability to express himself well and easily in both written and oral communications. His ability to handle verbal reasoning problems, while unexceptional, was within the limits of acceptability and, while some of his learning aptitudes were not as strong as these verbal skills, they were not prohibitively low.

On the balance, an acceptable person for key placement— from the purely intellectual point of view.

But there are other considerations. . . .

Mort's literary interest was extremely high. He had a strong interest in persuading others to his point of view and tended to see things pretty much in terms of black-and-white rather than shades of gray; all well related to his present placement as marketing chief.

But he was somewhat averse to working with quantitative data, and surprisingly uninterested in being of service to others. Now, since it is obvious that in order to obtain new and repeat sales it is absolutely necessary to have a concern for serving the consumer's best interest (without, of course, ignoring the supplier's profit motive) this was a minor kind of red flag.

Also, it quickly became apparent that he was not trying to develop a strong staff.

Company records showed he had hired a number of persons with questionable academic or employment records; people who, it would appear, knew very well they could not find comparable employment elsewhere. In short, Mort was obviously building his own little empire-within-an-empire, to protect his own job security.

Why?

Other aspects of his personality revealed by the testing and interviewing included a considerable fund of energy, personal drive and competitive spirit. He was the kind to make great demands upon himself—when he was truly motivated.

The Achilles heel, so far as I could tell, was a tendency to distrust others, to be quite suspicious (especially of those who might, conceivably, injure him either psychologically or in a business way) coupled with a strong dependency on the approval and acceptance of others.

This latter tendency, by the way, was so strong that he was unable to admit it—even, apparently, to himself—and, while consistent in his relationships with others, he compensated with a tendency to be outwardly direct, brusque, even a bit uncontrolled.

But while unable to admit dependency, Mort did seem to realize that what others thought of him was quite important to his psychological well-being, and this may have been his motive in acquiring the clique of inadequate underlings he had hired. They would accept his occasional burst of un-earned wrath and keep buttering him up and placating him. They had little choice.

With his peers in the company hierarchy, though, it was another matter entirely.

He was reasonably unpopular with them (as, indeed, he was with his immediate superior, the firm's general manager). His peers seemed to sense the fact that his ultimate goal was to collect enough of the reins of power into his hands to be able to manipulate the entire establishment from his own little niche.

What's more, a peculiar combination of circumstances actually made such a thing possible.

Mort's firm had very few customers, in absolute terms. Its product was technologically secret and so was the use made of it by the customers. For that reason, contact with the customers was pretty much confined to one individual: Mort, himself.

And that meant the company's future was largely in his hands.

Mort understood this very well—and, as might be expected

of such a personality, took full advantage of it. In short, he made things very nearly unbearable for almost everyone around him.

For a while, matters were permitted to rock along that way.

Mort's underlings smiled at his face, growled at his back, and sighed all the way to the bank every payday. His peers groaned and sweated, secretly wishing him a hernia. And his boss, the company's president, pondered the whole thing in silence.

Mort gained a false sense of security. Had he been a more sensitive person, perhaps more willing to consider the views of others, he might have sensed the slow approach of Trouble. But he was not, and did not. He had been so successful for so long in meeting his own personal needs that he had apparently decided it would last forever.

Even when the president, prompted at last to tentative action, suggested—quite tangentially—that the firm's marketing organization's staff might be improved and/or other persons be made privy to Mort's "private" store of information concerning customers, on a need-to-know basis, he simply rejected the proposals and went merrily on his way.

Apparently, however, that cavalier dismissal of an obviously reasonable suggestion had an unexpected effect upon the president.

It may have been that he realized—tardily, but at least in time to avert outright disaster—that his position was dangerous not only to the company but to him, personally.

It may have been, too, that he further realized it was his own lack of supervision which had allowed Mort to place everyone in such a position. If so, he must also have perceived that his own ability to handle the situation was at best questionable.

In any case, he took what I would call an intelligent action.

Quietly, carefully, he selected a new Director of Manufacturing from outside the firm, brought him into the organization and as soon as possible promoted him to a new post—general manager—which he created especially for him.

The new post was, in effect, a buffer between the rest of the management group and the president.

Mort, therefore, was no longer in a position to bamboozle the president as before. And his new boss didn't bamboozle so easily; in fact, he had apparently been hired because he didn't bamboozle at all.

Typically, the power-shift left Mort largely unmoved.

He had been in the East—living it up as "expense-account royalty"—when the new man's promotion was announced. It did not seem to occur to Mort that the move posed any threat. After all, his own position vis-a-vis the company's few and highly-classified customers remained unchanged. He still had the whip-hand.

Nor did the new boss's first move worry him.

The new man, fully capable of acting with boldness and precision, opened the game with a seemingly harmless ploy. Indeed, it may have appeared to Mort that the man was offering him a gesture of accolade.

What happened was that Mort was reassigned—with a new and exceptionally fancy title—to head the company's marketing in the eastern part of the United States.

Then the general manager hired a reasonably qualified professional to handle a seemingly innocuous portion of the marketing organization—nothing for Mort to worry about. The fact that this would give the new man, nominally Mort's underling, an excellent opportunity to become conversant with the situation, to meet all the customers who had in the past dealt only with Mort, and to tinker effectively with the marketing organization (including the upgrading of competent personnel and the termination of many of Mort's toadies) may even have escaped his notice.

Too late, he realized the true effect.

Mort found himself left in control of only two of the firm's eastern regional people—and a very small percentage of the business. He had been effectively lured onto a sidetrack . . . and the understanding, when it came, almost sent him into shock.

His last-ditch attempt at a power play was a dismal failure.

He threatened to resign over a miniscule inconsistency in the company's policy, a point by no stretch of the imagination worthy of important consideration.

To nobody's surpise but Mort's, the resignation was accepted without comment.*

To protect itself, to blunt the effectiveness of any campaign of complaint Mort might have launched with the firm's few-but-oh-so-important customers, the company issued an extremely warm and sympathetic statement that Mort had resigned voluntarily, regretting his decision and wishing him well.

And that was pretty much the end of the Crooked Strangler.

Oh, he got another job, of course. Sure he did. He went over to a competing firm. Tried the same tactics there. Was eliminated in a mere fraction of the time it had taken my client to identify and disgorge such a potential cancer.

The second termination, coming so close upon the heels of

---

*Without comment from management, that is. Mort, himself, did a lot of commenting—but I can't quote him here.

the first, was the tipoff for other potential employers. Mort found himself with a lot of time on his hands.

Darned if I know what *did* become of him. . . .

The saddest part of the whole story is that it might so easily have ended otherwise.

For the company:

True enough, a different end could have been a disastrous one for my client firm. Mort really *could* have succeeded in his underhanded bid for domination, and Lord only knows what would have become of the whole organization. On the other hand, strong and decisive action to head him off from his obvious Strangler tactics, if taken early enough in the game, might have convinced him that such jiggery-pokery was unworkable. It just *might* have forced him to concentrate on doing a real job for his employers; just *might* have relieved him of the temptation to become a Crooked Strangler.

And for Mort himself:

Well . . . how can a man be sure? My own experience with Mort led me to suggest to him that he try a rather healthier and more realistic approach and perspective on his environment and capabilities. I told him then, and I still largely believe, that an honest approach to the job and himself might have put him in a position to do really well—to maintain his tenure in the best job he ever had in his life, and to discover that he did in fact possess the ability to perform and to protect himself in the Executive Jungle without resort to questionable procedures.

But could he really have done so . . . being himself?

Even if he had *wanted* to delegate responsibility to others, it was pretty obvious that he couldn't delegate it to the kind of nonentities with whom he had deliberately surrounded himself. He would have had to begin by getting rid of most of them, short-circuiting the others, and bringing in really professional types who could perform.

And, given his particular emotional conditioning, such an approach to his work might really have been impossible for him. His need to "protect" himself—in a fashion which can only be called dishonest—would have mitigated against it. He could not have tolerated the presence of any competent person in a position of responsibility. He would have felt threatened, and this in turn might well have undermined the self-confidence which any really competent salesman must preserve at all costs.

Which leads us to the final word on Mort:

Regardless of the many plus factors observable in his character and personality, everything considered it would seem quite unlikely that such a man could change, could become anything but the Strangler he proved himself to be, without a basic revolution inside himself.

Such revolutions, in my experience, are sadly rare. Mort was what he was . . . it is unlikely he ever could change.

So there they are: the three Stranglers . . . smart, dumb and crooked.

John, the Smart Strangler, was honest, dedicated, pursuing success at whatever personal cost. A good man, on the whole—absolutely necessary to the original formulation of his company. But at some point, the "do-it-all-yourself" modus operandi which provided the basic life-spark *must* yield to an ability to delegate or face a future in which that same drive and dedication become malign.

Do You *Work for* a Smart Strangler?

Then your first order of business is to keep the boss advised and aware of the fact that your efforts in his and the company's behalf are effective, always with an eye to almost twisting his arm to convince him that you can be trusted with at least one individual responsibility. That one success can lead—ever so painfully, ever so slowly—to more and more. It's not an easy thing to do. But it is extremely exciting . . . and rewarding. The same goes, by the way, even if he's a Dumb Strangler.

Do You *Work with* a Smart Strangler?

If you're his peer in business, you might as well get set for it: you and he are going to wind up as competitors rather than neutral associates or teammates. This kind of guy can *not* resist the urge to make himself Head Honcho. If he's a friend, besides being a peer, you have an especially difficult situation on your hands . . . because such a man will not take easily to aid or advice; he really does want to play every single position on the team. About the best you can do is to nudge, or aid, him in starting an enterprise of his own. And again, much the same thing may be said if your peer is a Dumb Strangler.

Are *You* a Smart Strangler?

If you are, isn't it about time you took a little action in your *own* behalf? The first thing to check, of course, is the quality of personnel with which you surround yourself. Are they truly able in their own field of expertise? Flexible? Willing? Loyal? Do they have the self-starter ability that is needed inasmuch as you don't have time to hold their hands? Can they be objective about your approaval or disapproval? Can they accept sacrifice as you can? They'd better—you're a darn demanding guy! In fact, you are one hardnosed son-of-a-bitch, and the only way you can possibly dare delegate responsibility (and its attendant authority) is to have a man under you who meets such criteria.

If you do have such people—grit your teeth, hold your breath, forget the pounding of your heart . . . and *let the man do his job his way*. Let him do it. Or start looking for a buyer for the business before you throttle your productive infant in its crib.

In this eventuality, it just doesn't matter whether you're a Dumb or a Smart Strangler.

You had *better* be a lucky one. . . .

And that, sadly, brings us to the matter of how to deal with Mort, the Crooked Strangler.* Sad case, Mort. Sadder, by far, than the Smart or Dumb Stranglers, because for one thing poor old Mort is never going to know the satisfactions of honest accomplishment. The best he can ever do is to cover his own tracks and protect his own position . . . temporarily. God knows he might be able to do an honest job. But his own basic feelings of inadequacy and insecurity won't let him chance the attempt. So . . .

Do You *Work for* a Crooked Strangler?

If you do, and you're moderately bright, you may as well admit to yourself he's never going to delegate any responsibility to you at a high enough level to let you grow, in experience or confidence. And his ideas about what is to be done, and how, in any given situation will be pretty rigid. You'll have to get used to being a kind of robot,† giving

---

*By means, that is, short of outright mayhem.

†Inasmuch as a Crooked Strangler is a kind of robot himself, albeit an ineptly programmed one, I guess that makes you a kind of assistant robot. Eerie thought, huh?

nothing of yourself but merely following Mort's rather super-ficial orders and directions. You can polish the apple, of course; play down your own brightness and abilities, show you're awed by his ability, power and position. It might make you—and your ideas—more acceptable to him. But don't count on it, and even if he does decide to let you try it your way . . . be prepared for the moment when he decides you're "feeling your oats," and decides to chop you down to size. Or . . . get out the old résumé, update it, and start shopping for a new job.

Do You *Work with* a Crooked Strangler?

Well, don't ever forget this is a power-hungry, fearful guy who is quite a strategist. You can keep your mutual boss advised of Mort's activities—his successes as well as his fail-ures—not forgetting to drive home the point that they affect not only your own area of responsibility but the company as a whole, and never, *never* letting yourself be cast in the role of a "spy" or "snitch." Keep it objective; keep it docu-mented; keep it pertinent. Remember, too, that Mort con-siders himself a tough, line-oriented individual. He respects the same personality in others. He is, therefore, less apt to take liberties with a man who shows similar strength.

Are *You* a Crooked Strangler?

Don't answer too quickly. Mort would never have so identified himself. It requires a certain objectivity, an ability to see yourself in perspective which not everyone possesses. Ask yourself . . . how competent are the people you've brought into the company? How competent were the ones you drove out or let get away? *Could* you delegate any of your authority? To whom? For how long? How far could you trust him? Does your own position rest solely upon the fact that nobody except you has the knowledge, contacts or ability to keep the store in operation? Oh, really? Well, if so, why did you let it get into such a position . . . ?

Chances are, you *could* change it all, you know? Get a few really competent hands into the picture; give them small trials—and bigger ones if they measure up. It would lighten your load. Why, you might even discover you *like* running a smooth, competent operation. You might even find out that the things you were afraid of didn't really exist at all. How about it . . . ?

And now, one final word:

Does a Strangler—Smart, Dumb, Crooked or Whatever— *Work for* You?

Well, friend, you have well and truly hired yourself a problem. If you have, the first step is to recognize that fact. The second is to waste no time taking action. This guy's a potential tumor!

Suggestion, depend on it, won't work. Neither will cajolery, pleading or appeals to the guy's better nature. If he's crooked, he may not have a better nature; if he's honest, he'll think his better nature only means he should work harder.

Your choices are three: reform him (if it's possible; swift action and a forthright statement of the problem and the action you want will save the day . . . sometimes); transfer him (maybe he has talents, such as Frank's salesmanship or John's technical expertise which would fit him for another kind of job less administrative and more useful from his own and the company's standpoint); or . . . fire him.

A tough attitude?

Maybe.

But who ever heard of pleading with the Boston Strangler . . . ?

2
The Miracle Man, or You Can't Tell the Players without a Score Card

In attempting to understand what's wrong—or right—with any given company, the man to study first is always the Boss.

His title can be just about anything: President, Executive Vice-President, Chairman of the Board, Chief Executive Officer, Chairman of the Executive Committee, Chief Stockholder, Proprietor, Chief of Operations.* The title's immaterial; he is the man with the power. The final responsibility/authority. The man who calls the shots. The desk where the buck stops. The Boss.

Unless the firm's a very small one, he can't do it all alone,

---

*I knew a Boss one time whose title—right there on the door to his office—was *Head Bore*. Turned out it wasn't as crazy as it sounds. The guy was *anything* but a bore; on the other hand he had a distinct aversion to *being* bored. And he figured a sign like that would keep real bores away because they wouldn't know what to make of it. He let me in, though. I considered that quite a compliment. I think.

of course. The bigger the company, the more diffuse his actual power becomes as it filters down the executive pyramid.

Still, he remains The Boss . . . and the company he heads will, inevitably, become in large part a reflection of the kind of man he is.

Efficient, reasonable and smoothly running organizations with high morale and a respectable track record of production reflect the handiwork of able, experienced and intelligent men sitting at the apex of the pyramid.

Irresponsible, helter-skelter companies with a record of missed production schedules, spotty employee-relations and constant upheaval reflect leadership of a different sort.

Military organizations throughout history have had a rule about where the responsibility lies for failure or success, and it's worth remembering in this regard:

Only the commander can be blamed.

He can't be everywhere, all the time; it's his duty to delegate. And if it develops in the end that he has trusted too much to a subordinate who can't hack it . . . then it's his tail in the lawnmower.

Similarly, when the job gets done and it's decoration-pinning time, it's The Boss who makes the acceptance speech.

And so it is . . . or should be . . . in the business world.

Unhappily, the Executive Jungle always contains a few denizens who seem to think it need not be so; when things go well, it's "See what I accomplished," and when they go wrong, it's "Another nice mess you've gotten me into, Stanley."

Of this offensive breed, perhaps the deadliest to company and personnel alike is a species I call "The Miracle Man."

Don't take that title too literally.

This guy does not *do* miracles. He *expects* them—from his

backers, from his employees, from the world at large. And when he gets anything less, it's Katie-Bar-The-Gate. . . .

Examples of this peculiar Jungle-lurker are too numerous and too diverse to be really rewarding on an individual basis. But to clarify and identify the kind of man I mean, let's examine in general terms the recent career of a company president we will call

Irv, the Miracle Man

In the beginning, Irv looked good and so did his company.

For reasons which are not really pertinent, both had acquired an excellent reputation in a very short time—the kind of reputation which made it possible to attract some very able and competent people to fill key positions.

Sad to say, Irv found himself believing his own publicity.

So—flushed with early success—he decided he was God and could accomplish anything, literally anything, he set out to do. And as is so often the case in situations of this kind, he was an excellent salesman if nothing else. He bit off more than he could chew; took on a really rugged commitment— one better suited to a larger and more sophisticated firm. His board of directors received the "good news" with undisguised concern and called him to account. But Irv's luck and personality were in top form; he made wild promises, painted a glowing picture of the future in store . . . and obtained the directors' full backing and consent.

Reaction of the company bankers was similar to that of the board. But Irv talked to them—with great sincerity, citing his and the company's "excellent record"—and the result was the same. The bankers fell into line.

Now Irv's neck was out a mile.*

Now, as he told his subordinates at the factory, it was up

---

*And that'll give you a headache every time.

to all of them to "justify the faith" he had shown in them, by fulfilling the outrageous contract-schedule to which he had committed them all.

Only one voice—but, it should be noted, the voice was that of a man with a proven record of accomplishment who had recently joined the "team"—was raised in dissent. This man said he had a couple of questions. And when he asked them, it was obvious to all within hearing that the questioner was trying to see if there was some hidden card in Irv's hand; perhaps some production source or secret process of which he was unaware. Something that would make the impossible possible.

When it became plain that no such rabbit would be pulled from the hat, the questioner made a statement of his own. He told Irv forthrightly that such an operation as the one just outlined was out of the question.

And he was fired on the spot.

Other members of the plant "team" went ahead with their jobs.* As much as anything else, they were still under the spell of Supersalesman Irv. The Miracle Man would show them all how it was done. And back they went to their jobs, ready and willing to give their all to "justify the faith."

That proved more difficult than most had imagined.

The truth was that Irv the Miracle Man actually had no miracles in his repertoire—but he expected them of the loyal members of his "team."

No priority preference could be obtained from a supplier of wadgets? Nonsense! Who was in charge of obtaining those wadgets? Why hadn't the need for them been anticipated?

---

* A couple of them still believed in Santa Claus, too, as I recall. Touching, really. But a thing like that can lead to occasional disappointment. Especially if the Boss wanders around the place in an ermine-trimmed red suit. Whoever thought Santa Claus would tell you to clean out your desk?

Because no such production increase possibility had been mentioned heretofore? Well—in that case, why hadn't the situation been made clear to the supplier; after all, he's in the wadget business and wants to keep us as a customer, doesn't he? So what if the wadget-maker already was firmly committed to other customers . . . lean on him, Stanley! It's *your* job to get the wadgets. I trusted you; now do your job. . . .

What, a scheduling foulup? Assembly 932-WX isn't ready and it's holding up the whole show? Well, why *isn't* it ready, George? It is . . . except for the wadget that holds the frammis? Well, George, Stanley fell down on the job and didn't get those wadgets ordered when he should have. There'll be a big delay on them. But I know I can trust you to get the 932-WXes out anyway. It's your responsibility, George—handle it any way you have to, but have those 932-WX assemblies ready for the line tomorrow. I'm counting on you, George. . . .

Damn! I thought I'd hired competent people, and look at them; coming to me with every little problem. *Wadgets*, for God's sake. Can't they handle anything themselves . . . ?

The answer, of course, was a resounding *No*. At least so far as Irv was concerned. The Miracle Man had done *his* part. He had brought in the business and handled the niggling objections of the directors and the bankers.

Why wasn't the "team" prepared to "justify the faith" he had in them . . . ?

This attitude of disappointment communicated itself to the "team" in short order. The wadget crisis* threw the

---

*Actually, I don't think there really *is* any such device as a wadget. Webster's doesn't list it, and I'm pretty sure I never heard of one. That's why I used the term as camouflage for the real item manufactured by the Miracle Man. On the chance that there really is such a thing as a wadget, however, I would like to take this opportunity to say . . . oh, my *God!*

whole plant behind schedule, but it was a mere distant rumble of the thunderstorm to come. Little by little, the impossibility of the task they had been handed began to be clear to everyone in the place . . . except Irv.

Irv knew where the real blame lay.

He had misjudged the caliber of the lieutenants he had employed. They were irresponsible, incompetent, untrustworthy. They simply would not and could not do the job. Very well: Irv knew how to handle people like that!

Subordinates whose sections failed for one reason or another to perform were given flat ultimatums. Do it, or else! Since "doing it" was not possible for reasons entirely outside the subordinates' control, they were fired.

Irv replaced them with newly recruited people, many of whom were just as competent and just as eager as those who had gone before—and just as susceptible to Irv's glowing description of the future in store for members of his team who could "justify the faith" he placed in them.

They moved into the jobs with a full head of steam built up . . . and found themselves expending it against the same immovable reality-factors.

When they did not "justify the faith" Irv fired them, too, for the same old reasons . . . and brought in the next of what eventually proved to be a long, long line of successors. Toward the end of this little horror story, faces were changing around Miracle-Man Enterprises with such rapidity that the labor force whispered "you can't tell the players without a score card . . ."

That is not a new joke around various industries.*

---

*But it's a joke around a lot of new industries. And not a very funny one, either, I must say.

But it's a telling phrase, because it has about it the distinct ring of truth.

I don't know what finally became of Irv the Miracle Man. But I know what happened to his company. It finally ran afoul of the performance clause in that impossible contract the Miracle Man had negotiated and, after a brief but agonizing period of attempted reorganization and legal maneuvers, wound up as a Chapter Eleven bankruptcy.

If Irv's story were unique, it would be sad—but, as it is all too common an occurrence in the Executive Jungle, it is sadder still in direct proportion to its prevalence.

Not all such companies, by the way, wind up with a Chapter Eleven.

Far more common are the firms that manage, somehow, to struggle along year after year while the "live body" pool of typists, assemblers, machinists, mechanics, maintenance men, etc.—who do *not* move in and out because they are not charged with responsibility for meeting demands which prove unrealistic—gradually develop a somewhat cynical attitude toward the whole dreary business.

Every few months or so, they learn to anticipate the sudden and sometimes unannounced departure of a department head, sometimes taking with him the key personnel he brought into the shop; this departure to be swiftly followed by the arrival of a fresh, hopeful, dynamic newcomer who moves at once to bolster morale by outlining the big changes and improvements he has in mind.

Trouble is, the continuing employees have already perceived what he cannot because of his newness on the scene; they know his bright new plan has as much chance as the proverbial snowball in an equally proverbial hell.

Their attitude becomes cynical:

"Here we go again, gang! A new director of marketing; a new marketing organization, a new contracts man, a new advertising man . . . new everything. Next month, we'll have a new director of engineering, a new engineering change-order control system. What a joke! What a farce!"

The new ones come, the not-so-new ones go.

Only the parade is permanent. . . .

Of course, nothing is really permanent. One of two things will happen, even in a company which manages to avoid bankruptcy.

Either the entire local supply of executive talent will be exhausted, or the word will get around locally that a job offer from Miracle Demands, Inc. is bad news.

Suddenly, the local talent-pool runs dry.

If the company's still wobbling along, the next step is to try recruiting from more distant sources. Sometimes professional executive-finding organizations are hired to do the work. They usually succeed, too, for a while.

But chances are that this will be a somewhat short-lived approach. One or two non-local people bouncing in and out of an organization can raise eyebrows from Maine to San Diego; the competent personnel become wary (they do *not* need a short-term item on their executive résumés!) and in the end, only marginal and submarginal people can be imported.

Now the Miracle Man at the top really *does* have some justification for his constant complaints about inept and incompetent subordinates.

If that were all he wanted, he might count his efforts a kind of perverted success.

Unfortunately, his basic wants are not the real issue; his board and his bankers and his customers all want production—and he isn't giving it to them. They want to find out why. Peculiarly, it sometimes takes them a long time to discover the truth.

It shouldn't.

A constant and increasingly swift turnover at management levels close to the top should be a red flag, a warning sign easily recognized by anyone looking into such a situation.

The company, remember, reflects the top man's personality.

If the place is demoralized, falling behind schedule, experiencing a series of somehow unaccountable mechanical difficulties; if it is an in-and-out performer, sometimes brilliantly successful, sometimes astonishingly incapable, there is only one place to look for the cause.

Try the five-window corner office with the carpet and paneling.

The spanner in the gears will be sitting behind the desk. . . .

Another easily recognized red flag should be that same kind of company president's relations with his suppliers. Is he constantly late in paying them? Constantly assuming all bills are payable on a 180-day basis?

Does he manipulate them by holding out the carrot of increased orders ("I know it'll be a big risk of your time and money and resources, but that new squittlet we want you to develop is the key to a whole new and bigger program, boy! With all the add-ons, it'll be absolutely fantastic for you in terms of potential. So I'm asking a little sacrifice now—think of what it can lead to! *Give* . . . !") and then, when the developing has been done, let the supplier discover that carrot was made of plastic all along? That the market wasn't really there?

It's not a unique situation to find a supplier developing his squittlet only to find that his potential customer has "suddenly decided to do all the work in-house." That is . . . the customer-company has gotten hold of the supplier's proprietary product, made some slight modification to protect itself from legal reprisal . . . and started making it himself.

Legally, he's on safe ground.

But what kind of augury is this for the future of the company?

Another red flag might be your president's relations with his own customers.* They're counting on him; expecting delivery. They're maybe even making "allowances" for unforeseen difficulties which have held him up; may even make their own financing and engineering skills available to help him do the job he has told them he can do.

If the result is performance as promised, well and good.

But what of the president whose supplier-firm has let his customer tie up millions in inventory; gone so far downstream with him that, if this company is the sole source, he's in danger of being left high and dry? That might give your man a unique kind of leverage in renegotiating a more favorable price with the customer . . . but at what cost in reputation and future prospects.

Red flag! Red flag!

The Miracle Man may have boosted your profit picture for the quarter by these tactics, but the method he has used is one that has killed more potentially successful companies than all the tight-money policies, labor difficulties and government spending cutbacks combined.

So far, we've been talking about company presidents.

And in the main, the species of Miracle Man confines its activities to this very special area of the Executive Jungle.

---

*If one or more of them has raised a mob to storm the plant and burn it to the ground after hanging the president, it's usually a safe bet that they're dissatisfied.

Once in a while, however, you'll run across a member of the same breed in some other position.

The names may have changed—but it's the same old script. . . .

Say he's the head of engineering:

If he's lucky, and the designs on which his people are working contain no basic flaws, well and good. That may postpone, perhaps indefinitely, the day when he can be identified as a Miracle Man.

But woe to one and all when it turns out his people are working with a design that is faulty.

His engineering designer may be a darn good man, but he's playing a game he can't win. Lousy is lousy, and probably most of the best people under the designer know it as well as he does. But let's say engineering is pretty well committed to this poor design they've developed.

Still, it doesn't meet specification. Obvious solution: go to engineering management and say, "Look, we're 13 months into development and six months behind on delivery. It's not going to work. What we need is a new approach, based on new concepts. . . ."

Obvious answer from competent management: "Are you absolutely *sure*? Well . . . okay, then. It's a disaster and a damn bad break, but if it's really not going to work this way, we'll have to. . . ."

Obvious answer from the Miracle Man: "The *hell* you say! Well, buster, we're *not* going to start all over again at this late date, and we're not going to have you wild-eyed visionaries always telling us we've got to try something new. You *make* that damn design work, see? That's an order, and I don't want to hear any more about it. Put a patch on the balloon and *go* . . . !"

So the designer swallows the indignant retort that comes naturally to the tongue in such circumstances, submerges his best instincts . . . and puts a patch on the balloon.

When he does so, of course, one of the other components in the system falls out of bed, because now the whole system's incompatible. So he runs around to the other side and slaps another patch on there, only to hear the leaden clunk of some other hapless system falling out of bed.

He had allowed the Miracle Man to trap him in a vicious and recurring cycle of such patch maneuvers and to make this thing work now would require at the very least the ability to change water into wine.

Sometimes a really competent lieutenant actually can remain so fast on his feet and so ingenious in the manufacture of balloon patches that those devices actually are turned out . . . only, if he does manage to pass such a semi-miracle, you can bet they'll be coming out onesies-twosies, and every single one will be a custom job.

Trouble is, the customer is going to get the shock of his life when he tries to apply standard supportive maintenance in the field.

Those "custom" devices will be individualists; each will contain some specific problem not intrinsic to all the others bearing the same type and model number. Supportive maintenance will be absolutely unreasonable because every maintenance man will have to know all the various complications and subcomplications of each device and just how it differs from all the rest.

What a mess!

And the key to it all is the Miracle Man who holds the title of director of engineering. He and he alone could have refused to accept the flawed design; could have initiated the basic changes.

Instead, he promised—and demanded—miracles.

Which brings us to some important questions:

Do You *Work for* a Miracle Man?

Has your company lately developed any of the red flag warnings described above? It's time to worry when others for whom you have respect begin disappearing and their places are taken by a succession of ever-less-competent players. If you can't tell the players without a score card, maybe it's time to go to the Boss and work out with him some very specific goals and criteria so you'll know exactly what's expected of *you*. Then check those assigned goals against reality. If they are within the realm of the possible, fine and dandy. If not—see if they can be brought into conformity with the real world. And if they can't, well . . . maybe a change of scene is in order, before this guy decides your own ability to change water into wine is questionable.

Do You *Work with* a Miracle Man?

When one department of your company begins to develop the need for a score card to keep track of the personnel parade—and you begin to see it affect the performance of your own department because you're not getting, say, the needed prints in time—the first thing would be to get together with that other department head and see if a realistic program can be worked out. If he's a guy you can talk to (unlikely, if he's a true Miracle Man) maybe he could be led to see for himself the impossibility of his demands on his own staff. And maybe he can be encouraged, even helped, to bring it back to the level of reality. If not *I would yell bloody murder* to my boss and let him handle it. And I would make plans for departure if the boss could not or would not do so.

Does a Miracle Man *Work for You*?

If you're a major stockholder, major backer or responsible director of a company where the parade of personnel has reached the score card stage—I would be in one hell of a hurry to find out exactly why. And I would not ask the Boss, either. Maybe someone who has departed would be willing to talk; maybe I could quietly get a close evaluation of the program in progress and its relationship to reality. I would want to know his criteria for selection of personnel, for their placement and for their interfacing with the rest of the team. If I found any demand for miracles hidden in the context, my next step would be a quiet conference with the Boss himself. Maybe he could be made to see the situation as it actually exists. Maybe he could correct it himself; it is entirely possible that such a man has only momentarily strayed out of the real world. If he can be led or helped to find his way back, swell. If not, I would take immediate steps either to replace him . . . or to replace myself.

Are *You* a Miracle Man?

Ah . . . there's the tough question. Do your subordinates seem constantly to let you down? Do you hire apparently competent personnel who somehow never seem able to accomplish any of the goals you've set for them? Are you forever and ever having to replace them with "*really* competent" people—who in time (in some cases a very *short* time) must be discharged and replaced with more "*really* competent" people? Is it getting so you have trouble remembering the names of the personnel paraders? Do *you* occasionally feel the need for a score card? Well, brother—if this is the case, maybe it's time to back off and take an even strain on the line! Ask yourself: "Are the criteria *I established* for the recruiting and charter of each of these men realistic?" Did I get the right man in the first place, and did I ask neither too little nor too much of him? Maybe someone who has recently left the company—someone who has relocated, say—

would be willing to help. Ask the question straightforwardly: "Where did we miss the boat, Sam?" Remember, most people won't tell you their real reasons *when they're leaving*. It's too risky. Same goes for a period when they're trying to relocate. But when the emotionalism has faded, when they're out of the wet again and feeling better about it all, maybe they'd be ready to say what they really wanted to say when the going got rough. And maybe, my friend, their telling you off is just what you've needed for a long time.

Nothing like it for the Boss . . . when he's really in need of a quick, refreshing reality shower.

3 The Likely Candidate

So far in this survey of Executive Jungle denizens, we've dealt entirely with breeds who become dangerous to their companies and/or associates through their own errors in judgment or tactics.

So this time let's examine a different kind of problem.

Let's have a look at the hapless Jungle-dweller, more victim than predator, who winds up becoming a problem more as a result of another man's mistake than his own. I call him The Likely Candidate.

The trouble begins when a key position—usually in the middle-management stratum—suddenly develops within a company.

The company's manager wants to fill it from within.

Now, I have no fault to find with that *per se*. Certainly it is within the ranks of his own people he should look first; it is beneficial to morale in most cases to promote from within because the chance of promotion is bound to be a factor in any employee's feeling about his job, and because it is a big part of the manager's responsibility to help competent members of his staff develop whenever possible.

Further, it's bound to be a lot more trouble for management to find a suitable candidate from outside the company. First, the nature of the job must be evaluated to set up specifications the personnel department can use in its primary search. Then, even with excellent personnel department support in screening, the manager must accept personal responsibility for interviewing candidates referred to him. This interview must be in depth, and the manager may even have to handle some of the reference-checks himself— especially where technical questions must be asked about the candidate and his past performance.

In short, the whole thing's a drag and a busy manager, with plenty of other top-level decisions to occupy his time, can hardly be faulted for being annoyed with this frequently time-consuming and arduous task.

But sometimes it can't—or, at any rate, shouldn't—be avoided. It's up to a competent manager to know when these times occur and to accept the trouble and inconvenience when such a course is clearly required.

And when he yields to temptation . . . !

That's when he begins an absolutely outrageous process of rationalization. He allows familiarity with those about him, some half-crystalized half-opinions half-grounded in half-truths, and plain wishful thinking to bounce around in his mind. Of *course* he can fill that job from inside the company; these are damn good men he's got around him; no need to go through all that rigamarole of outside recruiting!

Let's see: who would be a Likely Candidate?

Before long, he fixes his eye on a specific employee. He kids himself—and sometimes the employee, too—that the man has acquired a lot of product knowledge on the job. He reminds himself that this guy has done very well in his present position. He bolsters his case with extraneous detail. And presto:

Another Likely Candidate is tapped by the Fickle Finger of Fate!

For a wonder, sometimes the choice even turns out to be a winner.* Men *can* grow and develop; the challenge of a really mind-stretching task has in fact been known to bring out latent qualities of leadership and ability in far-from-promising individuals.

Such cases, however, are sadly rare.

Far more often, a good and effective sergeant suddenly becomes a thoroughly inadequate lieutenant. And by the time this fact is recognized by those in authority, it is usually much too late to ease the man back into the position where he was doing a good job. In most such situations, he either is forced out of the company or quits in order to maintain his personal and professional dignity.

One of the sadder cases of this kind involved a man I always think of as

Fred, the Likely Candidate

Fred was the second eldest of three children (and the eldest male child) of a factory worker in the Midwest. His mother was also a part-time factory worker for most of her married life.

Fred had hoped to go to college, but enlisted in the army before he was able to graduate from high school. It is worth noting here that during his three-year army hitch, he never managed to advance beyond the rank of private.

After discharge, he took a high school equivalency exam,

---

*"Even a blind hog'll find an acorn *sometime*," as the sayin' goes.

got a General Equivalency Diploma, and was accepted as a junior college probationary student.

Fred enrolled in several science courses, concentrating on physics, but it soon became obvious that such a curriculum was too difficult for him. Instead of switching to another line of study, he abandoned his quest for a degree and enrolled in a vocational school for electronics technicians.

His employment record after vocation school was moderately stable. He joined a large aerospace firm as a "research technician"* and later switched to a smaller electronics company, where he worked as an electronics technician under strong supervision of a junior engineer. During a layoff from that job, he went to work for a smaller aerospace company where he worked at first in the standards lab, was moved to a position as inspection technician and finally had the luck to be installed as manager of quality control.

But this job, too, evaporated in one of the periodic aerospace layoff periods and Fred worked at a few interim jobs—each lasted a year or two—before joining the company which later became my client, as a test engineer. In short order he was transferred to a job as quality assurance engineer. And that's what he was doing when he suddenly became a Likely Candidate.

The company's quality control manager had been offered an outstanding position with another firm; there were only a few individuals in the department—and the others all were in jobs titled "technician" or "line inspector." How effective Fred was as a "quality assurance engineer" is open, in my

---

*Titles are one of my pet peeves. I have no doubt that Fred did hold a job with that title—but what did it really mean? Hell, I heard of one guy who was a "Traffic Direction and Coordination Technician." Turned out he was the fellow who paints the stripe down the middle of the highway.

mind. to some question. Nevertheless, the executive charged with filling the quality control manager's spot noted Fred's present outstanding title, noted the total absence of in-house competition, thought about what a hassle it would be to recruit anyone from outside—rationalized like crazy—and advanced him to manager of quality control.

Fred had actually held that position for *three years* when I made my evaluation of him.

The first shock I got was when I scored the several aptitude tests he took as part of standard procedure. His scores were low on more than a few. His IQ, for example, was below the national average. Puzzled by this, considering his progress not only with my own client company but with his previous employers, I retested him using an entirely different test.

Same general result.

There were no particular high ability spots in any of the areas tested, either. Fred demonstrated poor verbal reasoning ability, was apparently unable to express himself with a free flow of language—especially in written language, which was essential to his work. Yet with such an impediment, he was expected to interface not only with his own management, associates and subordinates but also with suppliers and customers.

His nonverbal abilities were also weak (though better than his verbal ones) and scored way below the average for people who perform well in middle management; his space-visualization, especially important in view of the engineering aspect of his job, was extremely low.

He also scored low—even by comparison to machine shop operators—on a very simple test of mechanical comprehension which, of course, was an area closely related to his company's products.

Fred's greatest interest seemed to be in scientific pursuits and for being around equipment and machinery, or for working with his hands. He also seemed interested in being of service to others.

His area of lowest interest was in literary or persuasive effort.

From the point of view of personality, I found him reasonably well adjusted. This, too, was a bit of a surprise, since a man usually obtains a sense of accomplishment only when he knows he is doing his job well, and Fred, while he had been able to exceed his potential a bit, actually wasn't doing his job very well—especially from an intellectual point of view.

Still, both he and his associates seemed to gloss over constant errors that resulted from his lack of ability to learn new situations, for expressing himself, or for comprehending subtleties or nuances. He was the kind of energetic person who always wants to get to work on things at once.

All in all, I must admit I found the whole picture rather surprising. . . .

But Fred was willing to accept everything I had observed about him without hostility when I played the results back to him with candor.*

Indeed, he seemed to think himself rather clever.

I asked him how he had managed to survive in such a situation, and he said he was no fool—he had been careful to staff himself properly or, when this proved impossible, to ally himself with people in the company who could supply skills required by his peculiar needs.

For example, he told me how he had produced a proce-

---

*In my line of work, you've got to be pretty candid—but you've got to pick your spots and employ as much tact as possible. Otherwise you'll get hit in the nose a lot.

dures manual by outlining the procedures (for on-line inspection techniques) to his *secretary*—who *wrote the whole manual*! He signed it, of course.

Opinions and counsel, he had discovered, were readily available from the fund of expertise possessed by the company's suppliers and customers. These were, naturally, accepted without question. Fred simply had no personal basis for evaluating it.

Perhaps most important of all, Fred's business peers were what he would have called "real good guys." That is, over a period of time, they apparently perceived his shortcomings and, while themselves performing acceptably, simply made allowances for him and operated their departments in such a way as to compensate for the quality control foul-ups, without ever carrying the problem to their superiors.

Maybe the company's management *should* have known.

There were enough clues; an informed superior might well have doubted whether such a man belonged in the organization at all. But few men like to admit a mistake in selection of personnel, especially when the person selected can "muddle through" it all (with a little help from his friends). Admitting the problem would only mean that the unpleasant alternative of outside recruitment would have to be considered again. Accordingly, when I confronted the company's general manager with my own evaluation, he resisted the knowledge—and the change—with the result that the bad situation continued for some time.

It was not, in fact, until the company itself was acquired by a conglomerate that the axe fell.

The new owners brought real in-house expertise to bear on the duties, qualities and capabilities of personnel in the quality control department. This quickly pinpointed Fred as a problem. In view of his present title and pay grade, there could be no question of reassigning him to a position low enough to match his ability . . . and he was out.

Rough on Fred. Very rough indeed.

And the hell of it was—the situation that produced his problem was not of his own making. He had contributed to it certainly; he had accepted a position and tried to maintain himself in it when he must have known he was basically unqualified.

But the major share of the blame must be dumped on the doorstep of the man who, unwilling to admit the truth that personnel available in-house were inadequate, turned his mind off and aimed a loaded forefinger at the Likely Candidate.

Assigning blame, however, is sterile work. An acceptable occupation, perhaps, for God. But as we are not God*—we must proceed to the far more interesting business (at least for us poor, fallible men) of dealing with our problems. And one of those problems may well be identifiable as a Likely Candidate who just can't cut it in his present slot. So ask yourself:

Do You *Work for* a Likely Candidate?

A man who finds that his superior is occupying a position for which he is unqualified is more than likely to discover that such an individual delegates authority pretty easily; leans heavily upon him for opinions and advice. Assuming, at least,

---

*Well, *I'm* not, anyway. Are you? If the answer is yes—maybe it would be a good idea to pay a visit to a friend of mine who has done some very good work in the field of clinical psychology. If it's still yes after that, perhaps several visits might be in order. And if it's still yes after *that* . . . well, whatever became of that pony I prayed for when I was six?

that the subordinate is himself qualified, such a situation can represent an unparalleled opportunity—if he's a man of real ambition. It can expose him to decisions and to experience that would otherwise be unavailable. Such a situation can be accepted, therefore, on a short or intermediate term basis. But beware: if your superior's position in the company is really secure (and it may be; remember what we discovered of the general manager's attitude when Fred's actual qualities were made known to him!) there is little real chance for professional growth—over the long haul—in such a climate. There is only so much you can learn or accomplish by remote control. When you've reached that limit, it would probably be wise to consider a change of scene. For those who can ride it out over a long period, however, there is the assurance that there will, in the end, be an accounting. And when that time comes, it is not at all impossible that a competent subordinate would find himself in line for a job he's actually been doing by suggestion and persuasion. Just make sure you don't yield to the obvious temptation of giving the superior's house of cards the "little, subtle nudge" that precipitates the accounting. Loyalty is loyalty, even when you feel it's not entirely returned . . . and it counts!

Does a Likely Candidate *Work for You?*

All right, then, who made the decision that put him in a position he can't handle? If it was you—shame on you! Make yourself no excuses; you owe the guy as much assistance as he will accept if you mean to keep him where he is. Help him acquire competent staff and advice that will minimize his failure to perform. If such a thing is realistically possible, help him acquire outside exposure to knowledge and/or training which would assist him in his work. And if, for one reason or another, you find you are unable—or unwilling to keep him where he is, you still owe him at least the decency of a straight-from-the-shoulder explanation of why you're (a) moving him back to his old job, in the unlikely case that such a move is possible, or (b) asking him for his resignation. In the latter case, see if you can't help the guy find a new position . . . but make sure it's not the same kind he has proved himself unable to handle. You've done enough damage as it is. And accept all the extra work and personal sorrow which result as a kind of moral chastisement: maybe it'll encourage you to take a little more realistic approach in the future. On the other hand, if you're presently considering moving someone else into a vacant slot—ask yourself this: am I kidding myself? Is this man really qualified? Does he really have background and other qualities demanded by the job? Or is my reason for promoting him merely a matter of personal convenience for me? And if you get a wrong answer to any of these (you know the *right* answer, don't you?) . . . keep right on looking.

Do You *Work with* a Likely Candidate?

Wellsir, what you do about it would depend, I should think, on just how much the Likely Candidate's work can influence the productive capabilities of your own area of responsibility. If such influence is minimal and you can "work around" the damage handily—why not let it go? No sense getting an undeserved reputation as a nosey critic; besides, don't forget it was your Boss who picked the incompetent. His reaction to having his judgment questioned is not likely to be a positive one, even if he secretly holds a similar view himself. On the other hand, if the Likely Candidate's poor performance is doing you real damage, you probably don't have much choice. You'll have to put in a beef; maybe a series of them. Just make sure they're well-documented, with an eye to protecting your own reputation and to encouraging your superior to rectify the situation. At the very least, you can use the situation to gain just a bit more leverage in terms of decision-making. But an advantage like that is likely to be short-lived. . . .

Are *You* a Likely Candidate?

Or are you in danger of falling into such a category? You know it would be foolish to accept a position that you know is really beyond your natural abilities and inclination to learn; it could be the mistake of a lifetime. The tendency of any ambitious person to accept a promotion is only natural; it's flattering, and for that reason if for no other it's awfully easy to kid yourself that you're going to "grow into" the job. But for such a decision to be based on reality, it is obvious that the man considering the move should have some background for it, a willingness to sweat through the agony of learning a great deal in a very short time, and at least a modicum of basic ability to handle the work. Anything less is an open invitation to disaster, for a man just can't help losing an awful lot of self-respect and personal confidence when he's stuck for any length of time in a situation where he really can't hack it. More, if he stays too long he will not only find himself on the outside—he will also discover that other prospective employers are quite dubious even about taking him on in the kind of capacity where he formerly was proven competent. They know the reduction in salary and prestige will be tough to swallow; that a reduced style of living will have an adverse effect on his morale; that he is less likely than most to stay on the new job.

Don't get me wrong—I'm in favor of ambition and growth. Certainly. By all means.

A man who finds, in the light of reality rather than wishful thinking, that he is capable of performing well in a higher capacity should discuss his desire for promotion with his superior, adding that he would like a chance to prepare for it by obtaining the experience and knowledge he needs.

He must be especially careful to do this if a promotion has actually been offered him that he feels he might qualify for in the future, but *not* at the present time. God knows the Boss won't be entirely happy about having his offer in effect declined; it's contrary to his expectations, leaves him with a slot still vacant, and could even be interpreted as a contradiction of his judgment. In such cases, it even sometimes happens that the refusal is the "kiss of death" to whatever future aspirations an employee might have inside that organization; a foolish reaction on the superior's part, but one that does occur. Even if the Boss *is* that kind of man, though, I would still recommend that the offer be declined.

You know, we would hope, that your own abilities and the whole course of your career—and your life—from that moment forward may well be at stake. Nobody ever promised you a rose garden; the Executive Jungle isn't one.

And the man who lets himself be pushed into a position where he becomes an incompetent Likely Candidate is walking directly into one of the more plainly marked tiger pits. . . .

4
The Manipulator

Consider the Panda. . . .

If you have young children or, heaven help you, a wife who just adores stuffed animals, you're probably familiar with the ilk; cute, cuddly little creatures with black and white fur—sometimes with the black covering just one eye, to make them even cuter. There was once an animated cartoon character named Andy Panda. He was cute and friendly, too. Everybody's pal.

And there's nothing wrong with thinking of them that way, either . . . so long as they're stuffed, or shadowing around on a movie screen.

If, on the other hand, you're considering a trip to the Himalayas, you'd better do what you can to get that image out of your head. Real, un-stuffed Pandas live around there and if you chance to get too close to one, that cute and cuddly fellow is more than likely to gnaw your head off with a single swipe of his cute, hairy paw.

Of course we're not talking about the Himalayas. We're discussing the Executive Jungle, a far different, far more dangerous—and, in its own way, far less well-charted—environment. But I couldn't help mentioning the Panda, because the considerable disparity between his outward appearance and actual nature always remind me of the Executive Jungle denizen we're going to encounter next.

I call this creature The Manipulator.

On the surface, he's usually one hell of a nice guy; a friendly, helpful superior, a pleasant and effective associate and a remarkably competent subordinate. More, he's the sort you're almost sure to find a worthwhile companion off the job . . . the boss whose fishing-trip invitation brings a smile to your face; the underling you automatically pick to have a wind-down drink with you at Alfredo's* when a particularly tough day has ended.

Also, there is seldom any question about his ability to handle any position in which you find him; his personal competency and the considerable "team spirit" of the people in his department are more often than not a source of pride (and, perhaps, no little envy) throughout the organization.

Just the kind of man you've been looking for?

Hold it . . . !

Before you phone personnel to see if they can get a line on a man like this, maybe you'd better hear the story of a man we will call

---

*Or Antoine's, or Gino's, or Harry's Palace Bar and Grill . . . if you don't care to pay extra for atmosphere. Personally, I prefer a place in my part of town called Jose's. They pour an honest Manhattan.

Hal, the Manipulator

I met him in the usual way, while evaluating key personnel for a client organization.

He was at the time a division manager for the firm, a good-sized company with a number of divisions, and I must admit I was for a time as much taken in as anyone else. Hal was—and is—one of the really detailed and expert role-players of my experience, and the role he had selected long before we met was a thoroughly disarming one. He'd had plenty of practice in it, and he was *good*.

To begin with, there was plenty of real and highly diversified ability behind the facade; enough, I think, to have made him in reality what he seemed content with only pretending to be. A man like Hal could probably have made it to the very top, had he chosen to operate in a simple and straightforward manner.

But he did not so choose.

Hal was bright, and one of his great strengths was in the area of social intelligence. That is, he could evaluate people accurately and in minimal time; could make himself seem to be "just one of the boys" when in fact he was in a position of great power and responsibility.

He could make people feel they were "not alone," that Hal was truly "interested" in the work they were doing, their personal lives, their future aspirations. Hal communicated this understanding and interest in terms not of the upper-level Boss relating to his department-manager-underling, but in terms that were real and valid to that individual.

Secrecy, on a highly personal level, was one of his chief instruments.

Let's say there was a war going on between two of Hal's department heads—marketing and engineering, for example.

These conflicts are frequent and natural* in industry; Hal's method of dealing with them was not.

His first act would be to take one of the combatants aside, perhaps in a quiet place not usually associated with business, and say, "Look, Bart—you know and I know we've got a problem with Gus. Believe me, I know exactly the kind of trouble you're having. But for the moment, we're just going to have to make the best of the situation. Bart, what I need is your *help*; join up with me and let's see if you and I can't help old Gus get the job done. . . ."

The implication is plain: Gus is not-quite-competent and the Boss is appealing for his far more competent and mature subordinate's aid in dealing with the problem. Flattering. Almost irresistable. And usually successful.

But what Bart—Hal's new friend, ally and confidante— doesn't know is that within a very short time after the friendly and mutually confident end of their little talk, Hal will be meeting with "old Gus" the supposed incompetent and taking him "into his confidence" too. And before that second interview is concluded, Gus will be allied with Hal in making allowances for the ineptitude of "poor old Bart."

Result: a restoration of interdepartmental harmony, plus a sudden and outwardly inexplicable attitude of helpfulness between two formerly antagonistic executives.

Further result: a vastly expanded and probably enduring sense of personal loyalty to and rapport with Hal, on the part of both men.

And it is this latter condition Hal was most anxious to arrange, for it is one of the many elements in the overall

---

*Two conventions, I think, are usually observed in such cases: No machine-guns in the corridors, no land-mines in the executive wash-room. With these exceptions, Brother, *anything goes!*

game plan he had had in mind throughout his tenure at the company—a power play aimed at assuming full control of the entire organization!

Hal's basic technical ability, his considerable and repeatedly demonstrated executive ability made him a skilled communicator with personnel of all levels. He could talk with much sophistication to a specialist on that specialist's own terms; he could deal with peers on their own level and leave them with a sense of camaraderie; he could show a full appreciation of the problems and possibilities at hand in the overall company picture when dealing with his corporate superiors.

And always, there was the personal touch. . . .

There were quiet after-hours gab sessions, usually on an individual basis, where relationships with wives, children and friends would be discussed—always with Hal in the position of exchanging, rather than merely accepting or giving confidences of a highly personal nature.

He was adept, in such instances, at implying—without ever directly stating—that there were considerations of magnitude involved in his own estate planning; to give an indication of his own financial success by suggesting that he needed to amass a great deal of money in order to send a child to a certain private school, to send another child to Europe, to send a third to a great university. All this, of course, to the end that the underling felt flattered by being made privy to the deepest concerns and secrets of the Giant . . . this Great Man who could discuss his own affairs as readily as the underling's own.

One thing the underling did *not* know: Hal was lying in his teeth.* The estate, the plans for the children, and all the rest

---

*Yeah—and I think the teeth were false, too.

were merely a figment of his imagination, intended to increase intimacy—albeit of a spurious sort on his end—and to give the subordinate a sense of Hal's own supposed greatness.

Your own confidences, of course, came freely after such treatment. You found yourself telling Hal all your troubles including those of the most intimate nature . . . and all with the assurance, unspoken but very specific for all that, of his interest and absolute discretion.

Further confidences—of a business sort and sometimes regarding interpersonal relations between Hal's subordinates —were further encouraged by his habit of "opening the bar" in his own office shortly after the end of the normal work day. There the "team" could get together, could mingle and react to each other, could generally let their hair down, all with that easy sense of friendship and camaraderie which tends in most cases to bind each to the others.

And, as in the case of the more private sessions, the free flow of talk would never be dammed or turned aside by Hal. Everyone was free to speak. They were all friends together. In fact, in time these techniques produced a rapport where it might almost have been possible for Hal to say "Lord but *we're* tired—bed's sure gonna feel good to *us* tonight!" after a tough day, or "Could *we* ever use a steak right now!" on a day when it was necessary to skip lunch.

Not that he ever voiced it just that way; Hal was an expert, and he never seemed to sound the wrong note.

Still, an occasional false tune did intrude from time to time. For Hal's "team" members, it was always "pie yesterday and pie tomorrow—never pie today." He demanded blind faith from all hands; his commitments to others were always positive, always inspiring. But they were also always not-quite-defined in terms of time or the exact reward to be expected.

The promise of the carrot was always there—but the carrot itself frequently turned out to be far smaller than promised, or actually nonexistent. When these disappointments occurred, Hal had what amounted almost to a genius for making the subordinate feel that he had done his best to obtain the promised reward, but this had been denied by circumstances beyond his control.

Similarly, he was clever at the business of avoiding controversial issues when they were raised. The line was usually something like, "Stick with me, George, I know just what you're talking about. In fact, I talked to Mac and Roger about the same problem and your point is well taken. But look—you know I've got a master-plan, and I can't tell you quite all of it right now. The strategy is just too sensitive. But when the time's right, we're going to incorporate that idea of yours *for sure*! So hang in there, boy. Hang in there! You're really going great . . . !"

Which, obviously, is mere placation.

But such was his charm and so strong were the personal elements in the relationship which he had established that the victim, more often than not, went away glowing with the implied compliment, the bond stronger than ever.

Even when—as occasionally happened—some member of the "team" would drop out, the relationship did not really seem to end. For one thing, the departing teamster never seemed to complain of Hal's tactics. Indeed, it seemed almost impossible to convince himself that Hal's sincerity and efforts in his behalf had been more apparent than actual.

And Hal never forgot his "old buddy" even when it was he, rather than the subordinate, who had terminated the relationship.

The reason, in my view, was comparatively simple:

Hal made them feel loved.

Weird? Not at all—if you think "love" is just some sort of catchword for the long-hair-and-protest-banner set, think again! Everyone needs love; half one's life is spent seeking it. A pat on the head from a superior whose good opinion is truly valued is as much an expression of love as the same gesture from a spouse or fiancée. A mother's kiss for her halfgrown offspring is no more valid in this sense than the Boss's half-glimpsed and secret wink of encouragement that says "I'm with you, buddy." Everyone needs love.

And, especially in cases such as Hal's, the need—and its satisfaction—work both ways.

This, I think, is the unhealthiest single factor in the whole unhealthy relationship which existed between Hal and his "team" of underlings. If they needed his interest and apparent support, he needed theirs *just as badly*. Boss and subordinates came, in the end, to lean upon each other in this respect—a mutual emotional dependency which, while perfectly acceptable in many cases where the emotional and personal content is relatively independant of other factors, is simply out of place in any realistic business relationship.

And when at last the going got rough, when things began to go wrong with the tightly-structured little card-house Hal had created in his division, it wasn't Hal alone who had to face the pressure.

"Boys," he said, *"we've* got a problem. . . ."

And it was the loyal "team" members who broke their backs, worked long hours, and felt somehow privileged to do so. This kind of thing could be repeated—over and over, with only the most minimal and tokenish sort of reward—until the team member finally lost his usefulness to Hal (even then, he was careful to ease the faltering member out of all meaningful situations in such a face-saving manner that they ended by "appreciating" his "kindness"; Hal was no fool . . . the guy *might* someday be useful to him once more) or until, as finally happened, Hal himself got the axe.

That happened at the company where he was a division manager when I first encountered him. Hal built the solidity of his bloc until he decided the situation and the time were right. Then he made his power-play.

It failed.*

Hal found himself on the outside, with a more than somewhat questionable entry for his résumé. And so did his loyal "team." Most of them had followed him out the gate *by their own choice!* And most followed him to the new position he was able to secure. For some of them, it was almost Standard Operational Procedure; they had *been through it before* . . . and must have known they might have to go through it again. But they remained "loyal."

Hal's approach when seeking a new position was almost always the same; in fact, it would remind an objective onlooker of the very techniques he used to sell himself to his subordinates: impress the prospect with his own past record of accomplishment, play down the actual circumstances of his departure from past positions, and do it all in a subtle—somehow self-effacing—manner.

Hal was even willing, in some cases, to admit he had been fired from a past position. Not the one in the immediate past. Not even one in the past few years, unless the admission was unavoidable. Typically, the admission would relate to a position held many years before . . . and then he would approach the subject with a kind of subdued pride, intimating that the trouble came as a result of him being "an innovator" and the previous superior "a staid old man who resisted innovation through fear."

---

*"Lead balloon" is the simile which comes most readily to mind.

Such an attitude was further validated by an almost immediate "accidental" mention of one or more of his *successful* innovations, thus apparently indicating that he had indeed been justified in the position he had taken.

And Hal really *did* have some actual accomplishments he could point to—that was the almost tragic part of the whole business; he was not really incompetent. He could have made it, in all probability, without the deviousness, politicking and manipulation.

(In relation to this, I think I'd like to mention one point developed in my own evaluation of the man. Reviewing his academic qualifications in the preliminary phases of the evaluation, I discovered he had been "kicked out" of one very tough university, and asked him about it. The reaction of pride described above flashed immediately to the surface. Hal indicated that he had been unable to live with the "rigidity" of that university's system. "I'm not that kind of guy," he explained. "I'm a real action-oriented kind of guy, and I can't *stand* that kind of nonsense." In other words: "You play the game my way, world—or I'm gonna pick up my marbles and go home . . . !)

At any rate, subsequent to his "severance of relations" with my client, Hal set up a consulting relationship with another very large corporation and I had, through an association which is not material to our tale, the opportunity of seeing him attempt to work out one of his typical power plays there.

The consulting deal was only an interim arrangement, so far as Hal was concerned. He wanted to sell the firm's chief operating officer on the idea that he could run the whole show. The technique was to give the appearance of not really caring whether such a position were offered him or not:

"Well, gee, Armand*—you see how it is. As it happens I'm pretty much in demand right now; I'd really have to have the salary figure I mentioned, to make it worth my while—but if you can't meet it, why, don't give that another thought! Maybe we can work it out some other time; for the moment I've got plenty of other propositions to think about. After all, I'm only making the offer as a favor . . . because I like you, Armand, you're a helluva guy and I think we'd work well together . . . but if it isn't gonna be, it isn't gonna be. No sweat here, really!"

I don't know whether "Armand" was unwilling or unable to make the deal Hal wanted. But I do know the deal wasn't made—so Hal moved in due course to what we will call the RST company, in a similar situation. There, he waited until he had what looked to him like a majority of the board members in his camp and made an open play for the firm's presidency.

He got the axe again, instead; and so did some of the directors.

With a shrug and an attitude of "it's *their* loss" Hal forthwith proceeded to go into business for himself. After all, it was the presidency of a company—the chance to do it all his own way—he'd been after from the beginning, wasn't it? Now at last he would have the opportunity of showing the world what Hal could do.

He had invested some of his own capital. He had borrowed

---

*That's not the man's name, of course—but I always thought names like that were kind of a plus factor. Stick in the mind, you know? For instance: how could anyone fail to remember a guy whose name was something like "Armand D'Arcy Guillaume Montmorency Cholmondeley-Featherstonehaugh VII"? (Oh, yes there is! And he pronounces it "Chumley-Fanshaw.")

a great deal more. He brought some of his loyal "team" members with him into the fledgling venture . . . and everybody lost.

The business went broke.

All parties lost time and capital.

But to Hal—and from Hal—it was the same old answer. "Gee, fellas . . . you know *we* did our best and you know it should have worked for *us*. But *we* just couldn't help what happened. . . ." Circumstances beyond their control . . . etc., etc. . . .

The loss of capital and prestige, however, were too serious to be scoffed or explained away entirely when Hal reentered the position-seeking arena.

He was able to find a job all right—with one of the same corporate giants where he had formerly been employed—but whereas he had in the past directed one of the giant's multi-million-dollar divisions, he now found himself heading a decidedly modest department, with a work force of only about 100.

Hal, however, was not to be daunted.

Patiently he began once more to build up the "image" he held of himself and any work he did; any team he headed: "We're the *real* brains of this operation, boys! Without us, nothing would ever happen. We're the only ones planning the entire future of this entity . . . !"

Needless to add, the minute the opportunity for a power play arrived, Hal tried the same old tactics again. With the same old results.

This time, however, the failure was serious. Hal was in pretty bad shape financially. Also, anyone looking at his job record just couldn't have avoided a certain amount of suspicion. Still, the old super salesman charm was there. He did not doubt himself.

The charm and persuasive ability of a true manipulator is never to be counted out; in time, Hal was able to move to a medium-sized firm located in San Diego. He came in as vice-president—and that's where he was when I saw him again.

He greeted me like a long-lost friend. We talked. And he told me all about his plans: how he was building a team of "real first-raters," how he was slowly but surely reeducating the firm's management to help them "really get on the ball."

And what could I possibly say to him?*

He was Hal, The Manipulator. He was himself. He was not going to change. Reality—the full comprehension of his situation and probable prospects—was never going to set in.

He was merely Doing His Own Thing. . . .

What motivates a man like Hal?

My answer would have to be a single word: insecurity. Somehow, Manipulators never appear to have a clear conception of their own worth. They never seem to understand that they can *make it* without all the maneuverings, chiselings, political Byzantinism and bloc-building. Despite all the surface assurance, they do not seem to believe in themselves. And that is a pity; that is a loss. For The Manipulator, especially one like Hal who possesses real ability, could so easily have the satisfaction of making the grade on his own merits.

And is Hal unique? Far from it! Manipulators prowl the Executive Jungle in numbers—their care, feeding (and avoidance!) are a matter of concern, or should be, to any survival-minded sojourner. . . .

---

*To be perfectly honest, I didn't know whether to laugh or cry.

Do You *Work for* a Manipulator?

If you do—don't trust this guy as far as you can toss a handful of cornflakes under water! Of course, one of the toughest parts of the whole problem is to *identify* the beast; his chief stock-in-trade is his ability to screen his actual nature. His glibness can fool—or sway—just about anyone, at first. But when weeks and months pass without notable improvement of the situation; when you find yourself more and more concerned about what *he*, individually, may think of you; when you notice that *his* toothache seems to hurt *your* mouth . . . well . . . maybe it's time to ask yourself: what did he say? What did he want of me? What did he promise? *Specific* questions like that are one way of pulling it all back into the frame of reality. If you are hazy about the answers to any of those specific questions—maybe you ought to ask him for a clarification. But do the asking in a *memo*. Do *not*, repeat: *do not* rely upon conversation. This guy's forte is changing words and their meanings. Write a memo asking it this way, perhaps: "Based on our discussion, are these the facts? Are these the criteria for our interrelationship? Is *this* our agreement?" And I would *insist* that he reply with yea or nay . . . in writing. And if the answer is *nay*, then he must be told: "Let's change it right now." Because if you don't, this is a guy who will use you for whatever good you are to him but never live up to his end of the bargain. Reducing it all to written form tends to make just about anyone more inclined to play it straight—and to increase their regard for you. One competent gamesman knows another . . . !

Do You *Work with* a Manipulator?

If, on examination, you find that a person of the above-described type is your peer in the corporate pyramid, the same primary caution should be exercised as if you worked for him—*trust him not*. No matter how friendly he seems to be, do not be deceived. This man is nobody's friend . . . not even his own. Again, I would take the precaution in every situation of interface to have him reduce his proposals or agreements to writing—and I would damn well not act on *any* oral agreement. More, if the man and/or the activities of his department were in a position to have a direct effect on the performance of my own personnel or my own department, I would do my damndest to show the world—and management in particular—exactly what kind of man they were dealing with. In fact, I think I just might do that anyway. . . .

Does a Manipulator *Work for You?*

Well . . . I've always tried to think of myself as a patient man, and in most cases I believe I can justify the image. But in this instance I guess I just wouldn't have the patience to put up with his nonsense for any length of time after I had once identified him as a Manipulator. *Out—now!* That would be the decision, I think, no matter how good a man he was in other respects. If you can't value a man's integrity, there's really not much else you can say for him. If he isn't playing it straight with employees, customers, suppliers and others—the hell with him. If I keep the guy on, the results of his operations will be haunting me the rest of my days.

Are *You* a Manipulator?

This is always the toughest question to answer; identifying yourself is never easy. The Executive Jungle is full of mirrors —but how many denizens can identify their own image? Still, if you are a Manipulator, self-identification can be—and usually is—the first and essential step toward the real success and achievement you have always desired. It won't be easy for you to change; since you can get so much of what you want by manipulation, it's easy to take that road instead of playing it straight . . . especially when you're not really convinced you have to. Is it worthwhile to try the other way? That depends on what you really think of your abilities. Try the same thing we recommended for dealing with others who fall into this category: reduce it to writing. What are your *real* abilities? What is your *honest* opinion of yourself . . . and remember, you don't have to show what you're writing to *anybody*. It's just between you and you, so you can afford a little honesty. If you find you really *have no* actual ability, of course, at least give yourself points for honesty—and maybe you'd better go right on Manipulating, if you're really *sure* there's no way you could make it honestly. But if (far more likely) you discover that you really could do the job without all the finagling and conning—why not give it a try? But watch yourself closely. Manipulators are clever, even with themselves, and the habits of a lifetime are no simple thing to break. A daily evaluation (Manipulation vs. Non-Manipulation) again on paper might actually be in order. Ask yourself whether you've really been intellectually honest with people; whether you're building real relationships, or ersatz one-sided ones. And be sure to keep the balance in the direction you want.

After all: Nobody really can get close to a Panda . . . unless he's stuffed!

5
The Late Bloomer

Not all the denizens of the Executive Jungle are malevolent.

A few—like Great Elk, or the zebras and elephants in more conventional jungles—are capable of defending themselves, but are non-inimical under normal circumstances. Their species are more to be encouraged than otherwise.

And it is such a breed I want to discuss next.

In a back room at the state museum in Vienna, there is a modern painting I always try to spend a few minutes with when occasion takes me to that city. It is a pastoral scene; a mountainside in autumn . . . with light and interest focused on a single wildflower in the foreground.

At first it is difficult to see what sets this particular flower apart from its fellows.* Usually, a moment or two is required to perceive that while it is of the same type as the flowers growing around it, this particular bloom is at a different stage of life.

It is no taller, yet no less tall; no lovelier, though no less beautiful. The difference is merely that, while the rest have reached the peak of their lives and are now showing the first signs of senescence, the flower in the foreground has only just arrived at its zenith.

The title of that painting, in translation, is "The Late Blooming One"—and I think about that every time I come across a counterpart in the business world. These Late Bloomers have an interest which is, in many ways, quite unique.

I think the best example of what I mean might be the case of a woman I think of as

Cathy, the Late Bloomer

Cathy came to me in a way that was, like her case itself, a bit unusual. A clinical psychologist of my acquaintance asked me for an evaluation such as I customarily perform only for business firms, because one of the members of a therapy group of his appeared to have some problems rooted in her occupational life. The member was Cathy, and her problems, on the surface, were pretty average ones.

Cathy was at that time a kind of Girl Friday in the office

*Especially if you've been tramping around the museum for about five hours on a "culture tour" that gives you only 24 hours to appreciate the entire history, scenic qualities and life-style of Vienna before moving on to Zurich. Next week: Rome, Milan, Florence, Venice and Toledo. Nobody can sort out any kind of impression of anything under conditions like that, unless you find it easy to identify an impression of complete confusion and sore feet. Next time, take at least *two* days to understand all about Vienna, huh? Well ... anyhow ... at least 36 hours. You owe it to yourself.

of a cabinet manufacturing firm. It was a small office. The Boss had many interests besides the business where Cathy was employed, so he found it necessary to leave her in complete charge for extended periods—in effect, left her to handle the show with only minimal supervision from him.

This kind of thing requires considerable confidence on the part of an employer, and in Cathy's case it was obviously not misplaced. I met the Boss on one later occasion, and he was frank to admit she would be difficult if not impossible to replace; he wanted to keep her as long as possible.

For Cathy, too, the arrangement might have seemed almost ideal. She was a widow with three children—11, 13 and 14 years old—one of whom had a serious medical problem. The nature of her job was such that she could pretty well set her own hours and was, thereby, enabled to spend more time with them (and on a more effective schedule) than might otherwise have been possible.

Further, it developed that she did not really have to work at all. Her late husband's insurance had left her with a sufficient income to provide for the children and herself. This gave her a certain independence with regard to employment; if a situation became distasteful or overly demanding, Cathy could simply walk out. She had, in fact, done so on more than one occasion in the past.

So . . . what was the problem?

Cathy. Herself. She felt somewhat trapped—at a dead end —in her present job.* Its obvious advantages did not seem to make up for what she considered a lack of challenge, of opportunity for growth. And growth, it seemed, was what she was looking for.

---

*"Complete wreck" was the phrase she used. A lot of people use phrases like this, I notice. Seldom justified, but in general use all the same.

I began the evaluation in the usual way, with standard tests followed by a depth interview and the development of a personal history.

The results were interesting.

Cathy's background had been a rather traumatic and limiting one. She was the daughter of a railroad fireman, born and reared in a Tennessee town of about 5,000 inhabitants; a somewhat isolated locale, cut off from most usual learning opportunities. Her early education would have been gained in the one-room Little Red Schoolhouse which has become almost a cliché in our time—and not too much of a drawback if everybody who attends wants to stay in a rural backwater the rest of their lives.

Cathy's burden, in such surroundings, was that she did not.

More, she was a bright, inquisitive child who was eager to learn, and that in itself must have set her somewhat apart from her playmates in that anti-intellectual atmosphere.

Her relationship with her parents and with her brother (he was the younger of the two) also left a good deal to be desired. While she indicated that her father was an easygoing, very patient man who tended to be positive in his view of the world and to give her what emotional support he could, her mother was an extremely unhappy woman, much given to complaint . . . even to outright nagging. Her husband had become rock-weathered, inured to the whine. Cathy never seemingly reached such an impervious state.

In addition, there was the lack of money; railroad firemen do not rate toward the top of the economic scale, even in rural Tennessee, and I suspect that a goodly portion of her mother's dissatisfaction with life was rooted in this fact.

And there was the fact that she was a girl. . . .

Rural society tends to be patriarchal; boy-oriented. Girls, even pretty ones, tend to be regarded pretty much as part of the furniture—nice enough in their way, but not really important. (There is a scene that springs to mind from *The Fiddler On The Roof* where parents are described as viewing a newborn baby girl and exclaiming: "Oh, isn't she pretty! Isn't she sweet! Isn't she wonderful! How do we get *rid* of her?" Believe me, such a scene could be set as easily in contemporary rural America as in the Russian Pale, circa 1900.)

In short, Cathy was bugged by her environment—without ever really knowing she was bugged.

Like most people, she tended to be somewhat uncritical of the attitudes of others. There were so many of them, so few of her; they *must* be right. *She* was the misfit, the one who was wrong. And there was simply no chance to talk these problems over with anyone. The rationalization had to stand, virtually unchallenged, in the secret part of the mind where human beings really live and feel. Except . . . Cathy simply *could not* accept such a judgment entirely; no matter how much she wanted to, she could *not* rid herself of the feeling that there was more to life and living.

It was a feeling which was to persist. . . .

Cathy graduated from high school in this little town. She stood in the top third of her class, and forthwith entered a nursing school in the same state.

Now, here was her first really serious error*—but it was not really one that could be laid at her door. Her choice of training above the high school level was severely limited, not only by her family's financial condition but more particularly by their view of the world and a woman's place in it.

A career, in their view, was something a girl went into if

---

*Well, second serious error, maybe. Her first was getting born into that family. But—what the hell can you do?

she was not married or about to be married when she got out of high school; something to be held in the background—or for emergency use only—if she *had* to work after she married and began to have children.

And there were "only" two "acceptable" career options:

A girl, in the view of Cathy's family and the general community of the little town where she lived, could become a secretary or she could become a nurse. Period.

Cathy opted for nursing and was doing extremely well at it (a thing both remarkable and expectable in the light of subsequent evaluation) when she was expelled.

She had been about two-thirds of the way through the course when one of her fellow students, a girl named Mavis who had been on the fringe of expulsion herself for some time, in an example of sheer destructive spitefulness informed the school authorities that Cathy was married.*

Mavis was being expelled herself and finked on Cathy not as an act of hostility toward her fellow student—but toward the school itself. Mavis knew the authorities there didn't want to expel Cathy; she was not only popular with students and faculty alike (which Mavis most certainly was not), she also stood fourth in her class.

But the school's rule against students marrying before graduating was inflexible . . . and out Cathy went.

Their regrets were more than matched by Cathy's own, for a number of reasons. First, while she knew by this time that she harbored no great and abiding love for the profession of nursing, it came as a considerable shock to her to discover that she might not be capable of carrying through on a

---

*As a psychologist, I would like to prescribe a brief but effective course of therapy for people like Mavis. It is known professionally as a "sharp right to the chops," and has been known to work wonders with otherwise treatment-resistant cases.

commitment once she had decided to achieve a specific goal. One of her great sources of inner strength had always been the feeling that she was able to do anything she "set her mind to." In addition, she was, I think, a bit shocked to discover herself thus betrayed by what she would herself have considered a "sacred" obligation to respect the confidence of another. Cathy had confided the secret of her marriage to a few girlfriends whom she thought she could trust.

Still, she left the school and embarked on a marital career with high hopes . . . which were, to large extent, again fated to end in disappointment.

Cathy's husband, at least as she later described him to me, was a man of considerable brilliance. (Such statements are usually rather questionable; we tend to exaggerate the good qualities of those nearest to us regardless of our emotions regarding them. In this particular case, however, I'd be inclined to place a good deal of credence in her statement. Cathy tended to see things pretty much as they are.)

From her description, he would have been an extremely able guy, IQ of 160 or so, pretty responsible in his attitudes.

Unfortunately, he was also a rather sensitive sort, thin skinned, anxiety-ridden and given to quick ups and downs. Their relationship had become a difficult one in the end because he apparently considered her his mental inferior and displayed a considerable impatience with her slower mind.

A redeeming feature was the fact that he was quite solicitous with respect to the three children, interested in their welfare and anxious to provide well for his family—even in the event of his own removal from the scene, as witness the insurance which gave Cathy a measure of independence.

At any rate, after leaving the nursing school, Cathy worked for a brief time (extra Christmas help) in a department store; this was followed by a four month stint of office work (the other job-career approved by her family) which ended when she became pregnant.

The remainder of her marital life is not too germaine to our story: she was still married, but several years had passed, when she accepted her next job—as a nurse's aid at a private psychiatric hospital. It might be argued that this showed a real interest in the nursing profession, but I doubt it. I think she just wanted to function outside the home, and fell back upon her nursing training because it was, in her mind, her only visible qualification. Still, she stuck at it until forced to quit because her husband was moving again (he was in a field where moving, due to changes of employment or promotion, are not uncommon) and when she again sought employment (seven years later) she worked again as a nurse's aid, this time in a geriatrics convalescent hospital. She left this job after six months when one of her children became ill; went back to hospital work for another four months the same year . . . and then her husband died.

This could be called a dividing line in Cathy's life.

Her marriage might not have been an especially happy one, but it was a central fact of her life until then. Now it was gone, and apparently Cathy decided to change quite a few things at the same time.

She moved from the East Coast, where she had always lived until then, to California. One of the reasons she gave was that the climate would be better for the children, minimizing health problems. But I strongly suspect that Cathy felt a complete change of scene was in order for her, too. She was putting thousands of miles between herself and the whole scene of childhood, school, marital and other memories—in effect, beginning a whole new life.

There were holdovers, of course. But they were dealt with in what I might call typical Cathy fashion.

For example, though she did not have to work, Cathy took a job within three months of her arrival in California—and quit one month later. That job was as a nurse's aid, in another convalescent hospital, and this time she made no excuses to herself or anyone else about quitting because of a child's illness or a husband's relocation. This time she said it straight out: she quit because she hated the hospital . . . and nursing.

She never worked as a nurse again.

Cathy joined an appliance-sales organization as a secretary, became bored by routine office duties and lack of advancement opportunity, and quit again.

Then she went to work for the cabinet manufacturer, joined the therapy group—and was referred to Rodman.

I said the results of the testing were interesting, and they were. Especially in the light of her job history. Cathy had, so far as I could determine, been working until now in two of the areas she should have most specifically avoided.

No one is a genius at everything.*

In Cathy's case, an examination of her strengths and weaknesses, abilities and disabilities, interests and disinterests showed a very sharp demarcation between what she did well and what she did poorly.

To put it more clearly—when Cathy was good, she was very, very good; when she was mediocre, she was awful.

Her greatest strength was in the verbal area; her vocabulary was superior to that of 90 percent of her peers, she could

---

*Albert Einstein, for instance, is generally regarded as one of the truly great geniuses of the twentieth century. He was also, I am told, a competent violinist and sailor. But if you're looking for a shock—cast an eye on some of his writings in the political field. The man may have known his abstract math, but in politics, he had the best mind of the fourth century. B.C., that is. . .

express herself in a free flow of spoken language, she had demonstrated an ability to handle the written word. (Cathy enjoyed reading; she had also actually written poetry—in high school and afterward—which was published.)

Surprisingly (especially to Cathy herself) she also had a considerable numerical reasoning ability. She could, for example, easily select the proper following sequence for a test set of numbers like 1,3,5,7,9 . . . or 3,9,81, etc. To do this, she had to be able to see the relationship between these real numbers. Her high score in this single portion of the non-verbal area of ability especially surprised her (the rest of her scores were low here) because she had always thought of herself as being relatively poor in the entire domain of mathematics.

She showed poor ability to perceive vectors in space and in maneuvering them mentally (space visualization) and re-testing confirmed this score. This was revealing, too; there had been two occasions since she left nursing school when she tried to continue formal education. She had to drop out of a couple of liberal arts classes during the early part of her marriage; more recently, she had tried a drafting course, and failed at it. Since space visualization is a necessity for a good draftsman, it would have been quite surprising had she succeeded.

Her interest (based on the results of an ipsative test, the kind where you are *forced* to make a choice of "most" and "least" from among three activities) ran highest in the area of persuasion—an interest in convincing others, swaying them to her point of view, selling herself—and only a little lower in literary effort.

Much lower on the scale was her interest in music (she had never played a musical instrument, had a rather sketchy grasp of music itself, though she enjoyed it in a subtle way.)

Her interest in things scientific was also slightly—*very* slightly—above average. But again, there was such a disparity between this score and the ones for literary and persuasive pursuits that it hardly merited a second glance.

At the far nether end of the spectrum: Cathy's smallest interest seemed to be in social service. Ministers, rabbis, courtroom-type lawyers (the ones who handle criminal and divorce and civil trials), doctors . . . *and nurses* . . . usually have an interest of this type. As I said, the fact that Cathy had (a) been able to do well in nurses' training and (b) that she had been able to function in actual hospital practice was a kind of tribute to her own determination and tenacity. Had she lacked such determination, results would have been far worse for all concerned. (She might have done very well, though, in nursing administration. That would have brought more of her persuasive abilities into play.)

Another low score was in computation interest. Cathy might do well enough adding a column of figures because she needed to know the result for some purpose of her own; merely adding figures because she was told to bored her stiff.

She scored a little higher in interest in the outdoors for the outdoors' sake; a bit higher still at working with her hands. But artistic interest (another of the qualifications she'd have needed for that drafting course) scored between social service and computation.*

Her aptitudes, needless to add, tied in pretty precisely with her interests.†

Cathy's personality was action-oriented; she had a sense of urgency to "get it done." She was a competitive type, liked

---

*That is, somewhere between none at all and damn little.

†People tend to be interested in what they do best. But the correlation is not always an exact one.

being boss, making her own decisions, anticipating problems, working under pressure. She was also a socially confident person; good at meeting people, exhibiting a large measure of grace and poise. She was a conversation-initiator, likely to take the lead in interpersonal relationships, more oriented toward people (though not necessarily from a "let me help" attitude) than toward things.

Cathy needed challenge—and people tended, for her, to be the major challenge extant in her world.

She also tended to be a bit impulsive; open and straight-forward in relationships with others (as opposed to subtle) and more apt than most to say what was on her mind. Fortunately, she was also pretty level-headed in most respects, and had this impulsiveness pretty well under control. Otherwise, I would have been worried about the number of bumps she was likely to get on her head. . . .

So . . . what did it mean, in terms of future benefits for Cathy? Where might she aim herself, for best results?

Here, a bit of care was indicated; Cathy was an intermediate-range planner; she was not a long-range type or a strictly real-time girl. Any long-range goal, therefore, would have to be hedged to a degree by others in the intermediate distance.

I told Cathy first of all that I considered her well qualified to become a lawyer.

She was certainly bright enough to make it through law school, to pass bar exams and become a successful practicing attorney—so long as she limited herself to areas requiring negotiation, persuasion, etc. Her low social service interest would mitigate against divorce work, civil actions, becoming the "defender of the damned." But she would be a fiercely effective legal infighter, a strong and competitive bargainer in corporate affairs.

That, however, was a long-range goal—and despite the kind of self-willed determination which had taken her through two rough years of training for a nursing career she really didn't want, I knew too well that she was just as capable of throwing up her hands and saying "the hell with it" should she become bored, or the goal seem too distant.

An intermediate-range objective, then, was needed—and the one that recommended itself most readily was the field of purchasing or of contract-negotiation.

Cathy was bright as hell; her intelligence was highly verbal, she enjoyed working with facts, had a high competitive sense, needed challenge and variety of experience, and could deal easily and well with men on their own terms. She was also a damned attractive woman . . . which wouldn't hurt her bargaining ability a bit.

Relative to this, I suggested immediate enrollment in courses of business law, purchasing, contracts. These could be useful if she decided to go all the way into the law career I'd suggested; if not, they would still help fit her for the business career she seemed most likely to find satisfactory.

One other comment here: a big part of the job, I said, was recognition that self-discipline plays a part in any worthwhile achievement. She was going to have to do a few things she did not like in order to get on to those she did; crap courses in college, for instance, that (usually for no really discernible reason) are prerequisite to those which really matter.

She seemed to accept this. . . .

In fact—she *did* accept it. I got what might be called "feedback" on the progress she had made a bit later in the form of a second visit from Cathy, this time accompanied by her boss at the cabinet manufacturing company, a man we'll call Wade.

Cathy said she was taking the first of those courses I'd

recommended, the one in business law, and was thoroughly fascinated by it. Couldn't wait for next week's class (working, of course, on that real-time basis that keeps the old motivation-juices flowing.)

Wade impressed me as a bit less than enthusiastic over the whole thing, though he gave lip-service to the progress she was making. He said it was "great."

In truth, he probably thought it was nothing of the kind.

Wade needed Cathy to run the office at his cabinet-making plant. He'd have been more than happy to see her stay right there; who ever wants to lose a really competent employee? The fact that he would doubtless have lost her anyway, the moment she got really bored, would have been a tough one to communicate since he lacked complete insight into her character and motivation.

Cathy was a late-bloomer.

Many people are—and I chose Cathy's case for a special reason: it's a phenomenon that occurs more often in our society with women than with men. Because there is considerable social pressure on girls to find mates at an early age, because the proper rearing of young children is an occupation generally assigned to the female parent on a full-time basis, and because—as in Cathy's case—there is pressure to enter the "traditional" fields of "feminine" endeavor (and against selection of traditionally male-dominated areas such as law, medicine and business management) many highly competent women begin the careers that really interest them and for which they are truly fitted rather late in life.

This is a pity. It is also a situation which may well be mitigated or even reversed in the future. But it does occur with a depressing frequency today. What I'm getting at is that it need *not* doom the individual to mediocre accomplishment.

Remember that late-blooming flower?

It grew no less tall, no less beautiful; it merely reached its potential a bit later than its fellows.

I think Cathy's got an excellent chance to make it.

She demonstrated the ability, in discussing her own situation with me and later in taking at least the first of several recommended courses of action, to be fairly objective about her own abilities and to comprehend what might be serious minus-factors.

She could, for instance, see her own need for self-discipline. Not necessarily in those words; what she said was, "I'm not always as reliable as I might be." She meant the fact that she was likely to walk away from a job that began to bore her, no matter how much she might know she was needed in it—and that she was, at times, pretty darn unofficial about arriving on time for appointments. If she really wanted to be there (inside, where people do not lie to themselves; not up on the surface where social pressure may influence apparent choice of what you "want" to do) she would be there. If not . . . well . . . don't wait dinner.

Her present boss might not be overjoyed at the prospect of losing the kind of Girl Friday who can run the office while he's away—but Wade's no fool, either. Seeing the possibility, even probability of such a thing coming to pass, he suggested to Cathy and to me that she might switch to another of his enterprises. He is a builder by inclination, and was setting up a medium-sized residential development. He wanted Cathy to try her hand at selling houses.

Well—how about that? Certainly selling would be a step in the right direction for Cathy, who has the competitive instinct and negotiating ability needed for such work . . . but I had some reservations about how well she might do in selling houses. Playing chauffeur to little old ladies (and little old ladies in trousers) who just wanted a day's outing with no real interest in buying, simply wouldn't be her kind of thing.

While I thought she might do well enough at selling real estate, I strongly suggested that she confine her efforts to industrial sales and commercial property. Cathy, with her directness and low quotient of subtle perception, would do far better in the kind of direct negotiation possible when dealing with businessmen—rather than with women, who all too seldom are willing to communicate directly.

She is at any rate headed in a direction which I feel must in the end give a happier result for her. She may attain that long-range goal of becoming a lawyer; may really hit the top if she sticks to corporate or contract law.

Or, who knows? She has, to date, made no apparent commitment in the personal area which would lead to a second marriage. But even should she do so, I think she would be extremely wary of entering into any relationship which could restrict the scope of her achievement outside the home.

A lot of things can happen. A lot of things do happen.

The medium-range goal of starting in a field which makes more use of her real abilities and interests is one which, I believe, will be achieved without too much stress and strain—while providing for her the kind of continued daily challenge and interest a person of her kind needs to find any kind of happy adjustment to the world.

In short . . . I think Cathy has now an excellent prospect for being the kind of woman who is at home in her own skin . . . !

So . . . what about the Late Bloomers around us? What do we do when we find one?

In a single word: *Encourage!*

Does a Late Bloomer Work for *you?*

Well—*don't panic*, even if, like Cathy, this is an employee whose continuance of function in his or her present position seems like a near necessity. Recognize this: if the late-blooming is real, trying to hold this one in position is a battle you've lost before you begin. See what you can do about lining up a replacement .. and consider the possibility that the late bloomer might be even more useful to you in another capacity. Be as objective as you can in helping this person assess the talents and interests and potentials available—get professional aid, if you feel you're missing some area of data needed for proper understanding. *Encourage!* Look: maybe you can restructure the job in some way beneficial to both of you. Perhaps the late bloomer can continue to work for you, on a part-time basis, say, if outside training and experience are needed. Keep this in mind, brother: altruism is fine, and part of what I'm saying here is on that basis—we are each of us, to some degree, our brothers' keepers; but at the same time, I'm speaking to self-interest, too. There are few experiences quite so rewarding as giving needed aid and encouragement to a person who suddenly "finds himself" even at a somewhat later time of life than average; also, I know of few businesses where a fully effective and basically happy individual can't turn into a true asset. *Encourage!* It's in your own interest . . . !

Are *You* a Late Bloomer?

Well, maybe you don't have the advantages Cathy did. For one thing, you may not have an outside income to give you at least a measure of financial freedom; for another you may not be able for financial or other reasons to obtain professional aid in choosing the best course of action for yourself. But there's still a lot you can do toward helping yourself. Begin with a question: Who am I . . . as a person, not as what I've seen myself as being before in roles I've played . . . not as housewife (or husband), not as mother (or father), not as any of the assigned characters I've been trying to impersonate.

Who am I as a person ... objectively, as divorced from all other considerations of present or past situations. What am I best at? (Not just what am I best at that I do all the time but what am I *really best* at?) What interests me most? (Not just what interest that I now am enabled to pursue do I like best, or what do I think I ought to be interested in, but what *really interests* me?) Time enough to assay the chances (vs. roadblocks) to pursue these interests and/or talents after they've been identified. And don't let yourself get away with any quick answers. (You are really *good* at sewing? Better than whom? You really *enjoy* music? Better than what ... and how often do you really take time to *listen* to music to the absolute exclusion of *all other activities*? Oh ... *really? Really* ... ?) Don't give yourself an inch, don't let yourself get away with a damn thing. Remember: this is for *you*, not for the neighbors, or daddy or mommy or your spouse. You don't have to make a public announcement until or unless you want to. The result of the questioning is your property and yours alone! Now, then: when you have an honest answer (and hopefully you *will* know when you do) you have taken the first step. Your course of action after that should be pretty plain. It will *not* be easy; bank on that. Few worthwhile things are easy. Sorry about that. But—well—my friend, it is the only game in town that you can possibly hope to win in any way that will be meaningful *to you*.

Do You *Work for* (or *Work with*) a Late Bloomer?

Same advice as for the boss who finds a late bloomer in his employ—same as for anyone discovering a late bloomer in his or her vicinity: encourage. Encourage! Help if you can—and encourage in any case.

That late-blooming one may prove to be the loveliest flower in the Jungle. . . .

6
Winning the Battle but Losing the War

According to von Clausewitz, "Tactics" is the science of winning battles, while "Strategy" is the science of winning wars.

There is a big difference.*

And one of the commonest (and least fortunate) of the denizens of the Executive Jungle is the breed that never seems to learn this distinction. He becomes so intent upon winning all his battles that he somehow loses sight of the real objective . . . and winds up losing the war.

As a prime example consider the case of

---

*Doubters are referred to the biographies of J. Caesar, N. Bonaparte, B. Arnold, S. Bull, C. Horse, K. Wilhelm II, P. von Hindenburg, E. Rommel, A. Hitler, L. Johnson, et al.

Charles, the Tactician

Perhaps I would never have discovered his Tactician status had I met Charles only once. Tacticians are a breed that seems adept at personal camouflage; they usually imitate one or the other of the more forthright species, while secretly (and usually without knowing it themselves) sabotaging their efforts in a way that shows up only on long-term assessment.

But I met Charles twice.

Both meetings were for the purpose of evaluation. The second time, when I was finally able to penetrate the surface appearance, he was a candidate for one of two pretty good positions with a client company.

One of the jobs, as manager of production control, was a line-oriented position and therefore likely to admit of easy and perhaps rapid upward progress.

The other, as program manager in the same firm, while nominally of equal pay, rank, and status, was more likely to show the way to a dead end and the rank of "Good Old Charley" than to the powerhouse-affluence end of the executive suite.

Unhappily (for reasons which should become obvious) the probable salary for each of the jobs had already been mentioned to Charles before our interview . . . albeit only in a tentative way rather than as a firm offer.

Charles was about thirty-five at the time of this second interview.

He had been divorced for about five years; had a son (to whom he appeared quite devoted) and appeared to be in good health. He told the prospective employer (and me) that he was stable in his present position with another firm, though not entirely satisfied and therefore willing to consider a change that could be advantageous to him.

I already knew most of his early background.

Charles' parents had divorced when he was pretty young; his feelings toward both were ambivalent.

He wanted and needed the love and approval of his father, yet rejected him because of what he considered neglect when Charles had been a child.

His mother, on the other hand, had given him love and had not apparently neglected him, but she had remarried when he was 15 (and moved the two of them from the eastern metropolis where Charles was born, to the West Coast) only to discover that her new husband was a drug addict. That marriage ended in a quick divorce, which would seemingly have suited Charles well enough—but the mother had proceeded forthwith to make him the object of persistent nagging (perhaps as a substitute for the former object, Charles' father.)

Charles graduated from high school and immediately joined the marines, where he attended a service school to become an aircraft engine mechanic. He attained the rating of staff sergeant, working at this specialty, but did not reenlist when his four-year hitch was up.

Instead, he went to junior college for two years and then switched to a state college, aiming for a teaching certificate. Along the way, however, he said he discovered teaching just wasn't for him.

Another man might have switched to a course more in line with his actual desires. But Charles did not. He stuck it out and got his BA in education. (Throughout his life, Charles seemed to feel that completion of *any* program, attainment of *any* goal—even one which has become worthless in the goal-seeker's eyes—was an accomplishment much to be preferred over nonattainment or switching to another line of endeavor, which he appeared to equate with outright failures.)

After graduation, his job history was not so good.

He was first employed in such capacities as administrative aide, etc.; later he moved into manufacturing support areas like material control, production control and the like.

In smaller companies, he sometimes attained positions of authority. But when I saw him the second time, he'd held more than a dozen jobs of that kind and most of them had lasted less than a year.

(At one point, I should note, Charles saw consumer sales as a "quick" road to success. It didn't work out. He was back in industry after a rather short time.)

Later in his career, Charles moved into management positions as chief of materiel and production control with a larger firm. He then fell into a series of line jobs with smaller companies, varied by staff positions with bigger ones.

Once he held a partnership (of dubious value, as it turned out) with a service-type organization.

But his partner in this enterprise proved just as aggressive as Charles himself—and at length the situation became intolerable.

Sometimes Charles got his knuckles rapped just because he was the kind of person he happened to be. Sometimes it was because he found himself confronting an opponent with more office-political savvy and general infighting ability.

I administered the usual battery of psychological tests; they showed him to possess sufficient basic intelligence to handle either of the jobs at hand.

More, he was quite sound in the verbal areas (fluency, command of language, verbal reasoning, etc.). He was in fact the equal of top management in this respect.

His areas of weakness were the nonverbal ones (i.e. numerical and abstract reasoning) and he showed a rather strong distaste for any kind of work involving repetitive detail.

Charles seemed to possess, also, a distaste for aiding in development of other people.* He was not even especially concerned for their welfare. (Exception: The strong ties with his son. Charles' marriage, I might note here, had foundered apparently upon the well-known rock of mother-in-law meddling; Charles' vanity may also have been wounded a bit by his seeming inability to compete successfully with an aggressive woman—the wife's mother—for dominant influence over his spouse.)

His social activities as of this second interview were confined in large degree to "playing the field" so far as female companionship was concerned. This seemed to cause him no personal or career difficulty; no scandal had ever resulted and his emotional ties to these women seemed not of the especially binding type. He seemed in large degree to hold to what might be called the "machismo" pattern common to Latin men—Charles loved to take a friend aside and brag a bit about his conquests.

Perhaps his strongest area of interest (as indicated by the tests) was in scientific effort; an anomaly, considering the fact that his abilities seemed to lie chiefly in verbal rather than nonverbal areas.

Charles' personality was urgent, possessed of singular drive.

He liked to *get things done* as quickly and efficiently as possible; liked handling a number of assignments at once. But on one point he was extremely rigid: he wanted to do these things *his way*.

---

*This was probably why he decided against teaching as a career. Good thinking on Charles' part! Unhappily, not everyone thus disqualified actually avoids the teaching profession. If you doubt this . . . brother, think back on some of the teachers you've had in your lifetime.

And he wanted total responsibility for them.*

Not surprisingly, in a person of his type, he was quite bold and aggressive in his relations with other people. He liked meeting people, it came easily for him and he seemed especially adept at relating to them. This capability, however, seemed to me to arise from Charles' need for social dominance rather than any real interest or inclination to socialize.

He was, moreover, a skeptic; he tended to distrust others and their motives (no matter what his surface appearance of acceptance). I think this may have been due to his own tendency (which I observed in his negotiating for the jobs at hand) to exaggerate the importance of jobs he had held and the salaries he had commanded in the past. Perhaps he was saying to himself, "I doubt I can trust you; I know I can't be trusted."

(Ironically, this very skepticism may have cost Charles dearly in relation to the job offered by my client; he tended to discount the firm's description of the growth potential of the job he was offered because he didn't think he could trust the data they were putting forward concerning it.)

In other respects, I would characterize Charles as reflective, cautious, sensitive (though extremely—perhaps overly—masculine in his makeup), persevering in what he had accepted in the way of responsibility, ambitious . . . and relatively unforgiving toward anyone he believed had "crossed" him.

One further insight: Charles wanted all the symbols and trappings of authority and importance, not just the increased

---

*Because he also wanted the glory. Fair enough! If you're willing to stand the heat when you blow it, you deserve the medals when you win. Only . . . how many people do you know who really play it that way? Really? Well, aren't you the lucky one.

income and actual power. He wanted the "right" office, with the "right" paneling, and the "right" carpeting and the "right" desk. And, by God, he wanted them *now*. . . .

The results of this re-testing, when compared with results of the tests I'd given Charles at our earlier session, were remarkable for their consistency . . . which surprised me. I had some rather vague and generalized notion that he was, somehow, far more capable in several areas than the tests seemed to indicate.

On the basis of evaluation, I had to recognize some risks inherent in offering employment to Charles.

Still, the man impressed me so strongly in terms of his personality (and that vague sense that he was more capable than the tests indicated) that I just may have been guilty of more generalization than was really reasonable.

Nonetheless, it was my feeling that his nonverbal abilities were not prohibitively low, that the rest of his abilities and personality seemed to fit him well for the production control (line-oriented) job, provided:

1. That his work be defined in such a way as to allow him to call his own shots within the confines of his responsibilities.

2. That management provide close monitoring.

3. And that management recognize and act upon his considerable need for approval.

And that is what I recommended to the client firm.

I also said that, if a stronger candidate *should* turn up for the line-oriented position, Charles could also handle the project manager position—though probably for a more limited time, since he was an ambitious man and did in fact have a line potential.

The company checked out Charles' résumé statements and

the ones made during interviews with some thoroughness . . . and discovered the exaggerations about authority levels and salaries.

God knows, that didn't precisely count in his favor.

Still, there seemed to be no more acceptable candidates and, regardless of the exaggeration, it appeared that he might be well able to handle the work. So the line job, as manager of production control, was offered him . . . but at a salary perhaps $2,000 below the first, tentative figure mentioned at the beginning of negotiations.

And that was when Charles revealed himself as a Tactician.

He turned the offer down cold. His attitude, it developed, was that the prospective salary had already been agreed upon and now the company was "going back on its word." (Remember I mentioned Charles was a skeptic?)

He was referred back to me for counseling, and I did my best.

I told him, in direct language, that he was being a damn fool. The difference in salary was comparitively minor and, after all, he'd hardly been honest in some of the claims he made regarding his own job history.

I further suggested that there had been a "misunderstanding" about the firmness of the first salary figure mentioned; that the company had been justified in revising the figure on the basis of its investigation.

And most important of all: the salary offered, even revised downward, was more than he was being paid in his present position while the job was of the line-oriented upward-mobile sort he needed (which his present position *was not*.)

Also, I pointed out, there was no one in the company at that time with the peculiar personality and abilities to be competitive with him for the next-highest spot, which was director of manufacturing.

All he had to do was show himself to be what in fact he was, a man of ability, and it seemed highly probable that, within a not-unreasonable time, he would have the opportunity to move up to that higher position since it was the company's set policy to promote from within whenever possible.

I added—as pointedly as possible—that it was also hard to imagine him finding a better job (and especially one with more advancement potential) anywhere else within the foreseeable future.

After which, Charles again rejected the offer . . . from his point of view, he had won this battle.

His reasons were simple enough: he figured he was arguing from strength. The company needed him; he considered his own position at the moment stable. If the company was looking for "just any live body" to fill the hole at the second figure, he would be a fool to accept it. He still didn't trust the company (or me, apparently) in our outline of the job and its potential . . . and was, I'm sure, secretly certain that if he held out (with his usual initiative and boldness) the opposition would crumble and the position would in fact be offered again at the original salary.

Perhaps he thought, too, that having held out would place him in a strength-position in the company when the deal was finally made, whereas giving in now and accepting the lower figure would leave him in a potentially unstable position after he became an employee.

Such was his gamble.

And such was his loss; less than a month after Charles rejected my client's offer, the job he felt was stable—his position of strength in negotiation—turned out to be far shakier than anyone could have foreseen. A slight business reverse resulted in a minor (*not* a major) personnel cut-back . . . and Charles was one of the people who got the axe.

In a sense, he was fortunate; he got another job in a short time.

But it resulted in considerable personal inconvenience; he had to move quite a distance—and thus be deprived of the close relationship he had previously enjoyed with his son.

And, ironically, there was an epilogue to my client's previous job offer (no, there was no weakening on the client's part; no further concession was made to Charles once he had finally rejected the position at the lower salary) of which Charles may or may not have been aware: within just *nine months*, that "next step up" position I had mentioned, as director of manufacturing, became available.

Had Charles accepted the company's offer, he'd have had a chance by then to show what he could do; he would almost certainly have been under serious consideration for the promotion.

In a way, I sort of hope Charles didn't hear about that.*

And in another way . . . I guess I hope he did.

So what does it all come to, not just for Charles the Tactician, but for all the other war-losing, battle-winning Tacticians of the Executive Jungle?

Is there hope? I'd say yes . . . for a few. Tacticians have been known to become strategists at last. But it is a rare thing. Oh, of course, we all occasionally find ourselves emphasizing tactics at the expense of strategy.

But the person who goes through this particular experience again and again—perhaps to the exclusion of winning any wars at all—is not apt to change at a moment's notice. The insidious fact is that the tactical sense, even when strategic

---

*I do hate to hear a grown man cry, don't you?

success is nonexistent, does give the surface appearance of
successful coping with the problems of life and/or the business world. A Tactician seems to succeed in *most* instances . . . and it is only over the long haul that his actual
orientation can be discovered.

Does a Tactician *Work for You?*

Careful, now . . . take a close look at the men under you
who *seem* the most successful in handling their careers and
their jobs. How closely does their overall history approximate
that of Charles? Have they "done well" in a number of past
situations, proven themselves shrewd and agile bargainers . . .
and then been deprived of the final prize by a seeming fluke?
Has this happened more than once? How often? What were
the circumstances? Was the issue that finally defeated them a
seemingly minor one? You know, having a fellow like that
work for you *can* be extremely worthwhile; he'll be a bit
hard to control at times, but if you once prove yourself as
tough and determined an infighter as he, chances are you've
got yourself a hell of a man there. Helping him, though, is
going to be a bit of a problem. He's a skeptic, remember; he
may easily mistake any overtures of aid as (a) a gesture of
weakness on your part, and you may have to show him the
Old Man is still in good fighting form before he gets the idea,
or (b) a ploy on your part aimed at some unknown but
probably inimical objective of your own. In any case, you'll
likely have to let the hardnosed S.O.B. go right ahead banging
his head and getting his knuckles bruised until you can get a
realistic appraisal of the results of his conduct through his
head. Maybe you can't do it at all; maybe he won't even take
such an appraisal from someone outside the firm. Charles
probably wasn't capable of such acceptance, remember. But
if he can once achieve a true recognition of himself, one that

will permit him to guard consciously against the kind of self-annihilation he's been practicing in job after job, then he will at last have some opportunity for personal fulfillment.

Do You *Work for* a Tactician?

Okay, pal . . . now you've got a real problem. Because it can easily limit *your* opportunity for growth. Still, the tenor of your own relations with such a man can do much to alleviate the situation. Remember, this guy needs (a) to feel *totally responsible* in his own domain. So take care to avoid even the appearance of threatening this condition. Make sure, too, that he gets the recognition and praise he's entitled to—from *you*, if need be, though you'll have to use your own judgment here; you can't afford to become anyone's hand-holder or lackey—when something he's handled turns out especially well. And above all, *let* him win the battle as often as possible. You can't manage the war for him; that's his job and his alone. But when a possible solution to a specific problem occurs to you, and you're fairly sure it will work, see if you can't get him to think the idea was *his*. He won't thank you for it . . . but he won't declare tactical war on you, either.

Do You *Work with* a Tactician?

If you do—and you'll be in about as good a position to identify the condition as anyone—pretty much the same advice would apply as if you were his underling. Allowing a peer to seem to win battles with you may be a little hard to stomach, but if you have a clear sense of your own worth (and feel fairly sure your superiors know it, too) the chances are you can manage it. Praise for his successes (albeit not excessive or effusive) costs little and may keep the interoffice warfare to a mild roar; care in seeming never to threaten his position is always advisable—especially if that's what you *really are* up to! (Note: The same would apply, by the way, if you happen to be dealing on a peer level with such a man, but working for a different firm. Particularly if you're a salesman or vendor whose business is at least to some extent dependent upon his continued goodwill. Never confront such a guy head-on; he has *got* to whip you, then. Drop the seed of the idea, walk away, hope he'll pick it up. If he's a man of real ability, chances are he'll do that. Chances are, too, that you'll have a bit of fun on your own, keeping score on how many times you can get him to buy something by letting him come up with the idea himself.)

Are *You* a Tactician?

You're the *only* person in this world who can really help you, in that case. You're too damn skeptical to accept such an evaluation from anyone else, even if you do feel that little inward twitch that tells you a shot has just hit dead center. So . . . look at your career (and maybe your personal life, too) as objectively as possible. You've had "bad breaks"? Maybe; but what was the history of the bad break—did your own survival-tactics in some way contribute to the situation? What is your *real* assessment of your own worth; do you find yourself worrying more than is really necessary about your "bargaining" or your "office-political" position in the company where you work? Does there always seem to be more infighting, more "politics" in your area than elsewhere in the firm? All these, friend, are clear warning signs. Assess them. Assess yourself. And remember: it's the war, not the battle, that's really important. Maybe the only thing you've needed, in every "bad break" up until now, was a clearer, more objective view of yourself . . . and your real goal.

The Duke of Wellington seemed to understand things like this very well.

Napoleon didn't.

7
The Messiah-Seeker ("I Want a Man Who...!")

When a vacancy occurs in a key position and management determines that it cannot be filled from in-house personnel* the usual procedure is to see who's available—and competent —outside.

That ought to be a fairly routine procedure.

If you're the manager, you know, or ought to know, what qualities are required to do the work. Oh, sure—maybe you'd like to see someone in there with just a bit more finesse than Good Old Joe who retired last week; maybe, too, someone with a little more potential for growth. Someone who could even flesh out to be a possible successor to someone in a still higher echelon. To you, even . . . when the time comes.

---

*This time, someone managed to avoid picking a Likely Candidate from those most readily at hand. Bully for him.

So the manager (or the personnel chief, if the task is delegated to him) becomes one of the hunters in the Executive Jungle. And usually, he manages to bag a man for the job.

Not, perhaps, an ideal candidate. But at least someone who could handle it with a few minor adjustments.

Only, sometimes it doesn't work out just that way. . . .

You've seen the kind of hunter who goes to the North Woods but would rather come back with nothing at all than a buck that has one prong broken off his antlers? He's looking for perfection, and he would rather waste the trip than accept less.

Wellsir . . . now and then (not, thank God, *too* often) you find a hunter abroad in the Executive Jungle with the same kind of hangup. He, too, is looking for perfection. He is seeking a *Messiah*. And unless someone finally takes him by the neck and shakes his brains up a little, he is also likely to waste the trip. For instance:

Ike, the Messiah-Seeker . . .

. . . was a man who knew (or thought he knew) exactly what he wanted in a man to fill one of the key positions in his firm.

"*I want a man who* has a degree in mechanical engineering from MIT," he declaimed. "He must have also a master's in business administration (I'd prefer a Harvard man, but it's not essential). He will need a particular expertise in thermodynamics, will have held positions of increasing responsibility for the past fifteen years, have a potential of becoming our vice-president for engineering (or even a more exalted rank), but he shouldn't be over thirty-three. . . ."

So help me!

That's what Ike wanted. Those were the specifications actually forwarded to the recruiters by a supposedly rational executive (no, *Ike* was *not* his real name) attempting to fill a key spot which had suddenly been vacated by death.

I don't suppose I have to add that the man who had died possessed no such qualifications, though he had been doing the work and doing it well for a number of years.

And I also don't suppose I need add the word that he never found the Messiah he sought. . . .

Sounds crazy,* doesn't it?

But Ike *wasn't* a lunatic, or anything approaching one. He was merely a peculiar kind of hunter—a Messiah-Seeker—who comes to the hunt with face shining, and goes home empty-handed because, suddenly, the game seems to have thinned and scarced out to nothing.

Why?

It's too simple to say the Messiah-Seekers are unrealistic. That's like saying pain hurts or water is wet. The reasons for a manager setting forth unrealistic demands may be as various as the individuals who make them. But I have noticed that, in the main, they seem to fall into three distinct categories. The Messiah-Seeker may:

(a) Have neglected to do his homework; taken insufficient time to add up the actual—versus the ideal—qualities needed to perform in the open position and turn these into real-world specifications for a man to handle the job. He doesn't discriminate between what the candidate must have as opposed to the frosting on the cake.†

(b) Actually expect disappointment; he may have been

---

*"Crazy" is a word not found in most standard texts on psychology. Don't ask me why. We substitute a lot of different words for it—but in this particular context, I can't think of any other word that will do as well.

†Frosting is nice but not essential.

burned in the past by setting minimum standards and finding that the candidates selected for interviewing undershoot even the minimal . . . and so tend to overspecify in the future in the hope of actually getting a minimally-qualified individual.

(c) Or be downright dishonest; have no actual intention of filling that slot at all . . . and so take care to specify a paragon who they are confident no one will be able to find.

(There *is* a fourth type. He's the guy who, far from seeking a Messiah, is apparently seeking a bum! He deliberately *underspecifies* requirements for a given job—and is willing to hire a man whose ability to perform he truly questions—just because he's afraid the right man, the qualified man, would want too high a salary . . . or would, perhaps, be capable of edging him out of his own job.)

(About this fourth fellow, however, I'll have nothing further to say here. My God—I don't even like to *think* about guys who feel they have to do things like that!)

So let's deal with these three general types in order.

First—the man who overspecifies because he really doesn't *know* just what he's after: his main problem may well be a slight confusion over the difference between ability and credentials, over the difference between what is important and what is not.

A map is *not* the country it represents.

And owning an Amati does *not* make you a violinist.

Typically, a recruiter who overspecifies—especially with regard to academic attainments—is secretly, perhaps unconsciously, harboring the notion that a degree in itself confers some sort of ability; that the embellishment of letters after a candidate's name are a kind of end in themselves.

Now, God knows I'm not going to quarrel with the custom of requiring formal degrees and training for certain jobs.

If a man is going to take out my appendix, I want to say

here and now I will feel a lot better about it all if I know as I slip under the anesthetic that he is entitled to use the initials M.D. after his name. If a man is going to fly a 707 with Rodman aboard from Los Angeles to Paris, I damn well want him to have on his person and fully authenticated the little scraps of paper which set forth his rating as an Airline Transport pilot.

But the fact that the doctor has an M.D. after his name doesn't necessarily qualify him to snatch my sweetbreads; the guy *could* be a radiologist (or, God forbid, a *psychiatrist*!) who hasn't had a scalpel in his hands for twenty years.

And a piece of paper setting forth his rating doesn't make that guy on the flight deck a 707 captain, either. He *could* be a superannuated throttle-bender with 20,000 hours on Gooney Birds . . . and five minutes' cockpit-instruction on multi-jet equipment.

In both cases, it's the *competency* of the man that interests me; I want to know if he can *do the job*.

The fact that a particular candidate actually has a BS in engineering—or an MBA—does not necessarily imply the ability to put either degree to practical use . . . or even that the degree itself involved training in the particular work he'll be required to handle.*

What's really needed, in setting up specifications, is a clear evaluation of the job to be done: the personality of the man

---

*Many years ago I interviewed an engineering candidate who impressed all the engineering management he had spoken to in my client's firm. This man, they suggested, knew all the latest techniques and programs they were interested in. Testing him demonstrated very low ability in areas where low scores such as he had would almost preclude success in engineering. What a dilemma. How poor could these test results have been? After all, the man claimed a Master's degree. In desperation I checked with his school—amazed to find he did indeed have a Master's degree—in music!

needed to fill it, the performance ability in specific tasks. (I have seen *nurses* who could do a more efficient job of appendix-lifting than the supposedly qualified surgeon they were assigned to assist!)

Job specifications should be flexible:

You've got to be able to trade off one kind of qualification against another. Has the candidate, for instance, special experience or talent—something in his military background, even a high proficiency at a particular hobby—which might be an adequate substitute for some engineering courses he lacks? Or, taking the opposite tack, has a man with an engineering degree that is fresh from the mill (and as yet unapplied to a real job) some academic training, some previous practical experience, some special talent or peculiar pattern of college courses which can be traded off for experience he is unable to show?

Are the qualifications themselves relevant?

Why, for instance, must a man have "at least a 10 year record of successful performance as a Corps of Engineers draftsman" in his background in order to qualify as chief designer for a private firm. Especially if that firm's not planning to handle construction for the Corps? (Could it be that the man who wrote the specs was *himself* a ten-year drafting-room veteran when he came to the company, and has always told everyone it did him "a world of good"?)

What are the *real* minimum qualifications?

And, in specifying more . . . are you naming qualities or formal certifications that are truly needed, or are you merely "covering all the bases"?

Which brings us to the second kind of Messiah-Seeker:

Some managers—men who really *do* know the real-world qualifications required for the job at hand—go right ahead and specify the moon and stars. After which, they sit back and wait for the disappointments.

Actually, of course, they don't intend to be disappointed at all.

In fact, as I mentioned earlier, disappointment is exactly what they're trying to avoid; they are overspecifying in the hope that a man not-quite-up-to-specs on the basis of their overestimate will turn out to be exactly the one they had in mind in the first place.

There are two ways a thing like this can go.

Either (a) in the end, the personnel recruiters trudge back into the office weary-footed and empty-handed, stating the obvious fact that there *are* no such people available, or (b) they sidle into the room and hem and haw a bit before telling the boss they have a guy who's *almost* right . . . well, not *entirely* up to snuff, you know . . . but, "Gee, B.F.—guys like that are sort of *scarce* these days, you know . . . ?"

The hell of it is, unless the recruiter's outright incompetent (in which case why on earth are you dealing with him?) or dishonest (same question) you'd have saved both of you a great deal of time and effort by playing the tune straight the first time without all that camouflage.

If he's come up with nothing, it's a total loss.

If he's come up with an almost-qualified man (who may be just what you wanted in the first place) you have still wasted time and effort and the only possible plus in the situation is that you have to some degree placed the recruiter at a moral disadvantage in future dealings. And if you're the kind who *likes* doing business that way . . . well . . . what can I say?

The whole thing is a big waste, even if you get the right man.

Also: aren't you being just a *bit* dishonest . . . ?

And that final query brings us, naturally, to the third type of Messiah-Seeker who, as it happens, is not really *seeking* a Messiah at all. In fact, if you brought him the man he said he wanted (miracles *have* been known to happen) the only effect would be to put him to the trouble of thinking up still more impossible specifications or picking some tiny flaw in the perfect candidate.

Because this guy is a real swindler.

He is prepared to sacrifice the time and effort of the recruiter (and his own; after all, he's the guy who made up the weird spec-sheet in the first place) in order to give the appearance of doing what he was not really doing at all.

Why?

Typically, such a man is responsible to someone (or some group such as a board) in higher echelons who wants some particular program implemented, while the operating manager is secretly opposed to the whole idea. His easiest out is to convince higher authority that such-and-such an individual is crucial to success of the plan . . . and then, after supposedly herculean struggles, be "forced" to give his own boss the "sad news" that such-and-such a man simply cannot be found. It's a delaying tactic that is basically dishonest. But you might be surprised to know how often it succeeds in the manager's prime objective—which is to halt the unwanted program before it gets off the ground.

Sometimes, too, the ploy is smoke screen aimed at the rest of the industry (or even at the boss's own staff) in an effort to hide the Head Man's private intentions.

He announces his company's intention to enter the Frammishandle field, for instance, and forthwith sets off with fanfare to hire the world's greatest Frammishandle-making executive (first being careful to see that so such man exists) while secretly negotiating for a firm cost-plus government contract for the mass production of Gleeblejits.

The hell of it is, while such a ploy not infrequently succeeds in distracting and confusing, it is seldom really necessary—and there's the poor recruiter with his tongue hanging out and his fanny making a third track in the dust, hot on the trail of a Man Who Never Was. Woe is him!

It's a dirty trick.

Also—whether the overspecification is honestly or dishonestly motivated—it's a sorry waste of time and effort, and in the end the only result must be at least a slight lessening of confidence in the Man At The Top. He's either a bit of a jerk, a cynic, or a crook . . . and no Boss can afford to place himself in such a light before the team whose morale is one of his chief responsibilities.

So how do we handle a situation like this?

Does a Messiah-Seeker *Work for* You?

If you see a parade of talent, but no applicants seem qualified for the job you've told this guy to fill, you may have one of these on your hands. Your first duty is to find out what kind of problem he's got. If he simply hasn't done his homework—maybe you'd better have him show you the specs for the job, and defend them to you point by point. (And if you find you have to go to this extreme, maybe you'd better give an eye to *his* qualifications!) If he's a skeptic who's *expecting* poor-grade material to be thrown at him, maybe you'd best have a talk with the head of your recruiting section; skeptics don't get that way by themselves. Maybe your personnel people have given the guy good reason for his jaundiced view. And if he's the dishonest kind, maybe you'd better have two looks: first at the program the new candidate was supposed to fit into (is it a good one; why does your subordinate have to take this tack in subverting it; are *you* riding off into the blue sky?) and second at the overspecifying manager; if the program's really okay, what has this guy got in mind? *Quid pro quo*, brother! Also *Quo vadis*! A guy who operates like this could turn out to be a real fink . . . !

Does a Messiah-Seeker *Work with* You?

Again, it's your job to find out the true nature of his problem. If it's one of the first two cases, no action on your part may be indicated (unless you're the recruiter) but it's always advisable to know if your co-worker is a fool or a cynic. Besides, he may turn out to be the third type, a smoke-screener—and in that case, you've got to get behind that screen *fast*!

Do You *Work for* a Messiah-Seeker?

Here, too, the first step is to identify the type. Especially if you're the poor soul ordered to find such a Messiah. If that's the case, you can save yourself a good deal of time and effort by going to the Boss and working through the specifications, item by item. If he's simply hazy on the real needs, this will fix things up; if he's a skeptic, chances are he really doesn't want to be one—and a demonstration that you clearly appreciate the situation will more than likely relieve his mind. At any rate, you've very little to lose. And if the Boss simply won't discuss the matter, then you'd better give close consideration to the possibility that he's being downright dishonest—throwing up a smokescreen—and act accordingly. Your options are to play his game; make an apparent scurry after the man he said he wants (while actually spending your time at the golf course) and then come back breathing hard to say the hunting was bad, or (my own recommendation) start scouting up another job for yourself. There is simply no use trying to work for a man you can't trust.

Are *You* a Messiah—Seeker?

No? Really? Hold on—take a closer look at the "Man Who" you said you wanted for that opening a couple of echelons below you. Does he *really* have to have a Ph.D. in thermodynamics? And be the former assistant head of the engineering department at Caltech? Couldn't he be a *little* older than twenty-five and still fit into the company insurance program? Does he really have to be a White Anglo-Saxon Protestant Republican? And what about a woman; yes, a *woman*, if she's really qualified to do the job? (Oh, *nonsense*—she could use the secretaries' john couldn't she?) All right, maybe that's a rather extreme case—but look at the qualifications you've handed down through the clouds to recruiting, anyway. Have you left the personnel people in a position to trade-off one quality for another? Have you made certain rigid specifications that could have been left flexible? If there's any doubt in your mind—any doubt at all—take it from the top, my friend! Have you really done your homework about that job you want to fill; do you really know what abilities and background are needed? Or were you in such a hurry that you used a scatter-gun technique, on the theory that a man with *those* qualifications could do *anything*? Or are you, on the other hand, expecting poor performance from the personnel recruiters? If *that*'s your worry, then it's probably time to Do Something About It. If the recruiters are your subordinates . . . set them straight or recruit a new recruiter. If they are your peers . . . scream like a wounded tiger to your own Boss, and make damn sure he corrects the situation. (And if you're the smoke-screener—or that fourth case I mentioned, the underspecifier who does so in order to forestall high salary demands or to protect your own shaky position—what can I say to you that would do any good? Maybe you *could* reexamine the situation and see that there is some more efficient and honest way to correct it; maybe you *could* count yourself again and see that you're a better and higher sum than you had originally computed. But it's unlikely. You've already made your decision. I'm just happy that it's you who will have to live with it instead of me.)

Hunter in the Executive Jungle: do you really know the shape of the game you are seeking?

Are you looking for food . . . or merely for a trophy?

And are you using a rifle or a shotgun?

Check it out!

Real, live honest-to-goodness Messiahs are getting harder to find every day. . . .

8
But I'm Doing It All for You...

As long as we're making this tour of the Executive Jungle, and classifying the denizens, perhaps it's time to have a look at the Nest. Or Cave. Or whatever . . . tastes vary.

Here we see Mama Denizen with the Jungle Babies, eagerly awaiting the return of Papa Denizen bearing the Kill for Dinner. He's due about 6:30.

When he doesn't arrive by 7:30, Mama will feed the Babies and tell them Papa's going to be late. He's working.

When he still isn't home by 10, she'll put them to bed with the same story. He's working. *Very hard.*

And when the Babies see Papa Denizen at the breakfast table next morning, perhaps one of them will innocently inquire:

"Papa, how come you work so late?"

And perhaps Papa will mumble:

"I gotta."

And Baby will say:

"Why?"

And Papa will reply:

"I'm doing it all for *you* . . . !"

And Baby will smile at Papa. And Mama will smile at Papa.* And that scene will be played, over and over again for years and years. Until . . . one day . . . that final "explanation" just doesn't seem to bring a smile to Baby's face. (Or Mama's, either, mayhaps.) Instead, perhaps someone will mutter some mild demurrer.

"The *hell* you say," is the phrase that comes to mind.

And Papa's eyes will pop open.

And he will voice some tactful query like:

"*Ethel* . . . what the hell have you been *telling* these kids?"

Chances are Papa will be asking more or less the same thing a few years later, too, when the Jungle Babies—now nearly fullgrown—inform him that (a) the Capitalist System makes them Physically Ill, (b) Papa makes them Physically Ill, (c) the Establishment makes them Physically Ill, and (d) they have come to the conclusion that Life is a Bamboo Tree.

"What's the *matter* with kids today?" is the way the average Jungle Denizen phrases it. "They've *got* everything in the world, haven't they? Handed to them on a silver platter? Didn't I give them everything they ever asked for? My God . . . I spent the last 20 years knocking myself out—*14 hours a day*, sometimes—and for what? Why, I was doing it all for *them* . . . !"

The hell of it is, the Jungle Denizen who says that is probably being as honest as he knows how.

He is interpreting the world around him, the world he helped to build, by the same yardstick he was using when he

---

*And Rodman will feel just a little queasy.

set out on his first sortie—ready to do or die. The idea that anyone, anywhere does not see the purpose of life as he did then (and probably still does) would be pretty hard to communicate to him. He really believes he did it all for the Kids.

So how do you give the guy an honest answer he'll accept?

Start with this historically valid fact: the youth "revolution" is not a phenomenon unique to our times.* Youth has always rebelled against the order established by its seniors— and a good thing, too, or damn little progress would ever be made.

Yes, but—what about the "generation gap"? What about campus riots, the rise of narcotics use, the apparent lack of responsibility evidenced by today's youngsters? Isn't *that* unique?

Not really.

It is unique to us because it is occurring in our time; in past decades, past centuries, the world was not so highly specialized. We didn't have the high dependency for *things* that others must provide us. We lacked the mass communication facilities which bring us in contact—on a real-time basis —with events actually in progress all over the world.

And there is a further complication: denizens of today's Executive Jungle fought a war—the greatest and most terrible this earth ever saw—between 1939 and 1946. It cost them years off their lives; cost them the last part of what should have been their late adolescence and early manhood.

When that war was over, the survivors felt somehow cheated.

---

*For ready reference, try a classical speech you probably had to learn in school. It begins: "O tempora; O mores!" (What times—what morals!)

They had lost the one irreplaceable commodity: Time. And they felt a great urge to make more purposeful use of the lives they had preserved through the war. The G.I. Bill produced a whole generation of young men technically trained and university-educated in quantity and quality never before envisioned. They emerged from their colleges ready to "make the world their oyster."

And by God, they did!

But it wasn't easy. Our social mores insisted they become husbands and fathers, yet opportunities for career growth that followed their graduation made them captives of the industrial shell. They were locked into a system, aimed at a goal, which permitted no deviation from the course once established.

An unfortunate—*more* than unfortunate—side effect was that their children were, by the very nature of their fathers' occupations and by the very magnitude of their fathers' success, deprived to a more or less degree of the personal warmth and attention they had a right to expect from a parent. The best their fathers could do, in most cases, was to offer the *things* that this material success could provide.

Tragically, as such families grew in years, they also tended to grow apart. And the problems that all adolescents face were considerably increased by the lack of a male image in the household—indeed, in some the female image was also lacking—with the result that, as preadulthood approached, the more dramatic problems finally became clearly apparent to the parents.

To them it must have seemed an overnight phenomenon.

Actually, of course, it had been happening for a long time; without their parents being aware of it, the kids had been impressed with standards which were in fact contrary to their own welfare.

The children were frightened. They were confused. Their supposed "rebellion" and "disaffection" with all their parents seemed to represent was merely a kind of final scream of hopeless frustration—a last appeal for the love and personal guidance their fathers had been forced to deny them, and had tried to compensate for with money.

Sadly, the attention they now obtained due to asocial behavior was not what they really needed or wanted.

Rehabilitation centers, social workers, clinical psychologists, psychiatrists and all their ilk suddenly found themselves faced with the task of trying to repair the damage done these youngsters; damage they all-too-easily—and correctly— identified as resulting from neglect, albeit not of the knowing or intentional kind.

Problems of this kind occur in many strata of our society.*

But the more apparent sufferers are the affluent kids, the rich kids, the offspring of successful and dynamic executives who would be the first to deny that they had ever "neglected" their offspring in any way; the first to say: "But, I'm doing it all for *you* ... !"

A solid case in point is that of a youngster we'll call

Don, the Jungle Baby

Don was about eighteen when we met. He was the preadult son of a highly successful aerospace technology executive; a man who had started his own company about four years earlier and who was already being singled out as an over-all winner.

Don was referred to me by an associate.

---

*The common laborer's kids are no less likely to give their parents a hard time than are the children of the affluent. And no more likely, either. It's just that the rich kids have more money to raise hell with.

At this time, he was home again after completing a thoroughly unsuccessful first year at a well-known university in a northwestern state. It was his father's alma mater, and there was little question that Don had been "pressured" into going there himself. His failure had been a crushing blow to all concerned.

Now he was just sitting around . . doing absolutely nothing and "considering" attending a local college.

He had two friends; one male, one female.

The male friend was about his own age, a dominating, rather cruel youth, who apparently took considerable advantage of Don's dependency. Presumably this "friend" would on occasion actually threaten Don with terminating their "friendship"—which would have left him with no friends at all—as a lever to manipulate Don into doing the things the "friend" wanted to do.

The female friend, on the other hand, appeared—from Don's own description of her—as emotionally mangled as he. In this case, too, he seemed to have developed a considerable dependency; a dependency which led him to join her in various kinds of nonconstructive behavior including use of marijuana and psychedelic drugs of a more dangerous nature. (Luckily, however, after initial experimentation he rejected the drugs—a hopeful sign, I thought, since it indicated the existence at least of a basic urge toward self-preservation, and a certain amount of personal courage.)

Don's relationship with his siblings was poor; two were a lot younger than he, while the one closest his own age had problems the equal of his own.

His mother was warm, compassionate and tenderhearted—but submissive and lacking in courage to support the children psychologically.

Maybe the biggest problem was that each of the children,

and the mother too, really lacked the emotional support of the father. Don, especially, considered his father an extremely reserved, highly controlled man, intent upon making what he considered unreasonable demands on him and other members of the household. True, the father demonstrated the same stern and driving attitude toward himself.

But Don wasn't his father. He was himself.

Waiting to begin a new semester at the local college, Don had a lot of time to think. He spent it reading and playing records. And he spent as much time as he could away from home—leaving the house every work day just before his father was due home from work, and not returning until he was sure everyone else would be asleep. He, himself, would sleep through breakfast (to avoid not only his father but other members of the household with whom he felt he could not interface properly) and spend the day in the usual way.

Tests of the usual type (the kind used to determine abilities and interests of executives being evaluated) were given Don.

They showed he had a general intellectual *capacity* above the national average. His scores on individual aptitudes varied pretty widely; he showed outstanding aptitude for word-knowledge and seemed able to handle detail with considerable speed and perfect accuracy.

At a lower level but still well above average for his peer group (college freshmen) he demonstrated a capability of dealing logically with abstract reasoning problems; did almost as well with quantitative data; showed a number ability about the equal of his peer group average.

Several areas of lesser capability were significant:

He had little affinity for perceiving vectors in space and manipulating them mentally (space visualization) which would have been important for anyone entering most engineering careers. (Don's major in his unsuccessful first year at the university had been engineering.)

While he fared well on understanding word meaning, he had little ability to express himself in a free flow of language (needed by writers or those planning to engage in verbal communication) and had trouble handling reasoning problems where words (as opposed to abstract or quantitative data) were concerned.

He did well, however, on his final test in the area of creativity (measurement of ability to arrive at unique or uncommon solutions to common problems.) In fact, he exceeded 64 percent of professional scientists and engineers in this respect.

Don's interests were strongly esthetic: music, literature, art—and all were supported in an active way by his avocational background. I could not, however, imagine him succeeding in any artistic pursuit due to his limited space-visualization (unless he limited himself to abstractions.)

In addition, Don showed some strength of interest in the out-of-doors as such (not only, I think for the intrinsic beauty there but as much, perhaps, for the opportunity to be away from other people) and in the area of being of service to others. (Despite his avoidance of most people due, I think, to the not-entirely-unrealistic fear that they might hurt him, Don was actually a potentially compassionate and understanding person, fully capable of considerable empathy with those who shared his plight.)

The least of his interests, by the way, was in working with detail (an area in which the other tests showed he had ability!) especially if they were repetitious and monotonous.*

---

*As who the hell does, you will say. And I will say, too.

Other low areas included persuasive interest, no predisposition toward selling himself or his ideas, or in meeting people formally. He showed little-to-no interest in mechanical efforts, in working with quantitative data or in scientific pursuits. (So much for the engineering course he'd been pressured into taking!)

Probing various aspects of his personality, I found him quite emotionally unstable.

He had a very wide variability of mood—rarely at the ecstatic level, more frequently at the depression level. On this latter point, I should mention that the extremely high level of control he found it necessary to maintain over himself was probably a major contributing factor to the depression, as were his inhibitions (i.e., hangups).

In addition to the self-restraint, I found his degree of reflection quite high; he was introspective; he had a flair for planning . . . and these controls, too, tended in many ways to contribute to the variability of mood.

More: Don was sensitive.

His feelings could be hurt by comparatively minute things, and he was extremely shy and retiring. He was frightened—actually *frightened*—of meeting people in new situations. And he was a "lone wolf" (as mentioned earlier) not because he wanted to be, but because he was easily wounded . . . which also gave him a great distrust of all other persons; taking people into his confidence constituted a tremendous risk for him because anything he told them could easily be used later as a weapon against him . . . a weapon against which he had no defense, and against which he could not fight back.

His sole defense posture, then, was avoidance.

I think I mentioned earlier that Don felt hostility toward his father. There were two specific causes for this: a long-range cause, in that his father had devoted such time and effort to his work (at the expense of his family, a system of priorities which Don interpreted as rejection), and a short-range one, which centered upon his father's insistance that he attend the college where he had set a high standard twenty or more years before (thus, in Don's view forcing him out of the home and also forcing him to compete with his father's long-ago college image. This last would likely have been a losing battle even if Don had not been hampered by his own personality problems.)

He was a person who took direction reasonably well (he could *not* strike back physically or verbally if wounded; he would merely have to drag himself away to lick his wounds) and he was, of course, unable to cope in any way except withdrawal from people who were more dynamic, aggressive or self-assertive than he—which meant just about everyone in the world.

One point worth remembering: Don's high level of tacit agreeableness was motivated by his sincere desire to be loved and to please others; a trait very much in consonance with his test-demonstrated sensitivity and interest in social service.

Don was also highly impressionable, easily swayed, lacked any great sense or responsibility, had little perseverence and in general was pretty "copeless" in dealing with the real world. If things got rough . . Don would just give up.

His *least* interest, I saw, was money—money for its own sake, for what it could buy, even for security it might offer. (That was his father's province. In rejecting money, he could reject his father at the same time.) Of course, it must be remembered that part of this disregard for money may have been based on the fact that Don had never in his life had to worry about money, either. . . .

And, while he was in the father-rejecting business, he also found time to reject another of his father's interests: power.

His father was a policy-maker, an authority figure directing the activities of a considerable work force. He commanded those symbols which the world usually sees as the hallmark of the successful individual. So Don rejected them . . . motivated in part by his apparent disaffection for his father and also, I think, in part by his own understanding of his inability to handle himself intelligently or maturely—a perception leading logically to the implication that he couldn't handle others, either.

His strongest feelings (he said) were in the religious area.

He professed a strong belief in God (though he had no association with any organized or orthodox religious body) and it developed that he felt he somehow "communicated" with God on a distinctly personal basis.

He even voiced a rather tentative intention to become a recluse and to spend the remainder of his life attempting to come to grips with the true nature of life and the world through prayer and meditation. (This, I think, was a function in part of his basic desire to avoid further contact with people.)

And he was also very curious: Don wanted to know the relationship between effects and causes, to understand the essential "why" of what he observed around him. He was also reasonably compassionate, a hell of a good listener, and able easily to empathize with people when hearing their sad stories.

Finally, Don was methodical: he had a low degree of drive, coupled with an extreme degree of caution which kept him from doing things rapidly. (He could allow himself to take no chance of making errors; that might draw criticism . . . and he couldn't cope with criticism.)

And such was the picture developed by my evaluation.

Discussing the results with Don was far more difficult an undertaking than obtaining them in the first place. He was so suspicious I felt I had to be careful above all to make it clear that (a) my recommendations were the very best I could make and I truly believed in them and (b) that my motivation in making the recommendation was *not* my own financial welfare. (My services are based on a flat fee; even if he wanted to call and chat with me later, there would be no further charge. I think I got *that* much across, at least).

Another objective, setting the stage for what I wanted to recommend, was to get him to admit—to me and to himself—that he *did* have problems, and that he was *not* capable of coping with them himself.

That was a big point. For what I told him was that perhaps the best chance he had of finding himself and developing the best relationship with the real world was through professional psychological help. *Not* an industrial psychologist like myself who deals primarily with the *identification* of problems rather than their correction but with someone professionally trained in the area of personal problem-solving.

Don rejected the idea.

Several years previously, he explained, he had had several brief sessions with such a professional—and had found the whole experience unrewarding. I tried to argue that while this might have been true *at that time*, the failure might have been a lack of "personal chemistry" between him as an individual and that particular professional or because the timing was wrong.

No luck.

Or, at any rate, so I thought then. Only a month later, though, in talking to the associate who referred him to me, I discovered that Don had, indeed, entered therapy with a practitioner I knew to be extremely competent . . . and that, in contrast with Don's earlier experience, the relationship seemed to be positive, and building.

That was highly satisfactory to me, not only from a professional standpoint but from a personal one as well. I liked Don.

Had he been the more typical pre-adult coming to me for evaluation, I might have made recommendations aimed at (a) getting him into the right school (b) selecting a satisfactory major study (c) planning his life's work, etc. But all these problems seemed to me to pale into insignificance when compared with the basic one of bringing Don alive into the real world.

I still think so. . . .

An unusual case? A bizarre one? Not representative?

Far from it: Don's story has become all too familiar to those who deal with the Jungle Babies—and the fathers who work fourteen hours a day because, of course, they are "Doing it all for"—the kids. And these cases will multiply, will repeat themselves, generation after generation, unless we here and now begin to achieve some kind of understanding.

Are You *"Doing it All for "* Your Children?

Oh . . . *bull*! Add it all up again, friend—this time without the self-congratulation and rationalization. A gift given in the knowledge that it was not what the recipient wanted is no gift; it is a salve to the giver's conscience and a demand-note on the receiver. What do your children—and your wife—*really* want? Is it such a simple thing as just you? Just you, yourself, unadorned by the trappings of great success and power; just you . . . and the certainty that you are willing and able to give *of yourself* in their behalf? That gift is known in the vernacular as "love," and a wise old psychologist once told me, "You can get away with an awful lot, if you give love." If you're a man like Don's father, you've got to stop kidding yourself about who you're doing what for. Brother, you are doing it *for yourself*! You have a burning need for success and its trappings; you are working like hell—and depriving your family of you—in order to fill that need, which is sometimes well-nigh insatiable. You are rationalizing ("But I'm doing it all for *you* . . . !") because the guilt if you look too closely in the mirror is more than you can bear. Try admitting to yourself that this is true—and that your own values in life are not necessarily those of the people nearest you. And try not to reach that understanding too late . . . children need love while they are growing toward adulthood, not later. Deprive the child of this at key points, and the need probably can never be adequately compensated. You say you are *willing* to *sacrifice* to give your *family* the comforts of affluence? Really? Well . . . did you ever ask them if they *wanted* the sacrifice? Or was it, as the youngsters today put it, "just your own trip . . . ?"

Do You *Work for* a Man Who Says "But I'm Doing it All for . . ."

Well, if you work for him, you probably *can't* risk contradicting him, can't take the chance of calling him on the lie. Unless you're planning to leave the firm—and don't mind doing so on a poor basis. But if your relationship with him is a firm one, just perhaps you can take the tack of introducing the smallest kind of doubt. Play it easy; play it by ear. But if he's really a friend—or a Boss you really admire—it may be worth the risk And much the same would apply if he's your peer in business . . . or just a good friend.

Are *You* a Jungle Baby?

If anything in Don's case history seems to ring a bell with you—well, hopefully you know your own case better than anyone else. If you feel personally capable of dealing with your own problems, by yourself—hooray for you! If not, I think I'd make the same recommendation to you that I made to Don: professional help from a professional problem-solver. Failing that (as I say, you know your own case better than anyone) perhaps it just *might* be possible to talk the whole thing over—in direct and realistic terms—with your father. Make it a private talk; make it at a time (by appointment, if need be) when he is not glancing at his watch, worrying about arriving on time for an appointment. And make it just as soon as you can. And if none of the above prove possible, then I guess the only thing I can suggest to you is. . . .

. . . do your *own thing.*

Rejoice in all mornings. Celebrate all sunsets. Look deep into the night sky. Wiggle your toes. Wiggle your fingers. Join hands and kiss. Laugh. Sing. Weep. Struggle. Hope. Believe. Live.

And love.

That man is not just your father. That man is not an ogre. That man is not your enemy.

Love him.

Love your mother. Love your brothers. Love your sisters. Love yourself. If you cannot love, pity. If you cannot pity, then for God's sake *have mercy*!

That man is more than your father. He is a man. A human being. As confused and fearful and trapped and frustrated . . . and as lonely . . . as yourself.

9
The
Right Actor
in the
Wrong Play

There's an old story about John Barrymore, from the days when he was the darling of Broadway. It may be apocryphal—but that doesn't matter.

Returning from a 20-hour revel with a group of moonlit companions including Gene Fowler (which should give you a fair idea of Barrymore's condition) and two ladies of the evening, the Great Profile checked his watch and found he was in imminent danger of being late for the 8:30 curtain. Accordingly, he demanded his friends' assistance in donning his makeup while their taxicab was en route to the theater (the role, as luck would have it, called only for contemporary street clothing) and, on arrival, ran full-tilt down the alley, through the stage door and onto the stage where (he was appalled to note) the action was already in progress.

Entering, stage left, he delivered his first line in a sonorous voice and was gratified to hear a swell of applause. He was less gratified, however, as toward the end of the ovation he heard the beginning of guffaws—a beginning which in moments became a general roar of laughter.

A quick glance at the costumes of the other occupants of that stage finally clued Barrymore into the situation: he had, in his haste, given the taxi driver the address of the wrong theater—one where another of his plays had closed a few weeks before. The audience had perceived the situation and acted accordingly.

Heaven knows, Barrymore was the right actor. The applause had been for him.

But he was in the wrong play . . . hence, the laughter.

Barrymore bowed deeply. And exited.

The curtain was still waiting for him when he arrived, 15 minutes late, at the right theater. But the incident became a Lambs Club legend before the night was over.

Unhappily, not all such situations end in laughter.

Trekking through the Executive Jungle with gun and camera* we come occasionally upon a denizen who is clearly misplaced. A giraffe, for instance, trying to hunt with a herd of elk; a hippopotamus functioning with rather limited success in a pride of lions, or a fox trying to boss a pack of hounds, are situations which might be analogous.

Their failure in such a milieu can hardly be charged to ineptitude on the part of the misplaced denizen.

They are capable individuals, in the main, but through

---

*I do like to keep my analogies straight—but I have always believed this particular phrase (encountered in numberless adventure books when I was young enough to be impressed by Frank Buck) needs a bit of amplification when speaking of the more specialized milieu of the Executive Jungle. Here, I truly think the phrase should be " . . . with gun, camera—and net." Oh, well.

circumstances of one kind or another they find themselves in an industrial setting which is simply unsuited to their talents, interests and abilities. Usually the sorry script develops something like this:

The prior success of an executive in a setting to which he is well suited makes available to him a number of opportunities for promotion or for lateral movement to higher-echelon jobs in other firms. Usually, the opportunities thus presented are jobs he can handle.

But sometimes—especially if the man lacks sufficient self-knowledge and objectivity about his own abilities, or has fallen victim to the all-too-common error of deciding his past success indicates that he can be all things in all situations—he accepts a job to which he is, in one degree or another, unsuited.

At first, he will find himself working enthusiastically and with characteristic new-broom success in the new position.

But as time passes, little things begin to crop up one by one and, day by day, everything seems to become more difficult—each new problem less and less soluble.

And he can't understand why. . . .

A particularly sad case in point is one I remember as

Orville, the Right Actor in the Wrong Play

I met him in the usual way; he was presented along with a number of other executives employed by a client firm, for evaluation with an eye to long-term growth potential.

It quickly developed that he was what I would call a born salesman.

Orville was forty, married for twenty years, father of four children. His mother had died when he was in his twenties; his father lived in a convalescent home. His present personal life seemed stable.

He was the youngest of a large family, was educated in the Midwest and had once considered a legal career, but finally took a degree in public administration at a midwestern university where (I was not at all surprised to learn) he had been highly active both in athletics and other extracurricular activities including campus politics and editorship of the school newspaper.

The job market was poor when he graduated, so Orville worked for a brief time for a local utility firm, then moved into the manufacturing field as a coordinator, being promoted to salesman within 18 months. In this setting, he performed admirably.

Orville's next few jobs were as general manager of a number of fabricating companies (he received a modest base pay, but his main income was derived from his percentage of the companies' sales.)

When he came to me for evaluation, he had been employed by my client for more than five years and presently headed the firm's marketing operations in the southeastern seaboard area as well as serving in a second capacity as manager of the company's modest assembly plant there. (This production capacity should not be overemphasized; it was a small plant and most of the items Orville was selling came from the home office; the satellite assembly operation was a convenience at best, really.)

In testing I found Orville to be a man of superior intelligence with outstanding capabilities in verbal or written expression, a free flow of language, acceptable vocabulary and verbal reasoning ability and sound nonverbal abilities as well. In general, it could be said that these abilities compared quite favorably with executives functioning successfully in the upper middle management level.

His highest occupational interests seemed centered around

his desire to sell—both ideas and tangibles—and his high interest in persuading others to his point of view fitted well, too. There was also a strong interest in literary effort (a good thing; he was responsible for all communications and report writing from his modest division) plus an appreciation for administrative effort far above that found in most managers.

His least interest was in the area of aesthetics* (art and music).

From the standpoint of personality, he was vigorous, driving and energetic, a man demanding variety and challenge in all that he did, with an interest in getting things done quickly. He was bold and aggressive in dealing with others (he could, unfortunately, be rather abrasive and overbearing, too, on occasion) and seemed motivated strongly to "be his own boss," to run his own show and be second-guessed by no one. This was a man who wanted to *win*!

In fact, his competitive instinct, while sometimes rather tactlessly expressed, was quite acceptable for his industrial milieu—which closely resembled catalogue sales. That is, Orville was basically a nuts-and-bolts salesman, selling items similar in kind and specification to those sold by his competitors. In this configuration, his tremendous drive and need to win were a high asset. It might also be noted that he showed considerable ability as a "ramrodder" of other regional marketing people who were reporting to him.

He was, additionally, a gambler: he was willing to take chances, had the ability to "read" others pretty well, and was a fine strategist in the sales field. Therefore, he and his sales people accounted for far more than their share of the firm's total sales.

But now we come to the sticking-point. . . .

---

*"The hell with that noise" was the way he put it.

Certain long-range plans of my client called for turning Orville's assembly-and-marketing operation into a ware-housing setup. The plan left Orville with some justifiable doubts about his own future with the company.

After evaluation, I recommended that he be retained as the firm's regional marketing executive in the Southeast (my client was already hiring new sales personnel for new territories there; the scope of marketing was expanding). It seemed to me he could do a fine job of ramrodding the sales crew, expanding volume, and that in such a position he could be of maximum service to himself and to the company.

Unhappily, for reasons I still don't fully understand, the company decided to bring Orville to its midwestern corporate center as assistant to the corporate vice-president for marketing. And that meant trouble, because—far from being his own boss—Orville now was working immediately under the vice-president (a hell of a salesman in his own right) and besides, this was basically a staff position and that was entirely alien to Orville's personality. He was the type to take the reins into his own hands, not to serve as consultant or counselor. And he could not stand second guessing. He was unhappy.

But he did not act impulsively,* managed to function at an acceptable level (though nowhere near his actual peak) for a few months—at which point the company made a second, and far more serious, error.

Orville was made director of quality control for the firm.

God knows, the firm's engineering sophistication was relatively low; nuts and bolts type operations don't usually

---

*That is, he did not actually assault anyone, and kept the criticism confined to words that were, more or less, printable.

require a high level of sophistication. Still, it *was* engineering, and quality control was an area of expertise entirely outside Orville's scope of training or education. More damning, a former department head had been promoted to general manager—and that worthy accordingly found himself not only trying to handle the reins of the whole division but having to make most of Orville's decisions for him.

I was shocked when I heard of this new placement, and made my feelings known—directly, but as tactfully as possible under the circumstances—to the new general manager.

But the die had been cast, so far as the company was concerned. For Orville, it was sink or swim.

He sank.

A few months after he moved into his new job, it became painfully obvious to all that he just couldn't hack it. The general manager discussed the situation amicably with Orville . . . and suggested he find another job, outside the company.

Result: a dead loss for all concerned.

The saddest part of the whole story, of course, is that Orville, while a rather uncomfortable person to be around socially because of his competitive and overbearing personality, had been a highly competent marketing executive. You don't have to "go to bed with" your work associates; you need not have them as friends outside the office—the only thing that really matters in the end is whether or not they can produce, and he *had* . . . as a salesman.

The company seems to have erroneously assumed that (a) a man who functions well in one job can function just as well in another (a fact by no means in evidence) and (b) that social graces can be equated with productivity.

Both parties lost—heavily—as the result of two very bad decisions; errors which could have been avoided by a clear appreciation of Orville's basic abilities and orientation.

Does the Right Actor in the Wrong Play *Work for You*?

Well someone—maybe not you, but *someone*—has made a serious error; one that can be damaging to the company and to the Right Actor. The guy must have functioned well in some capacity, or he wouldn't have been promoted . . . so what was his last job where he had a high degree of success? What were that job's requirements? What are the new job's specifications? If they don't coincide, the error's obvious. If they coincide in some points, miss in others, (provided they are not necessary conditions) chances are the coincidental items are just that—coincidence. Maybe the thing that made him good in the old job was something the new position lacks. If you can't figure it out for yourself, get professional help. If the man has been "forced" upon you by higher authority, and you had no immediate recourse, better let him do his best to function in the new job; if he makes it, well and good. If not—sit down and talk the whole thing over with him. Chances are he's just as unhappy with the situation as you are (though there's a chance he won't be able to admit it, due to considerations of status, prestige, income, etc.). Suggest he discuss the matter further (help him do it if needful) with the higher authority that miscast him in his present role. Help him, if no other appropriate position can be found inside the company, to get another job elsewhere—one more consonant with his talents. Be very sure that, if you don't (if the axe descends with the suddenness and finality it did in Orville's case) the sense of injustice the man will certainly feel must prompt him in the future to badmouth your company, to do it damage when he can*—and, as luck may determine, the day may come when the amount of damage he can do might be considerable! You *owe* this man something; the error was yours. Not his. . . .

Do You *Work with* the Right Actor in the Wrong Play?

If you can communicate with the man on a meaningful level concerning his obvious problems, well and good. Maybe an accommodation can be reached, at least on a temporarily effective basis, which will permit him to move gracefully back into the area of his own competence. If not, or if such communication is impossible, there's not much you can do except shut up—unless this guy's ineptitude impinges on your own area of responsibility. If the latter is true, then you've got to discuss the problem with your mutual boss. Chances are, the noise you make won't have to be a loud one. The situation will simply cry out for correction before much time has passed.

Do You *Work for* the Right Actor in the Wrong Play?

Well, then—loyalty (and channels) notwithstanding—you're going to have to go to the next higher level of authority to get most of the answers you need to do your job, especially if the work is of a technical nature. If you have no such option (if, God forbid, the guy *is* at the top level!) the situation is going to get damn frustrating before it gets any better. Don't act impulsively; don't act rashly. Wait it out if you can, in the hope that higher authority or the man himself will take corrective action. And if this hope proves hollow . . . well . . .

---

*Depend on it—he will go for the throat. Mess with a competitive type like Orville, and you've got a real problem. He makes a useful ally in sales; a deadly enemy otherwise.

there's always the old résumé to be dusted off and quietly shopped around the industry.

Are *You* the Right Actor in the Wrong Play?

Don't waste time agonizing about self-identification here. You know—in your guts—whether you are or not, regardless of what your own boss or associates may be saying. Chances are you've known it, really, since the day you sat down in the new office. Well, hell: it isn't the end of the world! Is there another opportunity, in the same company, that's more in your line? What are you *really* best at; where do your main interests lie; what's your strongest area of training, your most effective area of function? Staying too long in any situation for which you are not really suited can be terribly, terribly demoralizing. Even if there *is no* opening really suited to you within the company, the moment you are sure the one you have is "the wrong play" is the time to go to the Boss and say: "Look . . . I'm just not right in this job; it's working to everyone's disadvantage and it's got to get worse. Put me in (whatever field you handle best)." You should take such a shift—even if it meant a reduction in pay and prestige— because it is just about the only way you can maintain your dignity and self-esteem. Of course, if such a shift is impossible for one reason or another and if there seems to be no such opportunity within the company, especially if what you're looking for is growth . . . then it is time to go shopping outside for a new position. And this time, make damn certain it's the kind of thing you like and do best.

Delivering a line from Noel Coward in the middle of a Shakespeare scene is something only a Barrymore could bring off with any kind of flourish. . . .

10
Mama's in the Business Too

As in most wild areas of the world, denizens of the Executive Jungle usually have mates.

The true loners are a rare exception.

Hence, when an executive is selected by a company to fill a key position in management, whoever recruits him usually tries to find out just as much as he can about the executive's family. Especially his wife . . . for she's the most important single member of that family (except for the man himself) so far as the company is concerned.

The stability of the marriage, for instance, has a great deal to do with how stable (and effective) the prospective employee can be expected to be in his new job. A man in the throes of divorce is only in infrequent cases capable of putting forth his best effort. And a man with a nagging, or overdemanding—or even totally disinterested—wife may not be able to give his total concentration to the work at hand.

Even wives of what might be called the "optimum" type (respectful and aware of their husbands' career-demands; willing and able to bear a certain amount of social activity related to the job; sufficiently mature and self-confident to be able to trust the husband around attractive secretaries and female executives; willing to "keep the dinner hot" when he's unexpectedly late coming home; prepared to accept sudden travel demands, etc.) bear a bit of concern from the company's point of view. For the fact is that in hiring the man, you hire the whole family.

And in some cases, even the best-intentioned and knowledgeable of wives can constitute a hazard . . . sometimes for what might at first glance seem highly unlikely reasons.

A case that comes immediately to mind is that of a couple we will call

Sam and Stella

They were, to all appearances, a happy pair—especially since the company Sam headed had been their joint project almost from the day it opened its doors.

Sam was a bright and rather inventive engineer, highly motivated in the direction of personal success and willing to devote considerable time and energy to achieving it. After obtaining a good deal of practical and technical experience in one specific field, he decided to open a company of his own. And that wasn't too easy, since he had at the time very little in the way of financial resources to go on.*

---

*"Shoestring" was the word I was going to use. But I restrained the urge. Actually the situation was a little better than that. "Bootstrap" would be more like it, I think; or "arch support," perhaps. Something like that, anyway.

Nonetheless, he was an active and confident guy. So he dug into the work . . . with Stella digging right alongside him. Things were tough in the beginning. Stella served as Sam's bookkeeper, office manager, Girl Friday (and sometimes filled a post on the little assembly line as well) in order to conserve their capital. They worked 10- and 14-hour days in the beginning. But as happens more often than not, the work brought them together more than it tore them apart; it was a plus rather than a minus so far as the marriage itself was concerned—even though Stella's role was somewhat complicated by the fact that they had children who were an additional responsibility.

The fact is that, working alongside her husband, Stella never had the slightest reason to doubt that she was needed, appreciated, valued . . . and loved. Those days may well have been the happiest of her life.

But, because of the family, it was implicit from the start that there had to be a limit; Stella was only to continue her highly demanding schedule of working mother until the company was on its feet and Sam was able to hire people to take over the variety of jobs she was now performing in addition to her household duties.

That day came just a bit sooner than could have been predicted.

A larger firm, recognizing the potential Sam could bring to its overall effort and anxious to assure itself of a continued supply of the Gizzmo Sam's company was turning out, wisely invested in the smaller firm (in return for a percentage of Sam's equity) and, in a brief time, Sam's company was really away and running. It was "over the hump" financially and in most other ways. Stella was no longer required to be (as she actually had been at times) half the plant's "work force."

At that point, of couse, it was obvious to one and all that

Stella's place again was in the home. She returned thither with apparent rejoicing.

But . . . appearances can be deceiving.

The fact is that Stella could *not* divorce herself entirely from the company and its day to day activities. She was, not surprisingly, deeply interested—and exceptionally well informed—about the business. And her particular concern seemed to be centered in the area of personnel.

Especially *female* personnel.

The time came when Sam was faced with the problem of replacing a bookkeeper, who had departed for a higher-paying job. The candidates were three . . . and all female. And it was at that point that Stella took a firm hand.

One of the candidates was a woman of mature years, moderately rigid in her thought patterns, quite obviously suffering from the primary effects of the infirmities of age—and not especially experienced in the bookkeeping field (she had held a tangential job; her actual bookkeeping experience was several years behind her.)

Another candidate was a young girl, only a few years out of high school, possessing limited experience as a bookkeeper and pretty plainly uninterested in any job tenure longer than the period required to find a husband.

The third candidate, on the other hand, seemed at first glance ideal. She was a woman in her thirties, possessing considerable experience as a bookkeeper, a stable past job history and an obvious intention to find a job she could hold for a considerable length of time. She was, however, uncommonly attractive in a strictly feminine way, and a divorcée with three children.

Sam, not surprisingly, favored this third candidate.

Stella, also not surprisingly, raised hell.

It was obvious (to everyone but Stella, perhaps) that her opposition to the third candidate was based on something quite different from professional reasons. Stella felt "threatened" by this woman; threatened in a way she would not have been had the woman been married. She felt intimidated by her attractiveness and apparent availability (more apparent than real; the woman was for good and sufficient reason not particularly anxious to enter into another marriage). Indeed, Stella considered *all* divorcées a threat to the marriage contract—and made no especial secret of her feelings.

In fact, she made several far-from-indirect threats to Sam himself if he even considered such an applicant.

Result: the elderly woman was hired.

Further result: her work was substandard, her job tenure was brief (those symptoms of aging were more advanced than anyone had anticipated) and in the end the whole business of recruiting a replacement had to be done over.

Still further result: Stella had produced a strain in the fabric of her marriage to Sam; a strain which need not have arisen, and which was the precise opposite of what she had been—in her own mind—attempting to avoid.

Why the opposition to the divorcée?

What was she really saying to Sam? Could it have been something like, "I don't trust you around an attractive woman, Sam . . . because I don't trust myself?" And is it just possible that a bright and sensitive guy like Sam would understand this implicit statement, at least on a subconscious level?

Hardly a representative case, you will say.*

Still—it illustrates the extreme manner in which a wife, for reasons not directly connected with the business itself—may influence her husband's performance of his work.

---

*And I will say, too!

Wives of executives fall into several categories . . . and not all of them are negative, at least from the viewpoint of the firm that hires their husbands.

There is, for instance, the wife whose influence upon her husband is what I'd call the "supportive" type. She's no driver. But when the Old Man is wavering a bit, undecided whether to take a cut at something difficult (say it's the degree he needs to become qualified, or the next highest job on the executive ladder where the winds blow colder while the options get fatter) she manages to communicate the fact that she has *his* best interest at heart. She will encourage, she will soothe any fears he has, quiet the doubts; she is ready to move at a few weeks' notice, to aid when necessary and shut up when that's what's needed.

She is, in fact, one hell of a woman.

And then—there are the drivers. Support is not her bag, but she frequently "contributes" to the career of a successful executive by the simple process of making almost impossible demands. Her position "requires" a Rolls-Bentley; she couldn't "be seen dead" in a last-season's mink; they simply "must" move to a more fashionable part of town; the children "must" go to an expensive private academy, etc. And when all these ploys seem to lose their snap—there's always the final one: sex. Some of these ladies withhold it when, in their opinion, their husbands are not performing properly in the Jungle.

Another kind of driver, another type of demanding woman, can actually drive a fairly competent man into failure. She's the one who pays no attention whatsoever to her husband's actual potential and constantly demands that he perform and achieve on a level which is in fact beyond his best efforts. When he fails to reach the high goal she—not he—has set, the effect upon him is tremendously debilitating, creating a feeling of inadequacy which may well leave him unable to perform even to that degree of which he is basically capable.

Then, too, there is the "homebody." She is all-too-frequently married to a man whose job requires some specific activity on the part of his wife; she must accompany him to parties, to social functions of various kinds, sometimes must entertain business associates in their home. And she "don't wanta." She doesn't want to be involved in that kind of thing, she really doesn't care whether he makes $100,000 a year or $10,000—she wouldn't spend much more than she does right now if his salary were a million, because the whole thing would make her uncomfortable. A driving, ambitious executive married to such a woman is really in trouble because, say what you will, you really want a little pat on the head when you come back from a successful foray at Jabber-wock-slaying.

And there is the Clinging Vine. She's the one who is practically in tears every morning when her husband leaves for work; she's going to be "so lonely" all day . . . and, God help us all, this dame *isn't kidding*! She really *will* be! She has no outside area of interest, is at a loss to deal with the children without constant and close support from her husband, and will literally fall apart at the seams if anything at all goes wrong. She's the one whose telephone call interrupts a crucial sales meeting as she tells him, "You've *got* to come home right this *minute*! Junior has a temperature of 99.9!"*

The same woman, by the way, is Bad News when her

---

*There's a rumor that one executive whose helpmeet made such a call did in fact rush out of the meeting. Just what happened after he got home, no one seems to know. His son is all right; goes to school every day and seems in perfect health. The wife, on the other hand, hasn't been seen around for quite a while and there has been some flak about the new rosebed he planted in the backyard recently. I don't take any stock in rumors like that, though. Well . . . not *much*, anyway.

husband has a job where he needs to travel extensively, or on an irregular schedule. Knowing she's liable to let the house burn down if he's not there to tell her to phone the fire department is not going to make him more effective when he meets customers 1,000 miles from home. . . .

And then there's the Sweet Lady who finds it convenient to "drop in" on her spouse at the office because she was "in the neighborhood," or "downtown, shopping," and thought he might like to have lunch with her. Her visits are unannounced. And everyone in the office knows why she's there—she wants to size up the situation at the office, check the personnel for possible competition and generally "keep an eye" on everything. The general effect (a correct one, more often than not) is that she does not trust the Boss, the other people at his office . . . or herself.

Situations such as the one described in the story of Sam and Stella are, of course, dangerous from the word go. A wife who is presently, or was in the past, actively engaged in some part of her husband's business affairs inevitably becomes pretty well known to a lot of people throughout the firm— and any one of them (given a certain cast of character) is therefore in a position to attempt to further his own strength and strategic capability by currying favor with her. Everyone has an Achilles heel of some sort; with such a woman it may be her vanity, her loneliness, her avocational interest—whatever seems the best target of opportunity—and a skilled tactician unencumbered by a sense of ethics will find some way to take advantage of it.

There are, besides, a few wives (very few, comparatively speaking, for which thank God!) who actually, with malice aforethought, attempt to deter the progress of their husbands in the business world. They do this, usually, because of a real dislike—even hatred—of their mates which is strong enough to overcome their own instinct toward self-preservation.

And now and then you even find a wife who, apparently because of a rather low opinion of her husband's judgment or executive ability, will impose her own influence and her own decisions upon her husband . . . in situations where he, and he alone, should be choosing between alternatives. Even if the guy really *is* something less than brilliant, a situation like this is destructive as hell. And when the man really does have ability, but is forced by one pressure or another to defer to her will, it can end in nothing but disaster.

One further point:

While reality is and ought to be the standard of evaluation used in estimating an executive's chances of performing well in a given position, reality is not the *only* criterion to be applied to the executive's wife. Equally important—perhaps even more important, in a way—is the executive's *perception* of his mate; the kind of person he believes her to be.

She can be a bitch from bitchville . . . but if he thinks she's the greatest thing since sliced bread, it's worth taking into consideration; he's going to react to her on the basis of his own perception, not on the basis of objective reality.*

She can be a real angel, the *optimum wife* we mentioned above. But if he views her as the devil's grandmother, you've got to keep that fact in mind when you estimate the kind of influence she will have on his effectiveness.

Also, you've got to be more than a little careful in taking the man's statements concerning his wife too literally.

There *are* men who (a) find it necessary, for ego reasons, to tell the world their wives are paragons of every virtue— queens, whom they worship and serve with joy—when the truth is that the dame is one of the more devastating pains in

---

*Show me a guy who can be entirely objective about his wife, and I will show you a real nut.

the arse, or (b) regale friends and associates with tales of the woes and wounds imposed upon them by the shrews to whom they are wed, when the truth is that the stories are false, invented from whole cloth by men who are so happy in their marital lives that they actually feel shy about admitting the fact in public.

A sensitive ear for nuances is not only helpful in giving true weight to the husband's own perception of his wife—it is an absolute *necessity*!

And then there's the case of Rodman & Spouse. . . .

Oh, yes, I am well and truly married—and so is my wife. Believe me, the kind of strains imposed upon a marital relationship by the nature of my work could easily have been destructive on a total basis, if we were different people.

Thank God, we are not. That, of course, is pure good fortune—but in order to take full advantage of it, we were careful years ago to define the terms of our cooperation in marriage in the peace and quiet of non-emotional patterns. We each know the precise extent of our own domains and responsibilities.

And when one or the other seems to be—or is—imposing upon the relationship or venturing into the wrong areas, it is not necessary to express irritation with some phrase like: "God damn it, mind your own business!"

There's another set of words. We came across it years ago in an article we read . . . and it's been a part of our lives ever since.

"Honey: that's *my* side of the apple."

Apple? Yes, apple. The apple is our marriage, our friendship, our parenthood, our mutual responsibility functions. Each of us have our own side, and we know which is which.

You, my friend, should have it so good. . . .

Is Mama in *Your* Business?

The first question, of course, is to discover whether her influence is a negative one, or positive. And if, as happens, it's a little bit both ways . . . isn't there some way, some time, when you can discuss the matter with her, without "benefit" of emotion. I don't care how strained—or how happy—your relationship with Mama may be; the discussion *must* not be triggered, or surrounded, by emotional stress. You know the context of your relationship better than anyone; isn't there a time of day or a point in the week when, for a while at least, the emotional responses are at a minimum? Talk it over with her then . . . and *not*, for Pete's sake, on any basis of remonstrance or criticism. Lay the facts out, and *listen* (with as much sensitivity as you possess) to her own evaluation of the circumstances and her actions. It is possible, of course, that Mama doesn't really *want* to improve the situation; that she's enjoying it, finds it a satisfactory and successful approach to living her life. If so, then the problem may very well be insoluble and you have a choice between adjusting to it, seeking professional counsel . . . or visiting a lawyer, if the whole thing is *really* intolerable. Note the stress on "really." Before you go flying off to court, back off and take an even strain for a moment. Make sure "really" applies; that you're taking a step that will be satisfactory to you—not just one you think you "ought" to take. And, above all, keep emotion as much in the background as possible. Decisions made in anger or the depths of frustration are rarely valid ones.

Does One of Your *Subordinates* Have Mama Problems?

Then you have a decision to make: if it's not affecting his work too adversely, or damaging office morale in one way or another, the wisest and most effective course may be to keep your nose strictly out of it. You didn't take this man to raise;

you're not responsible for his success or failure in his personal life. And meddling in a marital relationship can be a terribly sticky business. If, however, the marital situation is in some way interfering with normal operation of your company, then the matter becomes your business on a very real basis . . . and the time to act is as soon after you have perceived and evaluated the problem as possible. Talk to them both, if you can; private conversations with either are usually subject to "editing" when related to the marital partner. Discuss the problem frankly and objectively, not in a tone of chiding or criticizing, but on the basis of responsible adults dealing with a very adult kind of problem. Do your best. And when you're done—leave the two of them to work the matter out, the best way they can. It's their business to handle that end of it. Your end of the bargain is to see what effect this has on solving the problem itself. If the situation is really improved, well and good. If not, and if the trouble is serious enough—well—maybe it's time to see about recruiting a replacement for this man . . . and Mama, too.

Are *You* Mama?

You're the only one who can really answer. If your husband is an executive, and ambitious, you are in a better position to help or hinder than anyone else in the world. But "help" means different things to different people. Your husband may need your aid, here and now, in the office itself the way Sam needed Stella. But when the day comes that this aid is no longer needed in that specific area—try to keep in mind that this is *not* rejection. Your "Sam" is displaying for your applause the prize he has won; telling you that you have helped make such a success of the work that now he can afford to give you the leisure and comfort he wanted to all along. *Accept it in that light*. And if your relationship to his business life is a different kind . . . see if you can spell out, for your own private information, the exact nature and responsibilities of that relationship. Then be careful. Pay attention to your *own* side of the apple; let him handle his like the responsible and loving man he is. Support him. Trust him. Love him. His future is in your hands . . . and so is your own.

11
Steady as She Goes...!

Not all the more successful denizens of the Executive Jungle attain their positions of power and affluence through application of the customary virtues of decisiveness, tough mindedness and leadership ability.

A calm, unflappable personality and the ability to inspire confidence can also produce entirely satisfactory results*— but only under certain circumstances. The situation in which such an executive succeeds requires (a) an established product-line in the field where progress and innovation are held to a minimum, and (b) the existence in a position just superior to his own of a "patron saint" or "big daddy" chief whose umbrella is wide enough for a subordinate.

---

*It can also produce a certain amount of rage on the part of stock-holders, especially on those occasions when they have to watch such a man express confident calm while testifying in a bankruptcy action.

Such denizens have their place in the Executive Jungle. And their course through the world is readily traceable by the oft-repeated and distinctive sound-pattern common to the species. I heard it loud and clear, for instance, when I was called to evaluate an executive we will call Mike. His voice rang sharp and true:

"Steady as She Goes . . . !"

He was in his early fifties when we met; happily married for almost thirty years and sire of a brood of eight children, in good health, and candidate for the senior vice-presidency of a client company. Mike was, above all, a very easy guy to like.

In assembling his personal background, I learned he had been the eldest of five children born in the metropolitan South. His father was a successful manager at the local telephone company, a permissive and hardworking man with a warm and even temperament; his mother was more artistically inclined but spending primary effort on her home, her children and the general support and nurture of her husband.

Mike was, by the way, singularly fortunate in having parents of such a stable and substantial type; it was obvious that he was trying his very best to emulate them both. . . .

In college, he had elected an engineering course. At first, his choice was aeronautical engineering. But this proved peculiarly difficult and he switched soon enough to electrical engineering. This specialty, it should be noted, was a far different thing in those days; there was no real sophistication (electronics, as such, was simply *not included* in the curriculum!) and he selected what was known as the "power option," a study concerned principally with power generation and transmission—the kind of expertise needed by public utilities. It is a relatively elementary variety of engineering, and one in which there is very little innovation.

Here, too, it might be noted that Mike's completion of the course was due in large part to the supportive and persuasive abilities of his wife; even such an elementary course proved peculiarly difficult for him, and he obtained his degree with a ranking far below the top of his class. He willingly admitted in later years that he "just wouldn't have made it" had it not been for her. *

Mike was drafted after graduation, spent three years in the service, and on discharge went to work almost immediately for a large and well-known electrical equipment manufacturer where he spent the next nine years as a junior executive of steadily increasing responsibilities and the following three as general manager of two different divisional entities.

And it was here that he encountered another bit of luck.

He formed a warm and productive relationship with one of his superiors in the firm, a highly regarded and influential executive whom we will call Henry. Their personalities were compatible; their admiration and loyalty mutual; and it is hardly necessary to add that in both the senior posts Mike held during his final three years with that company he was reporting directly to Henry.

(In discussing this time in his career, Mike chuckled happily about these two assignments. He commented with satisfaction that he was "lucky" in not having been faced in either case with the marketing and engineering problems

---

*"Luck" should have been Mike's middle name—he had it, in positively vulgar quantities, where people close to him were concerned. Parents, wife, etc. In a way, it's kind of a pity he wasn't born rich. He could have handled such a life rather successfully, I think. And that, if you read the newspapers carefully, is not at all as easy as it might sound. . . .

which confronted most of the firm's general managers; his divisions were concerned mainly with fabrication and assembly. . . .)

This phase of Mike's career ended abruptly when Henry suddenly moved to another firm—a well-known conglomerate. And he took Mike with him.

This was a break, again, because his immediate assignment was in the Far East (where he stayed for about six years) and his poise, charm, honesty and integrity (as opposed to the stereotype of the hard-driving and hard-driven, nail-chewing American executive) won him easy acceptance. Then the conglomerate promoted Mike to head a recently acquired company in the Midwest.

This acquisition was of substantial size. It held a well-known and dominant position in a highly competitive field. But there was nothing wrong with the firm internally (it was stable and well able to maintain its position and profitability) and Mike's three-year tenure there was characterized by an actual increase in profits.

And then came the promotion to group vice-president.

This might be called the watershed, or Great Divide, in Mike's executive career. It occurred while he still stood under the umbrella of Henry, his patron, and was a real venture into the thin-air reaches of the company—a distinct vote-of-confidence for him. But it was followed by two very serious developments:

First, Mike's umbrella moved out of reach. Henry left the firm and, in effect, set Mike adrift for the first time under no helm-orders but his own.

And second, the business itself took a distinct turn for the worse—not, I must emphasize, in response to Henry's action or to any misstep of Mike's, but because of a national downturn of business conditions—which put Mike very much on his mettle to handle the developing situation.

It was a time when stringent measures (even outright sonofabitchery) were very much in order; to steer his group through the rough times ahead, a firm and sure hand was needed.

Mike just couldn't hack it.

He could react quickly to a situation, but he couldn't make a decision and ram it through against opposition. He lacked tough-mindedness. He lagged in action and timing. He resisted the urgings—and, at length, even the outright demands—of his new superior for action. He just wasn't that kind of man.

So the situation finally became intolerable.*

Mike left the conglomerate . . . and forthwith did what can only be called a very foolish thing. He accepted a post as chief executive and board chairman of a smaller firm in a tangential product line, taking a considerable cut in salary in return for a big block stock option—gambling on a tremendous one-shot killing.

(He was motivated, I think, quite honestly; he really thought he could turn a losing company into a winner. And if he did so, the stock option would possess tremendous value. I think, too, he saw this as an opportunity to leave the dog-eat-dog atmosphere of rough competition forever; if he could make a seven figure number from this deal, he could be independent of everything and everyone in industry, once and for all.)

And all might have been well, had he been a different man.

The trouble was that Mike had failed to appreciate the definite pattern that had emerged in his last position; demands for a tough and self-disciplined approach to problems

---

*For Mike and his boss in almost equal degree. The boss's back was against the wall; he had to have real performance from Mike and Mike's alternatives were no less restricted. He could take strong, decisive action—or his departure. And he could *not* take strong, decisive action.

were, if anything, more stringent in the new job—perhaps because the organization was of smaller size—and, in the end, it was clear to one and all that Mike was not able to "turn the company around" as had been hoped. Three years after he came to the firm, the board asked for his resignation.

But his reputation as an executive, amazingly, seemed relatively untarnished. Ejected from the smaller company, Mike found himself the recipient of a number of tentative job offers . . . one of which came from my client firm.

Which is how I happened to meet him, and make my evaluation.

In testing Mike, I found him to be (on a basis of general intellect as divorced from specific qualities—one of the brightest individuals I'd met in some time; he literally "blew the top" off most of the test scores, placing within the top two percent of intellect and, even in comparison with his own peer group in industry, placing very, very high.

He had high verbal skills (especially logical word formation, drawing sound conclusions on the basis of data given and on *no more* than data given) and his knowledge of word meaning was extremely high for an executive.

But here we find a paradox: he had trouble expressing himself in a free flow of language when the structure was loose and the rules non-rigid. He did well enough, however, in tightly defined conversational situations, speaking calmly, with self-confidence and composure.

His nonverbal ability, too, was exceptionally sound, particularly when dealing not only with numbers but with symbols and other abstract data to arrive at logical conclusions; he handled details with speed and accuracy—but performed at only a mediocre level in a test for creativity, the ability to solve problems in an unorthodox or unusual way.

(These results, please note, reflect an interesting light on his academic attainment; that engineering school where Mike graduated was pretty mediocre—yet a man with his apparent learning potential had not been an exceptional student in even such a relatively undemanding milieu.)

So far as interests were concerned, Mike showed a high preference for art and for music (probably a legacy from his mother, who apparently encouraged him in this respect) but, while he had a good understanding of language, I doubt he could have met a really challenging situation in which writing was a factor—he simply hadn't that kind of fluency, unless the subject had been highly technical and specific.

Like most marketers and many executives, Mike had a strong interest in convincing others to his point of view; liked selling things, liked selling himself, liked selling ideas. He liked the outdoors, working with his hands, but was less interested in working with details of a repetitive type. He was interested in working with quantitative data . . . but it was still a low-level interest, for Mike.*

It's also interesting to note that he placed very, very low in the area of scientific interest (though he was supposedly an engineer!) but placed above the norm for executives in social service—being of assistance to others.

As a personality, I'd call Mike a pretty straightforward sort.

He was exceptionally capable in dealing with factual data, and of course possessed the high quality of intellect needed to handle such work. He was also a very positive individual—

---

*That was the peculiar part of the whole evaluation: this guy was an all-around high-potential type who simply had not performed in the exceptional manner which could logically have been expected, because of one or two defects which might have been called relatively minor. Like a space capsule forced to abort its mission because a single solenoid fails to function. *Chilling*!

an optimist, and therefore usually pleasant to have around even when he's not terribly realistic. To be blunt, this guy was Pollyanna in trousers.

And it was this trait, I think, which caused him in many cases to evaluate people poorly; his tendency was to take them at their word, to think the best of them, to evaluate their motives in that optimistic way. And not all people in this world are bright, conscientious and hard working; it is foolish to assume such qualities in everyone ... but Mike simply lacked the awareness to do otherwise. And for this reason, he frequently delegated authority to persons who could in no way justify the obvious faith he had in them.

Such a person is, obviously, highly vulnerable to the machinations of outright bastards, incompetents and/or loafers.*

He also lacked the ability to envision future developments. He could *not* project from present data inputs the probable course of industry and life-styles five, ten or fifteen years into the future. He was strictly a here-and-now guy. Couple this with his open-mindedness and Mike could easily be swayed by someone who could show he had a real argument—and he was a true babe in the woods with regard to attitudes, motivations and the nuances of interpersonal relationships.

He was a team-oriented kind of player, tenacious in striving toward short-range goals when he had made a factual decision, and able to stick with a decision reached in concert with a superior, however, his tendency to gallop off on tangents was something that cropped up only when the program involved long-range goals, five-year plans, etc.

His own interest, at this point, seemed centered on having an opportunity to help formulate policy—and to hold a title

---

*Strong words. But ... how on earth *can* you describe the sort of person who can take advantage of a guy like this?

which would command respect. (When you're the Chief Executive officer, remember, you need not be as forceful or aggressive as the man who operates as a first-line supervisor! And this is not only because you're dealing with a different level of people, but also because of the prestige of that title.)

In summary: Mike worked well as long as Big Daddy was on the scene; but when Big Daddy was gone there was no such relationship on which he could depend and his new boss just didn't have an umbrella to lend—while Mike couldn't function without one, and couldn't devise one of his own.

We talked about his future plans; I did my best to encourage him to accept an alternative position to the one offered by my client (no umbrella there!), especially one in the very stable industry where he had won his first laurels.

At least, I *was* able to influence him to the degree that he rejected the offer made by my client . . . which would have worked out no better for him than his last two positions had done. . . .

Do You *Have an Employee* Whose Cry Is "Steady as She Goes . . ."?

Then make sure your orders are precise, and that he adheres strictly to them. This guy can be effective in certain specific roles. When it is possible to work out a short-range program, working together with him for a specific goal, he can really do one hell of a job—and, chances are, he'll be one of the best-liked men in the shop. Close supervision doesn't mean you're "regimenting' the guy. It means you're protecting him from himself, maximizing his capabilities and minimizing his weak points. Long term plans, however, *must* be broken down into a series of sub-tasks, programmed on a three- to six-month basis. When he has accomplished one sub-task, then and only then do we throw him another. He can handle it on this basis. It is only when the whole, long-range job is dropped in his lap that he is apt to make what might be called a tangential course-correction toward a marked reef. . . .

Do You *Work with* a Man Who Steers It "Steady as She Goes . . ."?

Well—all things being equal and negative chemistry aside, it is a pretty good bet you really *like* this guy. And you can get just about any degree of cooperation you need by requesting it, in a calm manner and on a strictly professional basis. Remember to communicate with him in very specific terms; tell him not only what you want to do but what you *don't* want to do. This guy's not imaginative—so leave nothing to his imagination.

Do You *Work for* an Executive Who Steers It "Steady as She Goes . . ."?

Again, you're going to *like* working for him; he's really a decent and well-intentioned person—and working for him is a truly tremendous opportunity, because he is open-minded enough to give serious consideration to any logical proposal you make, so long as it is directed toward a specific end. He conceives of himself as being creative, but he's really not; he is apt to mistake enthusiasm for creative ability—so do what you can to keep him on the track. Support him, demonstrate loyalty in a real sense, push him, for he will give you freedom and will let you do almost anything you want so long as you stay responsible and have an intrinsic ability to contribute. Keep communications specific; tell him what you want to do, what you don't want to do, and why you feel that way. *Do not get subtle*. Spell it all out, so he knows where you are and why you're there at all times. Play it this way, and you can turn the situation into one of the most rewarding experiences of your business career—from your own standpoint, and from his, too. Sadly, it should also be noted here that the "Steady as She Goes" type of executive is also Cold Meat for the incompetent, the lazy and the malicious. They hurt him, hurt themselves, hurt the company—but under his aegis they will be apt to survive in their positions (and get away with pure *murder*) long, long after they should have been fired.

Do *You* Steer "Steady as She Goes . . ."?

Face it: you are *not* going to change yourself. But there are a number of steps you can take in aid of supplementing your weaknesses and maximizing your strengths. First, you're unlikely to be much of a judge of people—so get professionals to assist in picking personnel. Second, since you're probably not a long-range planner, staff yourself with visionary thinkers; then program all long-range plans on a chart that will allow you—visibly and constantly—to see just exactly where you are and where you're going. Break it all down into a series of individual short-range tasks if possible. That should help you avoid tangents. Third, don't confuse activity with problem solving; keep an eye on that chart, and if no movement is visible . . . get your team together and work out a real-action plan with them. Fourth, do your best to get really knowledgeable consultants in all fields where you'll be making decisions based on human inputs; all such inputs are subject to human error, and the consultants can be darn helpful in spotting the faulty ones. You *need* their independent advice. Fifth, *calibrate* those with whom you must deal; you tend to forgive too quickly, so keep a written log and evaluate each individual regularly. Sixth, since you are unlikely to be tough enough in handling people—try a "management-by-objective" kind of approach; talking about objectives rather than about personalities. It should make it easier for you to get them on the ball . . . and keep them there.

Which brings us to a final word about this particular denizen: Don't underrate the man who says "Steady As She Goes." I said he has his place in the Jungle—and I meant it.

It's not every business that *needs* a two-fisted empire-builder.

And nice guys do *not* always finish last . . . !

12
The Man in the White Hat

I still like to watch old western movies on the late show.

No pain, no strain—and no problem trying to follow the plot if you tune in late or get a phone call that takes you away from the tube for half an hour. The Bad Guy is always easy to identify; he generally dresses like a dude (with a little mustache, maybe, if he's *really* a stinker) and he smokes see-gars, and he has to wear a black hat all the way through to the final scene.

The Good Guy is just as easy to spot.

He's the Man in the White Hat . . . and of course everybody identifies with him, even when he kisses his horse.*

Which is okay, on the late show.

But in the Executive Jungle, the script doesn't always read

*Well, anyway, it seemed okay when Tom Mix and Gene Autry did it.

just that way. Everybody would *like* to be the Good Guy. Everybody would *like* to wear the White Hat, in every situation. But sometimes another kind of action is really required; sometimes that White Hat has to be sorrowfully—but firmly—hung on the rack, while reality sets in.

Trouble is, White Hats are kind of attractive.

And a certain kind of Executive Jungle-dweller can get so used to wearing one, he'd feel naked without it. And that means Trouble. As it did in the case of one man, whom we'll call

Roy, the Man in the White Hat

I met him when he retained me as a consultant, to perform an audit of the "human resources" at an aerospace company where he was president. And one of the chief resources, of course, was the Boss. . . .

His history was rather interesting:

Roy was well educated, had a university degree with honors, and he had served for a time after graduation as an instructor at one of the better business schools in the East, before moving into a job with a highly respected business consulting firm. He was successful in his work there because he was perceptive, supportive, constructive and a very pleasant guy to work with.

Consulting work, however, has its pitfalls.

And one of them is that the consultant, if he's *really* good at his job, may (a) "fall in love" with a company where he's assigned, and want to run it himself, or (b) make such an impression on the management of a client firm that they try to woo him into the company. Which is pretty much what happened to Roy.

I guess the firm that hired him figured, if this guy really knew what to do (as he certainly seemed to) and could come up with highly workable ideas on a consultant basis, he would be the man to implement them. Which, heaven knows, is a correct line of thought in some cases—but not in all, because there is all the difference in the world between a staff position and a line job.

In any case, Roy was hired as vice-president for marketing—and actually performed the job for a time, until (ironically, you might say) a *consulting firm* performed an audit of management procedures . . . which resulted in Roy getting the axe!

Actually, it wasn't quite the way it sounds. . . .

The consulting outfit had actually made about twenty-five recommendations, including the ouster of a number of executives who'd been around the firm for quite a while. But of those twenty-five recommendations, the *only* one the president of the company saw fit to implement was the axing of the marketing VP.

Why?

*Because the company's president was a lot like Roy! He was the Man In The White Hat, too, and—since he'd paid $50,000 for that management audit—he felt he had to follow at least one of the recommendations. So Roy, because his tenure was shortest and because the Boss knew Roy was "too nice a guy" to fight back, found the Fickle Finger pointing at him. **

Roy took it like a little gentlemen—no recriminations for the Good Guy, you know—and went back into consulting work for a while. No great time had elapsed, however, before a consulting group with which he became associated selected

---

*In the previous chapter, you may recall, I said nice guys do not *always* finish last. And that's true. But don't forget: they do not always finish *first*, either.

him to take over as president of the firm where I was later hired as personnel consultant.

The company Roy now headed was, at the time he assumed the Corner Office, a loser; there were five divisions, and two of them were having a financial hemorrhage that was bleeding the one profit-maker to death while the others were holding their own.

Roy perceived the problem at once—and took corrective action.

One of the losing divisions was totally eliminated. The other loser was reorganized in such a way that it needed no additional cash (it later regained its health enough to begin to make money again). And the third, profit-making division, (albeit a meagre profit, all things considered) was able to use its financial strength to increase its competitive position and to go into product development, which had previously been lagging badly because of the drain to the two weak sisters.

All this, remember, was done within a very short time after Roy assumed the presidency. He came into the firm with no past loyalties, no personal ties with in-house personnel; he could therefore afford to take the hard and determined actions which were necessary to save the situation, all without soiling that pretty White Hat.

Time, however, was *not* on his side.

Before long he had made quite a number of friends within the organization; he had formed relationships which were almost without exception warm and personal. More, he had set several programs in motion which he felt would produce profits over the years—and, he sincerely believed, had adequately briefed the men in charge of those programs on just what he wanted, and how he wanted it done.

He had plenty of solid engineering and accounting backup and the marketing and manufacturing managers (who were in considerable degree responsible for the ill-health of the firm when he took it over) had had the matter "explained" to them thoroughly (Roy *thought*) and had (again, so far as *he* knew) proved amenable* to his suggestions.

But these two section heads were not White Hat wearers themselves. They were in fact men who ran very tight ships and tended (like the Stranglers we discussed in an earlier chapter) to keep to themselves bits of information which were of vital concern to Roy and to the company. They were, moreover, quite adamant—no matter how amenable they may have seemed to Roy—about changing their modes of operation. They were not about to do so. Especially since they seemed to sense that Roy would be a bit hesitant in exerting the force needed to make them do it.

Roy was a gentleman's gentleman . . . and it showed.

He never *became* angry. He avoided any situation which might have brought him into direct confrontation with a subordinate. He did his best to handle any problem with patience and in a circumspect manner calculated to avoid abrading the feelings of the people involved.

When he did bring himself to "discuss" a problem it was always by indirection. When he wanted to give an order, he could not bring himself to do so directly. It always took the form of a "suggestion."

Still, there was no doubt his actual intention *was* known to the people with whom he tried to communicate. They simply chose to ignore the "suggestion" because it had not been a direct order—again, with the assurance that no drastic corrective action would be taken against them.

---

*That is, they were smiling after he talked to them. I have a hunch those smiles were an unconscious response to their innermost thoughts: they were wishing Roy a case of terminal halitosis and twelve extra weeks in purgatory.

In addition, there were a few people surrounding him who were in fact so obtuse or insensitive themselves that they simply misinterpreted his intentions. The "suggestions" he made were not always entirely clear to them. They wanted to do the job his way, but they were confused as to exactly what that way might be.

(In fairness to Roy, it should be noted here that his business background and training were simply not of a line-oriented type, and not strong in the very fields he was attempting to handle by indirection through his subordinate-managers.)

This situation continued and worsened, little by little, as Roy became better acquainted in the firm.

When it finally became apparent to all concerned that Roy was simply not capable of acting to weed out an incompetent or even openly malicious subordinate, the effect was to cause even the good men in the organization to have second thoughts about the Boss.

"What am I doing here?" is the question that would enter their minds. "Why am I saddled with people I can't use, can't fire and can't transfer—just because Roy wants to be a nice guy? How long am I going to have to put up with a situation like this?"

And, on a slightly different level of personality:

"Why should I knock myself out? Roy treats everyone just the same—competent or incompetent; energetic or lazy. Your performance doesn't make a bit of difference. I must be out of my mind to put forth any real effort . . . !"

In lower echelons of the firm, of course, Roy must have looked like Santa Claus.

It was well known that he always "kept his door open" to listen to troubles of *any* employee. (On one occasion, a meeting with an important customer was actually postponed in order to give Roy time to help deal with a family problem encountered by a secretary in the organization!) But . . . Roy was the Boss—not the chaplain!

The result was that Roy's early good work for the firm gradually was eroded, its effects slowly nullified by the creeping paralysis that attacks any company where active and disciplined management is lacking.

Not that the business actually began to lose money.

It didn't. The company stayed "in the black" throughout Roy's tenure there. But merely making "a profit" instead of running at "a loss" is hardly a criterion.

In case that's not clear: Look at a business as though it were a tree—a tree with an established growth rate of, say, a foot per year. That's the average growth which can be expected of the tree. All right . . . now, here in the orchard we have a number of trees that seem to be growing at pretty much that established rate. But one tree isn't. It's growing at a rate of only *one inch* per year.

You can look at the tree and say, "Well, it *is* growing."

But the truth is that the tree is dying. . . .

Say you manage to show a profit for the year of one cent per share. It's easy enough to say you "made a profit" and thus congratulate yourself for having done the job. Last year the books revealed that you showed a *loss* of one cent a share.

Tremendous!

You're back "in the black."

But the truth is that the difference between last year's loss and this year's profit is only two cents a share—and it's possible that the profit both years should have been a dollar a share.

I was brought in, as I say, to do an audit of human resources. And I did it. In fact I maintained a working relationship with that company for some time. Roy was, properly I believe, solicitous about the employees' reaction to what I was doing; he made it very plain that "no one's job would be threatened" by the kind of evaluations I was to carry out.

My job, he explained, would be to discover how the "team" could work best together, what combinations succeeded best, etc.

And in general this was so.

But there were frustrations* which became apparent along the way. No recommendation was ever implemented if it would result in any negative feeling on the part of any employee. And of course I was never able to be much help on what was, in short order, apparent as the chief source of management problems:

Roy himself was unable to lay aside his White Hat long enough to put into effect a program which would have maximized his *own* strengths—while minimizing the weaknesses which were costing him effective control and the ability to implement measures he really knew were required to keep the firm moving in the right direction.

In the end, it was Roy himself who suffered.

His company was acquired by a group of financial investors who had acquired the controlling interest of his company's closely held stock. And the new management evaluated the situation in his organization with the same

---

*One of the better-known psychological experiments involves teaching a rat that if he runs a maze correctly, he will find cheese waiting at the exit. You condition him to this reward for a while—and then put him in a maze that *has* no exit. The usual outcome is that the rat runs around until he finally is sure there's no way out; no corridor that leads to the cheese. Then he lies down and chews his toes. I didn't do that, of course. Haven't been able to get my toes to my mouth since I was a baby.

accuracy as Roy had displayed when he was a consultant, and when he took over the firm.

His inability to take action when he knew action was required was diagnosed for exactly what it was.*

And Roy was out.

The story is a sad one. It would be sad, of course, even if Roy were a fool or an ignoramus who simply didn't *know* what ought to be done to keep a company solid and growing. But when you're speaking of a man possessed of Roy's qualities of mind and business acumen, capable of giving highly effective advice to others in a management position, it almost reaches the level of tragedy.

The Greeks, remember, conceived the tragic hero as a great man with a single flaw that destroys him.

And Roy's single flaw—his Achilles heel—was his honest desire to act as father-brother-guardian angel to the whole crew; he simply could *not* bear to have anyone think him less than a saint.

Does a Man in the White Hat *Work for* You?

The first thing to decide, in that case, is just how much you value this individual. If he has real perception, business ability, etc., and you want to keep him in the organization, then you must insist that he accept a mode of operation which can be both effective and acceptable to him, personally. You can't, for instance, simply tell him to, "be tough-minded." It's like telling a penguin to fly, or a rooster to swim. You *can*, however, present him with alternatives which

---

*Roy could have diagnosed it just as easily himself . . . if he'd been a consultant, rather than the company president. In technical terms, this condition is known as "proximate myopia." Or: "There's better seats in the back of the auditorium, folks!"

are less acceptable than continued inaction. You can point out that, when good men in his organization see him patting an incompetent on the back, they wonder if the Foulup is blackmailing him in some manner; you can advise that in failing to take action against the single bad apple in his basket, he is impairing the good opinion the others have of him. The lesser evil, then, will be doffing the White Hat for a moment, to deal with the problem. You can also suggest a program of management-by-objectives (which I'll detail a little later in this chapter).

Do You *Work with* a Man in the White Hat?

Such a guy may not be your direct responsibility; you didn't take him to raise. If his ineffectiveness doesn't affect your discharge of your own responsibilities, perhaps it would be best just to let nature take its course—unless, as is not unlikely, he's a friend of yours. It's pretty easy to be friends with a man like that. So, if you *must* take some action, you're going to have to *push* him—in much the same way his own boss might push him. Giving him a choice between lesser evils, in a friendly but firm manner, is one way of handling it; helping him select objectives or goals in the near future for his subordinates and needling him from time to time to see if they've accomplished them is another. One thing to beware of is his inability to fire people. He'll *transfer* them instead of giving them the well-deserved axe, if he's pushed to extremes—and a guy who is transferred by the Man in the White Hat is worth observing with a rather jaundiced eye. He's almost *got* to be an eightball. You can't let him get away with that, friend or no.

Do You *Work for* the Man in the White Hat?

If you're a bright guy yourself, just starting your business career, working for a boss like this can be a real treat. He's the kind of guy who will delegate responsibility easily; all you've got to do is show you can handle it and are willing to accept it; he'll always give you the benefit of the doubt—and he'll never be peeking over your shoulder. This gives you a hell of an opportunity to learn your own job. But there are pitfalls: you've got to be careful never to take on more than you can handle; the Man in the White Hat can't protect you from that. And you may fault him a bit for not recognizing your superior performance as it relates to the performance of others, and for not rewarding you more than Joe Blow down the hall, who can't cut it. Still, this kind of boss will offer you challenging problems and let you use your own approach. Just make sure your *own* goals and plans are clearly defined, especially as they relate to those of your co-workers. And don't expect the Man in the White Hat to help when you have to deal with a peer who is frustrating your best efforts. He just can't do things like that.

Are *You* the Man in the White Hat?

Well, pal—let's not kid you: the chances of you changing yourself and putting that Hat in the closet for good are just about nil. People *can* change, or *be* changed. It happens in psychosurgery. It happens with the Sudden Revelation. (Remember Sgt. Alvin York's account of how he was turned aside from his early carousing ways by a bolt of lightning that knocked him off his horse and bent the barrel of the shotgun with which he had intended to kill a man?) But you know, bolts of lightning are a fairly scarce commodity; you just can't count on one for yourself. If you really want a more effective modus operandi, however, certain techniques are available to you—things you *can* do while continuing to wear the White Hat. First, you must assemble a staff of able and action-oriented managers; tough-minded types to whom you delegate responsibility—and be careful and selective in making your choices for this team; remember, you are *not* capable of firing them! Then, try management-by-objectives. Suppose, for instance, you have a subordinate who is not quite cutting it. Censure him; chew him out? Forget it! No matter how hard you try, this kind of personal exchange is simply not for you—so try it this way: bring him in and lay it on him in the form of a specific goal. This isn't censure; it's giving him a charter for an objective. You want, say, to increase sales by *x* percent. Okay, that's the goal. Then you tell him what resources will be made available: what kind and number of staff, what time-period, budget, etc. Together, you work out a detailed timetable, a series of limited objectives, to be attained along the road to the overall objective. Now it's not just your own idea, Mr. White Hat—now it's your *joint project*, one he agreed was feasible—and the breakdown timetable gives you an adequate day-by-day progress report to see how he's doing. If he continually misses the individual task-goals, you'll have to prod him. But it's not a *personal* thing now; it can be discussed in terms of objectives gained-or-missed rather than personalities. *That* you *can* do. Alternatively, there is the technique of making someone else wear the Black Hat for you. Get yourself an "executive officer" to stand between you and the individual subordinate-managers. Let *him* transmit your orders; do the chewing out. (But for God's sake, make sure the guy you tap for the job doesn't share your fondness for pristine headgear!) Or, if no such person is available, tell the subordinates it's the decision of your board of directors—*they're* the ones who said performance must be improved . . . or the axe is set to descend. If someone simply must be shown to the door and the boot applied to the posterior—chances are you simply *can't* handle it yourself. Try it, and he is as likely to emerge from your office with a *raise* as with his pink slip! For situations like that, you'll probably have to have someone do the work for you. That could be the executive officer (translation: hatchet-man) if you've got one, or if not, maybe you can borrow his talents. One method would be to hire a consulting firm to survey performance and make recommendations; if they really know their job, they'll probably come up with the same answers you did—only *this* time you're just implementing their findings. You're sorry as hell about it, of course (the White Hat is always sorry about things like this) but after all if you've paid good money for advice, you'd be a fool not to take it. In short, while you can't change your personality, in all likelihood, you *can* alter your *techniques* to get the job done.

Remember: there's a Man in the White Hat lurking down deep inside every single one of us. Nobody likes to be thought a Bad Guy. Nobody likes to think of himself as a Bad Guy. Nobody wants to wear the Black Hat.

But the main survivors in the Executive Jungle more often than not will be wearing hats which, if not actually Black, are seen on close inspection to have a distinctive cast of Gray . . . down close to the sweat-band.

13
The Right Answer at the Wrong Time

One of the biggest single factors in the success or failure of any plan is that of timing.

A potentially successful battle plan is worthless if it is arrived at a year after the war has been lost; schematic drawings for a modern television set would have been of very little value in the time of Queen Elizabeth I.

Similarly, a man who proposed a modern airline schedule to the Wright Brothers—on the day after their first successful powered flight at Kitty Hawk—would have been dismissed as a screwball of purest ray serene.*

Nothing wrong with any of the plans, understand.

They are the right answers.

---

*Comedian Bob Newhart based one of his funniest routines on a situation like that. Anyway, it was funny to most people. I wanted to cry.

But they are proposed at a time when nobody is ready to listen.

Which is pretty much how it was with an executive I evaluated on two separate occasions not so long ago. I remember him as

Jerry, the Truth-Avoider

My first evaluation of Jerry was performed in behalf of a client firm which was considering him for a key position in middle management, during the early 1960s.

At the time of this first evaluation, Jerry was in his early thirties, married about six years and the father of three-year-old twins. His wife was a college graduate, the daughter of a prominent midwestern executive.

Jerry was the elder of two children. His father was deceased; he had been a highly successful corporation lawyer. His mother was also a college graduate, interested in the field of law. Jerry had been reared in one of the more exclusive residential areas of a large midwestern city, had graduated from a high school there and was popular among his classmates. He had, in short, been born with the proverbial silver spoon in his mouth; no particular unfulfilled wants or needs. He had been taking a course in mechanical engineering at a midwestern university when he was drafted and spent two years in the Air Force—most of it in Europe, apparently having a ball.

Back in civilian life, Jerry returned to college at an Ivy League school and switched his major to business, specifically, the field of marketing. He took three years to get his BA, but held 3.4 grade average, a respectable mark and one not precisely commensurate with the "Gentleman's C Average" which might have been expected of him.

On graduation he obtained, largely through the efforts of his father who was widely known and respected, a position with a small but progressive organization in the Southwest, where he ultimately headed the customer relations department. He stayed five years.

So far, so good.

But at that point, the first crack appeared in what might have seemed a rather easy and successful life: Jerry departed from that organization under what might be called a "slight cloud." The exact nature of the difficulty was never entirely explained, at least to my satisfaction.

Neither, I might say, was what happened on his next job.

He came back to his home town with his wife and family, joined a large industrial firm as staff assistant to one of the line managers . . . and was out in just six months.

And that was where matters stood when he became a candidate for my client's opening.

Testing disclosed a superior grade of basic intellect, supported in the main by exceptional reasoning abilities (both numerical and verbal—especially in the realm of the abstract).

These findings would have placed him well at the level of upper middle management. But his vocabulary, both written and verbal, seemed mediocre . . . though he handled himself well enough in direct conversation.

He had moderate ability to handle detail, though not with any especially high degree of accuracy; his ability to perceive vectors in space and manipulate them mentally was also mediocre (though of no direct consequence, considering his career orientation) and he showed some capability of arriving at unusual solutions to common problems (creativity).

(A word about this last-mentioned ability, however: he had a fluency of ideas, all right . . . but many of them were obviously worthless. To put it another way, he might be able to think up a new way to solve an old problem, but the new way might often be unworkable on a practical basis.)

Jerry's occupational interests were clearly defined: he

liked selling ideas (and himself) as well as selling products. He also professed a strong interest in artistic effort (again, with no space-visualization aptitude to support it) and a liking for working with his hands.

His least area of interest was working with administrative detail or quantitative data.

His literary interest was below average, and his interest in being of service to others was only slightly higher.

He showed about average interest, though, in scientific pursuits and musical activity.

In summary, a fairly sound and substantial citizen—if test scores were to be accepted at face value.* This was, in fact, precisely the sort of image Jerry was trying to project; he described himself as a person interested in dealing with facts rather than emotions—one capable of arriving at logical conclusions, free from his own personal hangups.

Jerry saw himself, therefore, as an action-oriented guy; a success in most of the things he attempted, willing to take risks when commensurate gains were in prospect. He indicated he wanted to "run his own ship" and not be second guessed—and under those circumstances would "put his shoulder to the wheel."

I saw him on the other hand as a man easily capable of

---

*If I were going to do *that*, I'd hardly need professional qualifications; anyone, after a brief course of training, can take a set of test scores, profile them, and tell you in general what kind of person the profile is supposed to indicate. And you'd get some pretty sorry surprises, too, if you relied entirely on the results. And so would the client, had he relied on the pseudo-personality Jerry had managed to project in the tests. Maybe, someday, a test will be devised that is absolutely reliable and gives you answers that mean something in terms of the individual being tested *and* the people with whom he will be working. When that day comes, I think I will take up knitting and Good Works. But for the moment, the possibility seems remote.

fooling himself; in fact, I could see indications that he had been doing so for a number of years. I had the distinct impression that this young man, exposed to nothing but advantages and easy success in early life, had never lived in the real world at all; had fantasized much of what the real world was like.

This suggested to me that he was perhaps not ready to *deal* with the real world, that whereas he considered himself an independent sort, able to handle himself and others, he was really projecting a false image—one he accepted himself at face value—which would disintegrate in short order if even a part of the facade were pierced.

And that's pretty much what I said in my evaluation report to my client.

Of course I said the same things, as tactfully as possible, to Jerry himself. That's part of the "playback" I give all examinees, sharing with them as much information about themselves as I think they're capable of accepting.

I told him he probably didn't really understand the impact he had on others; that they perceived the basic insincerity and potentially manipulative tendencies which underlay the personality he was trying to project—and that these perceptions would not be likely to inspire confidence in a peer, subordinate or boss.

I suggested either that he expose himself to professional sensitivity training or to an in-depth effort with a clinical psychologist or psychiatrist who could, hopefully, help him obtain an insight into himself and his actual relationship to the real world.

I'm afraid it wasn't much help.*

Jerry had a very strong desire to maintain that facade behind which he was hiding. His ideas about himself—and the

---

*Obviously, the Right Time had not arrived.

world around him—while they may not have coincided with reality, were firm and he was not ready to place them in hazard. I think—at any rate, I suspect—that he had at least an intellectual appreciation of the value of the suggestions I was making. But he rejected them emphatically . . . if in a socially acceptable manner. And went his way.

My client didn't hire Jerry, and I didn't see him again for several years.

When I finally did see him again, it was obvious that the situation had worsened in several areas to a considerable extent. For one thing, his personal life was in pretty bad shape.

He had found another job after being turned down by my client . . . but this job was one that involved a great deal of travel; a national sales program for which he bore major responsibility (which, for a man with his lack of self-discipline and reality-perception, was about the worst he could have picked.)

Traveling, with none of the accustomed restrictions on his conduct, he had become increasingly dependent on alcohol.

As time went by, there were missed appointments, coming in late to work, trying to work with a severe hangover which—even if he did manage to meet a client on time—precluded any really effective contact. And it became a vicious circle: the reduced effectiveness increasing dependency on the bottle; the increased alcoholism reducing his effectiveness. The end of that down-spiral is always the same.

And Jerry was no exception.

He lost his job and all sense of personal worth at about the same time—an event followed closely by the departure of his wife, and their children, to live with close personal friends in another city.

Jerry had been cited for drunk driving after an auto

accident, and had lost his driver's license (for a period of one year) shortly afterward. Now, even had there been an opportunity for gainful employment, it was likely that the information that he was legally prevented from operating an automobile—and the reasons for such a suspension—would have mitigated against such a job offer being extended.

He was being supported by his uncle, who provided only enough for sustenance—not enough to buy alcohol—and his feelings on this subject showed a considerable hostility. But he was willing to pay for a new evaluation by me, in an effort to help Jerry get on his feet again.

My re-testing showed some adverse developments.

For one thing, he tested lower in confidence in people and money-interest (though it was still pretty important to him), coupled with a higher level of introspection. His level of objectivity had dropped; he was extremely thin-skinned on this second meeting and the meeting itself seemed far more anxiety-producing than the first—not because there was any greater or lesser risk involved, but probably because of the adversities which had clouded his life in the intervening period.

His strong interest in persuasion and artistic effort remained, and he did show a somewhat stronger apparent interest in social service activities. But I use the word "apparent" here because I also noted an increased sensitivity which was still not focused on his impact upon others or his compassion for them, but rather on feelings and circumstances which he felt had been imposed upon him. (This is about the same way an infant feels toward the world: baby at the center, with mother, father and others circling around him like planets.)

His drive level was still above average, and he had retained a fair amount of social self-confidence (or at least was able to give the appearance of having done so) plus the moderate predisposition for risk-taking.

But his frustration tolerance had dwindled, and there was less tenacity.

He was, in short, going right down the tube. . . .

His willingness to meet with me might, of course, have been a hopeful sign. But it wasn't, really. Jerry gave me some reason to suspect he was really no more willing to accept objective evaluation than he had been at our first meeting; I had a feeling he was doing it more to placate those in "authority" around him.

He still had not reached his own "bottom," that maximum depth to which an individual will permit himself to sink before he can begin taking the steps that will be effective. Until that "bottom" has been reached—and the subject knows it—a recitation of the right answers is ineffective on any really useful level.

Until then . . . it's still the right answer at the wrong time.

Is there an answer for him?

Yes. Oh, yes! I still think it's the one I suggested on the occasion of our first evaluation-playback. Professional psychological help would be a first step . . . but only if Jerry were prepared to open himself to it.

And is he ready?

Only Jerry knows the answer to that. . . .

Everyone in this world has problems; the business of living—the usefulness of the human mind itself—comes down to a matter of solving, or at least dealing effectively with, our problems.

But the time has to be right, in terms of the individual.

Nagging, repeated suggestion, aid of any kind whatsoever is simply of no use at all until the individual has reached that "right" time. Indeed, help extended before that time is as apt to cause further damage as not.

Does a Man in Need of the Right Answer *Work for* You?

Then you've darn few alternatives. You can bring him in, under the least stressful circumstances you can arrange, and talk it over with him on a strictly personal and strictly friendly basis. You can try to get across to him your interest in him as a human being, quite aside from your other obvious interest in his qualities as an executive and as your subordinate. You can do your best to overcome whatever skepticism he has (and it may be quite a hell of a lot!) But if you do so, you must first and above all recognize the fact that you are *not* a professional counselor in this area—and also keeping in mind that entering too deeply into an employee's personal life can be a considerable risk for you as a manager.* But if the man's habits and life-style are adversely affecting his work, you will at least have the unpleasant duty of giving him the choice between taking the steps necessary to rehabilitate himself—or the steps necessary to find a position elsewhere. To get this clear with him, you will have to set some kind of time limit in which he must make his choice; meanwhile, make him understand that you'll take every opportunity at your disposal to support him in every possible way. Getting too deeply involved, however, could be a serious error from everyone's point of view because in that case you would, to some degree at least, become partially responsible for his problem, become an actual party to it. It would compromise your own position, and make it far more difficult for you to be objective. If the man agrees to try to help himself, you'd be well advised to ask him to document his progress: show that he is, truly, consulting a professional, medical or psychological. Try to know who they are; see if there is some

---

*You stand in grave danger of becoming the Man in the White Hat, whose difficulties we detailed in the previous chapter. Woe unto you if you let *that* happen!

manner in which you can be in touch with them—not to meddle, but to be sure a workable approach to the problem has been initiated.

Do You *Work with* a Man Who Needs the Right Answer Now?

Logically, you could be expected to be far less sympathetic to his situation than an employer or even a subordinate; you've your own problems, God knows, and you're depending on this guy to pull at least his own weight in the management team. Well, then, perhaps some subordinate can "bridge the gap." Maybe there's someone through whom you can filter needed information on possible steps toward solving the problem. If your mutual superior is a knowledgable guy and *is taking* constructive steps to solve—or eliminate—the problem, perhaps you might be willing to wait (and extend yourself a bit, maybe) because it would be the fair thing to do and this may be a basically good and sound man who has simply run up against something he's not prepared to handle. If nothing is happening, though—you must assume that it's still the "wrong time" no matter how "right" the answer may be—in which case you will have to force the issue. You have, after all, responsibilities to yourself, to your own subordinates, and to the company. You will have to take the position that something must be done . . . not at some indeterminate future date, but *now*!

Do You *Work for* a Man Who Needs the Right Answer?

His condition will, most likely, give you an opportunity for increased responsibility if he can't function adequately. That's great for you—but you'll have to be a pretty decisive and self-confident kind of person, though, to exist for very long in such a situation. You really can't depend a hell of a lot on your boss for guidance or direction; even when he's physically present, he is unlikely to be much help. It's an opportunity, all right. But if you're the kind of person who needs close direction of a supervisor—or you're new in the company—the lack of this guidance can give you some really serious problems. In such a case, maybe you can communicate, directly or otherwise, with your boss's boss, explaining that you're not absolutely sure what needs to be done and asking guidance. Dirty pool, maybe. Perhaps a real gentleman of the Old School would try talking to his boss to see if it might be the "right time" for the "right answers." But one thing for sure—you're taking your career in your hands when you do this; if the time's not right, he's going to interpret your approach as a threat, and God help you if he does! You know your situation, and your relationship with your superior; you must make your own decision based on the facts as you know them. An alternative would be to ask for a transfer of some kind—or to look for another position elsewhere.

Do *You* Need a Right Answer?

Then you—and you alone—know whether or not it's the "right time" for that right answer. If you haven't hit your own "bottom" yet, chances are the time is *not* right. Everyone has a slightly different "maximum depth." When you hit it, you'll *know*, brother! The problem at base is one of *knowing yourself*—and if you think that's any snap, think again. You know the steps. You know you may need professional help; probably you do. You know, at the very least, that your conduct and your perception of the world and its reality have thus far been faulty; they have injured you in numberless ways. The first step is to stop fooling yourself about that single point, consciously or unconsciously. Once you take that step—the rest ought to follow in a pretty natural course of events. Consult a professional. Nobody is going to *force* you to do it; nobody is going to *force* you to accept what he tells you. But you owe it to yourself at least to consider his words and their meaning. After all: what have you to lose—and are you really prepared to lose it just because you failed to take a step as necessary and obvious as putting a splint on a broken leg?

14
Hooray for Me and to Hell with You

When a politician makes a campaign promise, it surprises almost nobody when he later finds some way to avoid honoring it. We have become a nation of skeptics when it comes to things like this.

Similarly, when a couple are married it seldom really surprises either when the "campaign promises" are broken. Courtship is one thing—married life is something else, and if they are really mature enough to consider marriage at all* they probably understand this well enough.

In both cases, the promises are really a statement of ideals; they are goals to be striven for . . . not bond-guarantees or demand-notes to be presented for instant payment.

---

*Nobody *really* is. And people usually don't *consider* marriage at all. Which, in a way, is probably a good thing. We can ill afford, in these times, to have a bunch of Justices of the Peace out of work and adding to the unemployment problem.

But industrial "marriage" is something else. . . .

If it is to succeed, if the company is to be happy with the executive it has in effect "married," and if the executive is to be both satisfied and effective in his newly acquired position, the "marriage contract" must be honestly entered into by both sides and the terms must be observed.

It's a simple issue: the industrial marriage must *meet the needs of both parties* or it will shortly become an industrial divorce.

It has no chance at all if *either* of the contracting parties is secretly thinking, "Hooray for Me and To Hell With You!"

And by way of illustration, I can think of no more explicit case than that of a man we will call

Miguel, the Deceived Bridegroom

I met him just a couple of years ago, and I've always felt a bit bad about the part I played in his deception—though I certainly was not aware at the time that false promises had been made to him.

We met in the usual way; he was a candidate for employment by a client-firm and I was to evaluate his potential.

Miguel was, in *almost* every way, a true gem.*

He was twenty-seven, married for just two years and father of an infant daughter. His wife was a native of the United States, but she had been reared in a very tightly-structured Mexican-American community, spoke Spanish as her first language—and with an idiom readily comprehensible to Miguel, since her parents had come from the same part of Mexico where Miguel had been born and lived most of his early life.

---

*Note that word "almost" and the fact that it's in italics.

They were well suited to each other, those two, and good friends in addition to being lovers; I knew almost from the first that, whatever problems Miguel might prove to have, they would *not* be of the marital type.

His own background was quite sound. His father was a college graduate, former mayor of a small city in Mexico and now retired. He was a quick-tempered man and ferocious in his anger (according to Miguel) but just as quick to recover when the anger was discharged. Miguel's mother was also a bright woman, but of limited education, a kind person and extremely supportive to her six children, of which Miguel was the youngest.

Miguel held a bachelor's degree in mechanical engineering from the University of Mexico and had spent one year (compulsory) in the Mexican Army as a second lieutenant. After the army service, he moved to the United States and managed—despite a language handicap, of which we will speak further—to obtain a master's degree in just eighteen months, completing thirty-six semester hours with a grade point average of 3.5. (He later began work on another bachelor's at the University of Washington; I think he was really after a master's in business administration. He stayed only a single semester, however, because the climate didn't agree with him. He moved back to Southern California, but in our subsequent interviews Miguel indicated he still intended to pursue the business degree.)

While he was earning the master's in engineering, Miguel had also worked as a research assistant on a project which required him to construct mathematical models for hydraulic flow systems.

This work tied in pretty directly with his first full-time employment, which was with a manufacturer of hydraulic components for industry. He was a project engineer, working with seven other similarly qualified men designing components, analyzing designs and testing them.

His work in this field subsequently became known to a very large company which was active in the same general area. The big firm "pirated"* Miguel away and he worked a year for the giant as supervisor of two lesser-degreed persons plus a draftsman. (He was doing this while working toward that second bachelor's degree.)

Leaving the larger company (his health troubles with the northern climate had more or less coincided with a general layoff in which that firm had to drop a good two-thirds of its total work force) and arriving in Southern California, he set about looking for a job . . . but not just *any* job.

Whether he had always had such an ambition (the pursuit of the business administration degree in Washington would seem to indicate so) or had been inspired in that direction by his tiny taste of administrative work with his second job I'm not absolutely certain. But by the time we met there could be little doubt of Miguel's intention: he sincerely wanted to be a manager—first, perhaps, in the technical area where he had started, but ultimately in the area of general management.

And that, it seemed, was what had attracted him to my client.

The firm's chief designer was quite anxious to get Miguel aboard. And he had good reasons over and above the normal interest of any firm in obtaining the services of a qualified and competent engineer.

---

*Not the word the larger firm would have used, of course. *They* call it "vigorous recruiting effort."

The company bloody well *had* to find someone like Miguel!

I didn't know it at the time (and the subsequent discovery shook me up more than a bit, I can tell you) but the technical competency of this company was not only a bit questionable—it was really frightening. In fact, it was a shambles. Somehow, that outfit had managed to pick up every castoff, eight-ball and foul-up in the industry; the few who did possess legitimate engineering degrees were unable for one reason or another to do the job . . . and a great many more had simply falsified their records (no reference checks had *ever been made!*)

So the chief designer told Miguel what he thought Miguel wanted to hear:"Come into our engineering department, fella, and as soon as you've got your feet wet and see the situation, we'll bring you along into management."

Well, it sounded good.

How was Miguel to know the man talking to him was a well-known whitewasher who would have promised him the moon and stars if necessary to beef up that disastrous engineering department of his? Miguel bought the whole line. . . .

And I began the testing process.

The tests disclosed the presence of a remarkably agile mind, able to go from one task to another without loss of motion. He could work with numbers extremely well, handle detail with speed and accuracy, and his reasoning ability was absolutely superb in both the verbal and nonverbal areas.

He could perceive lines in space and manipulate them mentally without any trouble. Tests of his creativity showed that, while he had little in the way of spontaneity of thought he was able to come up with workable solutions which were quite unusual for solving common problems—especially in the technical area. Such a man was of the type who usually enriches any company where he works by producing patent disclosures that offer his employers a proprietary advantage over its competitors.

Like many engineers, he had a strong interest in working with quantitative data, in artistic effort, for being around equipment and machinery and for working with his hands.

He was also interested in administrative detail.

Miguel showed far less interest—the lowest of his scores—in the fields of the outdoors, for music and for literary effort. (Peculiarly, since he was an engineer, he also scored low on interest in scientific effort; ideas, as such, really had little interest for him unless they could be put into practice.)

He was serious, sober-minded, conscientious, tenacious and competitive in the sense of accepting the challenge of a problem rather than competing with other people. He was the kind of runner who competes against the stopwatch . . . not against other runners.

He could analyze well; could see "the big picture" rather than getting himself hopelessly lost in detail; analyze the component parts of the picture and thus establish priorities for effort with respect to complexities, lead-times, his own resources and the resources of the company. Developing as a manager was, besides, his recognized and professed Main Drive. He sincerely believed himself to be a potential leader* and he possessed some apparent interest in such tradition-ally-accepted leadership qualities as convincing others to his point of view, being a seller of ideas (and, conceivably, of tangibles as well) while *not* being the kind of person who would willingly detract from the earned recognition of others. He had confidence in himself.

---

*Don't we *all*? But Miguel really meant it, and had the stuff to back it up.

In short, Miguel was pretty close to being the ideal candidate for a managerial spot . . . except for one little defect:

He absolutely could not speak English for sour apples!

Now, there's a lot of flak flying around these days about that particular point. Some people, for obvious reasons, would like to convince the world that the United States is in fact a bilingual. nation, where Spanish is as acceptable as English so long as the speaker is fluent in the language. And that is, or ought to be, true enough—so long as the persons with whom you must deal speak the same language.

Unhappily, not everyone in this country *does* speak Spanish.*

English is the language of the vast majority; the lingua franca of business and most of the professions. The inability to speak it fluently and understand at the same level places an absolute limit on any person's future in almost any line of endeavor. If you doubt this, ask yourself: How many presidents of major corporations in the United States are unable to speak English? How many major politicians? How many teachers and education-administrators? How many top-ranking doctors or lawyers?

Miguel *could* communicate in the very simplest forms of English; he could understand at about the same level. He was doing his best—on a self-education basis—to eliminate the handicap. But at the time of my evaluation, he simply was *not* a good transmitter of information and occasionally had trouble receiving as well.

Understand—for all I know, the guy could have had a shade on Cervantes *in Spanish*.

But in English, he simply couldn't hack it.

Which was why it was so obvious (at least in retrospect)

---

*Yeah. But not everybody speaks English either . . . including a lot of people who *think* they do.

that he had been deliberately misled by the chief designer who recruited him. Without a command of English, Miguel was going *nowhere* in that company's management area.

The hell of it is, the company really missed a good bet here.

Miguel was honest and fair, could delegate responsibility without breathing down the neck of a really capable subordinate; was willing to gamble (how else would you describe a man who takes the risk of emigrating to a new country? who kept an open mind, etc., etc.) Potentially a hell of an executive.

With a mind of the caliber he possessed, it was not at all unthinkable that he *could* have mastered English to a degree which would have eradicated his single drawback.

But the company paid no attention at all to that, had no interest whatever in Miguel's legitimate aspirations, or in the fact that certain outright promises had been made to him.

Once they had the guy on board as a designer and operating effectively, the rest of the program which had been outlined to him seemed to fade into the mists of lip-service. He was to have had the opportunity to get initial management responsibility early in his tenure and then grow in that area on a specifically outlined program.

He never got any of that.

And in a while, even the lip-service encouragement evaporated; the company said in effect, "Look, Miguel, why don't you just do the engineering and we'll keep the paychecks coming—it's all you're entitled to."

Or, to put it another way:

Hooray for Me and To Hell With You.

Miguel put up with that crap for six months, until he was fully convinced that the chief designer had been lying in his teeth and there was no mistake. Then he handed in his resignation, declined politely to reconsider it . . . and went his way.

That way was to a much smaller company.

It had a couple of drawbacks: for one thing it was in a rural area of Southern California rather than the metropolitan milieu in which Miguel and his wife were accustomed to living. For another, the smallness of the firm meant that Miguel's career advancement there would be somewhat limited, since the top wasn't all that far from the ground.

But it had two definite plus factors for Miguel: it was industrially oriented from the product-line point of view. And he was *in management*. He was chief design engineer, reporting to the chief engineer. Since the organization was so small, this title actually meant he was supervisor over only two or three persons. But it was a start on the kind of career Miguel wanted; the promises made him were fulfilled.

Funny. You know, such simple management responsibilities as Miguel was called upon to discharge with this smaller firm were of a kind which *could* have been provided by my client. It would have satisfied Miguel, at least for the time being, and at the same time the firm could have retained a highly talented engineer whose services were desperately needed. Moreover, as Miguel's language skills improved, I'm personally convinced he would have been first-line talent in the management area.

What a waste.

And what a disappointment for Miguel, the Deceived Bridegroom in this abortive industrial marriage!

Actually, he handled it all very well, I think. The new job has had its trials, of course; I heard from him quite recently, when one recruiting decision of his own had turned out badly—an apparently qualified man had, on employment, turned out to have a kind of personality which just didn't fit into the company at all. Miguel was depressed by this, and hopeful that his new employer would also retain me to evaluate future applicants. Which was as nice a compliment as I've had from an evaluee.

I think this new industrial marriage of his will work out fine.

Pity about the first one, though. . . .

All of which is merely a single illustration of the point I'm trying to make here: you are being fair neither to the prospective employee nor to your own firm if you expand a job picture beyond the bounds of strict reality.* The industrial marital contract is—like it's more personal counterpart—one that must be satisfactory to both contracting parties. Or in the end it will be null and void, and both of you will be the losers.

Of course, in all justice, I've certainly got to add that this "Hooray for Me and To Hell With You" attitude can be found on *both* sides of the hiring fence.

The world is just full of job applicants who whitewash to a fare-thee-well when talking to a recruiter about their ultimate aspirations and their intentions with regard to job tenure.

The recruiter is apt to hear a lot of malarky about how the applicant wants to be president of the firm some day, wants to find "a home; someplace to stay and grow with the company" when in reality he's looking for a stopgap job until he can find an opening in another field where he really intends to locate.

This is just as much a breach of the marital understanding —as much a case of "Hooray For Me and To Hell With You"—as the misrepresentations which were made to Miguel.

---

*Or, to put it another way, call them as they are.

Are You the Kind of *Boss* Who Says "Hooray for Me and to Hell with You"?

Then I'm sorry for you, my friend. Like Miguel's employers, there's a good chance you're overlooking some pretty good bets in a lot of ways; mistreating and in the end losing employees who could and would have done a hell of a job for you if you'd only been a bit more honest in your dealings with them. Nobody's suggesting you "hold the hand" of any subordinate; nobody can object to a tough-minded manager so long as he's fair and keeps his promises. But when you deliberately play fast and loose with the truth in dealing with an employee, whether in recruiting him or in handling him after he's aboard, you are building up serious trouble for yourself in times to come. Remember, when these guys leave the firm, there's a good chance they'll stay in the same business under other auspices. And there's no competitor more fierce than one who has a justifiable sense of being wronged by his former employer. Don't oversell a job just to get a man you want. Try to be as flexible as possible in meeting *his* needs and, if you really know they can't be met—for heaven's sake (and your own) *tell* him so, frankly. At best, he will find a little flexibility of his own and decide to see if what you offer isn't a satisfactory substitute for what he wanted. At worst, you'll part friends. And that, brother, is better than a hit in the eye with a sharp stick!

Do You *Work for* (or with) Someone Who Has Been Misled by a Management That Says "Hooray for Me but to Hell with You"?

Tell him. Don't soften the blow or be too indirect about it, either. Just set forth the facts as frankly and clearly as you can . . . and then be as supportive as possible in the ensuing talk. Maybe there's more than one way to skin a cat; perhaps the thing he's been promised isn't really impossible—perhaps some additional qualification on his part, or a quiet change of approach, will effect the changes necessary to put the desired goal within reach. And even if it really *is* impossible, perhaps there are still some plusses to be attained in the present job. At any rate, you won't have the burden of working with a man to whose deception and ultimate disappointment you have passively contributed.

Have *You* Been Misled by the "Hooray for Me and to Hell with You" Boys?

Don't be too emphatic in your answer until you have asked yourself the following subordinate questions: What is my goal? What chance have I of attaining it with my present employers? Were any promises made to me when I was hired which have not been kept? If so, was the defaulting a matter of unforeseen circumstances—or of deliberate misrepresentation? Realistic answers to those questions should give you a summary answer to the main question above. And if your answer is "yes," then you have a number of alternatives to consider. First, is there anything you can do—any additional academic or other qualification you could obtain, any line of conduct you could adopt—which would provide access to the spot you had in mind? Were your own stated aspirations realistic and legitimate? Is that still the route you want and need to go? Here, again, the answers to these individual questions provide a pretty clear picture. And they *should* point to the course of action to be taken . . . because if there's nothing you can do to attain your own goal in the present job and promises made to you were not kept, then (if you still are headed in the same direction) the industrial marriage contract under which you've been operating is in effect nullified. You must act accordingly. And if you don't

—wellsir—you are in the position of the guy who knows he's got a lousy marriage, but won't take any action to repair it or to dissolve it, either. Pitiful, perhaps. But not worth anyone's pity. . . .

Not all marriages are made in heaven.

Not all industrial unions are legitimate.

But the man who says "Hooray for Me and To Hell With You"—whether employer or employee—is in for trouble in either case.

15
Bright-Eyed and Bushy-Tailed (But Very Ineffective)

Observe the male lion. . . .

Note the noble stature, the mighty roar, the handsome ruff of fur about the head, the bearing that makes him heir to the title King of Beasts. Note that a group of his species are called a "pride."

Note also that he's a coward, a dummy and a lazy bum.

Any competent zoologist can tell you the score on him—that handsome, confident-looking hunk of male is a born lout and would very likely starve to death but for the hunting and protective activities of his mate, the quiet and competently hardworking female of the species.

I bring this up, not to discredit lions (if there are any lions in the reading audience: please, *forgive* me!) but to drive home a specific point: appearances can be deceiving—in the

Executive Jungle, perhaps, even more than in the lion's natural habitat.

I'm speaking, now, about one particular kind of executive; like the lion, he's impressive as hell. He is physically handsome in most cases, well dressed, has much poise and charm, a bearing that virtually exudes confidence, warmth and understanding.

And *energy* . . . !

He has energy to spare, 24 hours a day. You can almost *hear* his motor running when you're talking to him; if he's not actively "ramrodding" something or other, you can be sure he's deep in "analytical planning" and if anything really *should* go wrong in an area where he bears responsibility— depend on it! This guy will have a *perfect* explanation!

His only drawback: nothing *ever* seems to get *done* when he's around. . . .

A near-perfect example of this kind of executive, I think, would be a man we will call

Mac, the Magnificent

I encountered him when he was a key candidate for general managership of a division in one of my client companies . . . and he certainly looked like a Man On The Way Up. Management had singled him out as possessing top echelon qualities. And God knows he *looked* the part.

He came, I discovered, from a rural community in Washington; attended college on scholarship, graduated with honors, and was supported while doing graduate work by the same company that hired him the moment he had that M.A. in hand.

His employment history was stable, and exemplary: in twelve years he had worked for just two employers; the first four years with that original company, the next eight with the second, an aerospace firm where he headed a group of about 450 persons in a highly sophisticated area of technology.

This was a big firm, but management thought Mac—out of the tens of thousands of persons in their employ—was one of the dozen or so destined for really high-level policy making positions.

But one of my client's people somehow learned of Mac and his apparent abilities. He was approached, proved willing at least to discuss the opportunity for career growth which might be offered by a change in employment and came to me as part of the Red Carpet treatment. My evaluation, I think, was expected to be the cherry on the top of the frappé.

And God knows it looked that way in the beginning. . . .

Mac's background was encouraging; he was one of three children born into a stable, happy family. His parents weren't rich, had supported and encouraged him in all that he did, to the end that he had been able to obtain the scholarship that sent him on his way.

He was married; his wife's family background was similarly stable, and they had two children. Everyone in good health; everyone friendly and seemingly quite happy.

Testing showed he had, as expected, a good basic intellect. His verbal capabilities were particularly sound, and his interests suggested affinity for areas which were real and practical. He tended to be a bit of a tinkerer; liked to work with his hands; enjoyed sailing (owned a modest sailboat) and enjoyed the scientific milieu.

Unlike the stereotype of the engineer, however, Mac had the desire (supported by his excellent verbal abilities) to sell and to persuade others to his point of view.

His least interest was in details; he seemed to abhor them. This was apparent in his evident aversion to administrative effort and to working with computational figures. There was, too, a low interest in the welfare, training and development of others.

His personality seemed stable as a rock.* Mac was quite consistent in his interrelationship with others; had no history or evidence of depressions; showed a consistently positive turn of attitude—apparently always riding the crest of the emotional wave that most people ride up and down.

Complementing this was his confidence in his ability to perform his work well; Mac felt he could lick the world, yet this was not mere pomposity. His optimism was sincere and he had a record to justify it.

In addition, he was energetic, liked handling a number of assignments concurrently and seemed to enjoy the variety.

But here a telltale chink appeared in what otherwise might have seemed a virtually flawless executive personality.

Despite the energy and the willingness, Mac seemed to a large extent to lack any sense of urgency about getting things done. He appeared to have the notion that everyone was dedicated, conscientious, self-motivated and purposeful. Therefore, he seemed little inclined to push anyone . . . in any way.

More, his capacity for accepting frustration seemed higher

---

*Now, there's *another* simile that irritates me. Some rocks are stable. Some are not stable—especially here in Sunny California, where back country roads are lined with signs that say "Watch for Rocks." The darn things come tumbling out of nowhere and squish someone in a car who happened to be at the wrong place at the wrong time every now and then. "Solid as a rock" my eye!

than might otherwise have been surmised,* since his spontaneity would have indicated a much greater sense of urgency than actually existed.

Mac's primary concern would always be for the immediate as opposed to that which might happen in the middle or far distant future.

And he was objective—even to the point of insensitivity, a trait related for him, I think, to his preference for what was real and tangible (as opposed to that which was ideational). Such a man *had* to play things straight.

He would never be able to lie effectively over any length of time, since his memory was not sufficiently retentive to keep track of what he might have said two weeks before to different people. (And this, in most cases, is an admirable trait—as was the fact that success, for him, had to spring from exercise of his own merits, in order to be valuable to him. He could never have accepted success achieved by cutthroat, underhanded, or dog-eat-dog tactics.)

Money was important to him; oh, yes! But not disproportionately so. Perhaps his strongest motivation to become a manager was to become a shaper of policy.

It was for this reason, I believe, he was willing to listen to the offer made by my client. It was a chance to take a Giant Step upward, in his view; to achieve that kind of corporate title to which he had always aspired.

So . . . Mac took the job.†

As division manager in my client's firm, his early record was nothing startling. But then, no one had expected it to be.

---

*This guy could have smiled and exuded assurance while the Hindenburg burned.

†Oh, *bummer!*

Mac's division had been for years operating with a pretty good profit ratio; it was in a highly competitive position in what could only be called a dying industry. Technological developments had actually superseded that division's basic product . . . but the replacement item had not as yet gained much popularity due to price and other considerations.

But the time of change was coming.

And so was Trouble. . . .

Little by little, the complexion of the field changed; the new item gained just enough popularity to force the little "garage shop" operations—which had competed with Mac's division and other major manufacturers in the field—out of business. The immediate effect was twofold: the major firms' share in the market increased, and so did their competitive effort.

The cutthroat competition eliminated one or two of the weaker competitors; again, the survivors had a bigger slice of the pie; and the competition got even hotter.

The trend was obvious . . . to everyone but Mac.

Others—even Mac's peers and subordinates—were able to comprehend the situation; they knew the field itself was dwindling until at length there would be *no one* left. It was obviously time to switch, either to making the new product that had left the present line antiquated or into an altogether new field.

But getting Mac to understand and take action was another matter entirely.

He would listen with his usual affability, nod, agree that the warning sounded had merit—and then try to placate the speaker by citing wondrous improvements in the division's position which might be expected if some minor point were to be corrected. He would answer clear warnings amounting to *End Of The Road; Detour Ahead* with some meandering statement which, analyzed, became, "We might lose a few dollars on each unit shipped, fella, but we'll sure make it up on volume if we can just get a little bigger slice of the pie . . . !"

One by one, Mac's key personnel became disenchanted. And the division itself slipped, by almost imperceptible degrees, from profit into loss.

Unfortunately, Mac's superiors (who might have forced him into corrective action) were too involved at the moment in a program of acquiring new corporate entities to give much attention to what he was doing. They saw him in motion *getting things done*, they noticed that he was still smiling, still affable, and assumed the situation was under control.

Mac thought so, too. He made plans—immediate and intermediate—for *things to be done* to increase efficiency in making, shipping and selling the antiquated item. Not much came of these plans, but he remained optimistic. He issued statements indicating that certain steps would be taken. They didn't seem to get done . . . but he always had a ready explanation; more immediate and necessary difficulties had cropped up; the program had been postponed, but not abandoned.*

Some of his key personnel became discouraged and departed.

As time passed, these defections increased.†

But when, at length, top management finally was forced by an ever-increasing loss picture to take a close and realistic look at what was going on in Mac's division, there was a great reluctance to do anything about the situation. After all, Mac was a person of substance, exemplifying most of the qualities considered "best" in a human being; he still had the admir-

---

*With guys like Mac, nothing is *ever* abandoned. They just sort of fade away.

†"General Exodus" is the phrase that springs immediately to mind.

ation and respect of many people not only in his own division but elsewhere in the organization . . . and even among competitors.

He was still Bright-Eyed and Bushy-Tailed. . . .

(Besides, even had they taken a firm stand, demanded that Mac develop a real plan of action and adhere to it, there were a few who wondered—albeit privately, I think—whether he would really be able to deliver.)

So when action of some sort could no longer be postponed, instead of asking for Mac's resignation, they *promoted* him!

Mac moved up to a level even closer to the corporate top, apparently in charge of his own former division, and another which had a somewhat similar product line. At the same time, however, he was ordered to hire a results-oriented manager for both these divisions.

But that manager would serve, heaven help us, *under* Mac. . . .

And Mac, in time, found himself beaming approval over the whole affair; the new manager did in fact manage to put both divisions back into the black and set them in motion toward a really workable and forward-looking goal—while Mac sighed and told himself *he* was responsible for it all.

He still believes that.*

His friends in top management have, for the most part, even convinced *themselves* that it is true.

Mac's career continues, full-blast.

And one day, if all continues to go well and the company never hits a point where a real financial bind forces objective and realistic appraisal of his actual worth, he will sit at or

---

*Lewis Carroll said it:". . . sometimes I've believed as many as six impossible things before breakfast!"

near the apex of the corporate pyramid ... where his basic
ineffectiveness can smile the firm right into bankruptcy.

Does a Bright-Eyed and Bushy-Tailed Character *Work for You?*

Come on, now: the truth! Sure, you like the guy—who
could help it? But let's get a bit realistic. If he's always
smiling, always in motion, always full of plans ... but
nothing seems to get done ... you know damn well that's
what he is. So what to do? Well, chances are you *can't* fire
him. It would be like giving Mother a hotfoot and insulting
her Apple Pie. The alternative, therefore, is to see to it the
guy is staffed with competent people in all his key positions
—and that they have the *authority* to get things done. Then
you've got to lean on Bright Eyes a little; demand a workable
and comprehensive plan from him, break it down into separate day-by-day or week-by-week goals, and enforce adher-
ance to it. This is a real-time guy; he wants to know "what
did we get done today?" All right ... you can feed it to him
this way. It's management-by-objectives. And it's an approach that will work. If *anything* will.

Do You *Work for* a Man Who Is Bright-Eyed and Bushy-Tailed?

Well, it's a plus, really, if you're sure of your own competence. (And, unhappily, it is also a true haven for the inept.)
For the able, it provides (usually) a chance to do what you
want to do, the way you want to do it, without tight control.
You can learn a lot, and you can make errors (and learn from
them, too) without attracting too much criticism. The Boss is
a positive guy, an understanding guy. He's sure to understand
what went wrong and why you won't do it that way again. In
the end, of course, you'll have to leave. No matter how bright

the picture may look for the moment, the outfit is in trouble; when a real problem crops up as it inevitably must, the Boss not only won't be able to direct efforts to cope with it— chances are he won't even recognize its existence, no matter *who* tells him. *Unless*, that is, the problem is recognized by Bright Eyes' own superiors, in such a case the opportunity for growth and experience may be even greater, because if the head of the firm decides to retain him, the major part of the real responsibility—and authority—will have to be delegated downward. Meaning, probably, *you!* If that happens, call a spade a spade. Tell him, in detail (and probably in terms of step-by-step goals) what's got to be done; obtain his support, then go ahead . . . and do it.

Do You *Work with* a Man Who Is Bright-Eyed and Bushy-Tailed?

Then you'll have to be as tough on him as you can bring yourself to be, especially if his responsibilities and his discharge of them can affect your own performance. If he just *won't* listen, if he just *can't* seem to take the necessary steps—then it's time to take the whole thing to the top. The outcome there can be one of two things: either top management takes effective action and gets this guy on the stick . . . or you'd better dust off the old résumé. You *can not* afford to sit around making allowances for him and watching him foul up your own operations. A failure produced by such inaction on your part is chargeable, my friend, to *you*—not to Bright Eyes. And if you let it happen, you truly deserve anything you get.

Are *You* Bright-Eyed and Bushy-Tailed but Not Too Effective?

Chances are, you'll *never* believe it. Not, at any rate, unless the word comes from someone you have reason to respect—

or who has the authority to make you listen. But if you *do* at length decide you have some of these qualities, your first step is plain and inescapable: you *must* support yourself with subordinates who are intellectually honest, competent, and willing to say, "Mac—you're fulla beans! Here are the facts; *this* is reality!" And you've got to do *more* than listen; you've got to act on their advice. These people must not only tell you the truth as they see it, they must help you stay honest; help you set up specific real-time goals. They must not *let* you evade the issue or mistake motion for action. If you're not willing to do *that*, brother, a time of reckoning *is coming*—whether you can believe it or not—and the Man in the Pan will be *you*!

16
How Young Are You?

Just about everything today is aimed at the young.

Clothing styles, music, art, automobile designs, literature—all devoted to the proposition that youth is the best time of life and that any sign of aging is, somehow, a kind of social error.

Only . . . not everyone really *is* young.

Not everyone even wants to be.

And the problems that pop up in the lives of Executive Jungle denizens about the time they reach their late 50s and early 60s are *not* a social error—nor are they to be dismissed as unique situations unrelated to the rest of life.

They are just problems.

Like any other problems.

Some can be solved, some can't. Some that could be, won't be—and that is usually because the approach, far from being the kind of intelligent, realistic and workmanlike sort of thing which might be expected of a seasoned and able executive, tends for one reason or another to be either sloppy or totally out of character.

If a man really *wants* to sit on his front porch and rock, well and good.

But few people really do; most of us are accustomed to busy, active and meaningful daily lives. We are too young to sit around dying by inches; too healthy to settle for complete inactivity; too interested in the world not to want to take part in it.

But . . . what part?

And how?

Here's the story of how one man arrived at what seems to be a meaningful answer in his own life. I call him

Peter, the Man Who Was Too Young to Quit

He came to me at the suggestion of one of his superiors, shortly after he had elected to take early retirement from a job he had held for more than a quarter century.*

Peter was at this time sixty-one years of age. He had been plant manager for his company on the West Coast. Recently, because of a study and recommendations he himself had made, the firm had decided to close down the West Coast manufacturing operation; turn it into a warehousing deal.

That meant he was, in effect, out of a job.

His company was a good one; it recognized its responsibility to him and his demonstrated ability. Several options were forwarded for his consideration.

---

*A real anomaly for guys in his age group. Or *most* age groups, for that matter. Hell, in the aerospace industry, it's not at all unusual for some people to have an average of one change of employment every year!

If he wanted to keep right on working, the company said it would be more than happy to have him come East; he could be of considerable help there, helping to consolidate the manufacturing and marketing systems, until he was eligible for the regular company retirement plan at age sixty-three.

On the other hand, if he wished, he could take an early retirement which would pay him about two thirds of his present salary for eighteen months (this would have come to about $1,000 per month, or $18,000) until he was sixty-three, at which time he would collect a slightly reduced retirement income.

Peter and his wife were pretty much alone; their children were grown and out of the nest; the retirement income (augmented at sixty-five by Social Security) would be quite comfortable for them. So he elected to take the early retirement plan.

But . . . Peter wasn't really ready for that rocking chair.

And again, the company offered to help. Which is where I entered the picture. The company paid my fee for an evaluation of this valued and valuable man, to assist him in rearranging his life in a way which would best suit his new needs.

His personal and work history had some unusual aspects.

He had, for instance, worked for *only one* employer in the entire course of his career. His father had been a steel mill manager; a typical horny-handed bear of a man who had battled his way to the top and remained king of the hill most of his life from what I could gather.

Peter, his eldest son, had graduated from high school at the top of his class in 1924, obtained an engineering degree from Georgia Tech (while working each summer) and joined the firm from which he was now retiring shortly after graduation in 1929. He married about that time, too, and had always enjoyed a solid and friendly relationship with his wife and with their two children. They saw the kids, and the grand-children, not quite as often as they wished; Peter hoped, in retirement, to see a bit more of them. But he knew he had to have *something* more to occupy his mind.

He seemed quite robust and healthy, but I learned that he had suffered an apparent angina attack (which I privately noted as a probable true coronary) a dozen years before. It had put him out of his job for about a year, during which time he pared off a lot of excess weight and devoted real time and effort at getting into good physical shape. If he con-tinued this, it seemed likely to me he would outlive many a man who had had no such definite "warning."

Peter's employment history—with the single employer— was obviously stable. For his first five years in the firm he had been an engineer in Indiana. Then he had spent another three years as a sales engineer, then two years as a chief inspector, followed by three years as superintendent of pro-duction, all at the same place.

He was subsequently promoted to assistant factory man-ager, and held the position for the next six years (during which the war kept the plant running at full capacity and then some) until being moved up to the number one job as factory manager.

Then he was taken into the firm's corporate offices on a special assignment, dealing with market surveys and analysis. He investigated possible improvements in product lines, the prospects for new lines (and even the notion of dropping some present lines) in order to meet present and anticipated market requirements.

That assignment lasted two years, after which he came full circle: he was factory manager again . . . at the West Coast plant. And that's where he was when he made the survey that resulted in the West Coast operation's termination.*

As a personality, I found Peter to be a kind of hard-nosed guy, competitive, and used to seeing things in blacks and whites. I also suspected he had developed a certain amount of rigidity, having worked so long with a single firm and within the bounds of a certain set of established policies.

He was decisive, energetic, direct and purposeful in his communications with others where verbal or written.

His analytical powers were good, and he was not impulsive, but he was an action-oriented person able to establish practical priorities on any problem. He also was the kind of man who would keep a couple of alternatives in mind, if something came unglued with his original solution.

Peter had, besides, the gift of being able to size up situations—and people—with much speed and accuracy.

Accordingly, I suggested he become an industrial consultant.

One reason was that, while Peter was still an energetic and dynamic person, I didn't get the impression he really wanted another full-time job. What I figured he had in mind (correctly, as it turned out) was something that would let him, in effect, keep his "hand in" without being committed on a full time basis; something that would give him the opportunity of occasional bursts of activity, varied with periods of relaxation with his wife and family.

I further suggested that—rather than hang out his own shingle as a consultant—he make a connection with an estab-

---

*Right there, I decided Peter was a really solid citizen. How many people (with an intellect above the hopeless imbecile level, that is) can imagine turning in a report that says, in effect, "put me out of work"?

lished consulting firm, to work for them only at intervals on a "call-in" basis, on tasks that required his particular expertise.

(That would, also, be a very good deal for the consulting firm that took him on. No overhead, you see; no salary to pay when he wasn't actually doing a job for them. An ideal setup for any consulting outfit—times always come when they find themselves shorthanded—for which his work could only be pure gravy. And a good deal for Peter, too, since it fitted his own plans so well.)

By the way: I advised strongly against his going into the consulting business on his own hook. Such a move would have required him to do a lot of promotional work, selling his own services, and I just couldn't see him being happy spending his time in such a way. It would turn into a full-time occupation—and that was not what he wanted.

We prepared a résumé for the consulting firms where he thought he might make such a connection, stressing the advantages to their firm by having him on call on a "single assignment" basis (with no pay except during the times he was in fact performing billable services) and stressing the breadth and length of his experience in the industrial field.

How does a firm turn down a deal like that?

Answer: it doesn't.

And didn't.

Peter did, in fact, make more than one connection—a situation which I suspect may lead to a bit of trouble in the future. I'm hopeful that he'll be able to handle it; I think he will. The trouble with being on call to more than one company is that there might be some conflict of interest there; I think the best solution is for him to hook close to just one firm with a clientele large enough to provide fairly regular assignments.

But that's Peter's *next* problem.*

For the moment, the problem he brought in has been solved—and to his eminent satisfaction. . . .

So why am I telling *you* all this?

Well, believe it or not, my friend, every tick of the clock brings you nearer to the spot where Peter found himself. One tick nearer, every second, whether you are twenty or fifty. Unless you plan to commit hara-kiri at age fifty, it is a problem you must expect to face sooner or later . . . so why not start mulling a couple of ideas over in your mind *right now*? Workable ideas, that is; ideas which would apply to *you* . . . not to the guy you'd like to think you are, or to my friend Peter, or to someone you know who did it such-and-such a way.

Ideas that would satisfy *you*.

And if the ideas still seem pretty hazy—why not talk it over with someone with a bit of professional expertise in that field?

Face it, brother—total, rocking-chair type retirement is probably just not in the cards for you. The fact is you'd be going up the wall before long.

What's *Your* Age?

How young are you, anyway?

I don't mean in terms of years—I mean in terms of health, general activity and personality. What's your approach to living?

A guy like Peter (to go back to the illustration above) is simply not ready for full retirement. Navy records show that

---

*Yeah, and that's life, buddy! A problem-producing and problem-solving process. What else did you *think* it was, anyway . . . ?

life expectancy for a man retiring after thirty years of service is a lot lower than it is for most people in other lines; the Navy guys seem to have a lot of trouble making the adjustment. They seem to lose the will to fight and to accomplish which sustained them during their service careers.

It need not be so.

Not for them.

Not for you.

But whatever course you do decide upon and at whatever age you actually retire, the program you set up for yourself must be one that suits you . . . not ten other guys named Joe. That requires realism; the ability to see the world and yourself as you really are.

You've probably still got a hell of a lot to offer.

If you don't seem to find any takers on the horizon—it's a good bet that you're either looking in the wrong direction, or that your evaluation itself was faulty.

Get help. Get going. It is *not* later than you think; it is earlier! Do your own thing . . . and the years to come may be the best of your life.

Part 3
Pitfalls, Miasmas and Fevers

1
The Circle Machine

Carousels are a lot of fun.

They were invented, you know, by the Persians—for the training of their cavalrymen. Slaves turned the machinery that spun the merry-go-round with its horses (the horses were geared to go up and down as they moved, just as ours do today) and the apprentice warriors rode the painted steeds, carrying lances with which they tried to spear a ring off a hook located near the rim of the wheel.

The need for such a training device has, of course, pretty much disappeared. But the apprentices had so much fun (the slaves, I suspect, didn't think a hell of a lot of it) that the device was retained for the amusement of one and all. No carnival, traveling or stationary as an amusement park, can exist without at least one such ride. And a great many other, supposedly more modern, rides are based on the carousel principal.

They'll probably always be popular.

But for a man attempting to survive in the Executive Jungle, anything that moves only in a circle can be a real hazard; the kind of pitfall he must identify and avoid at peril of life and career.

And the Jungle is full of them.*

Every now and then (actually a lot oftener than I like to think about) I find a very capable man with all the capacities which should lead him along the trail to the better part of the executive suite, who has had a whole succession of very similar jobs in very similar environments—all of which have led him nowhere in particular.

It isn't that he's really *failed* in any of them.

It's just that none of them seemed to lead him anywhere; his personality for one reason or another didn't seem to fit with any of the companies, and he kept moving on—whether at his own discretion or as a result of the previous employers' suggestion—*and on, and on* . . . never quite finding the opportunity he was seeking when he entered the Jungle.

Don't *pity* him.

Help him!

He is riding a Circle Machine—one of several models now on the market—and unless someone shows him how to get off, he's going to go right on riding it until he's so depressed, disappointed in himself and generally despondent that his life will hardly be worth living.

A good case in point is that of Jason, a man I encountered

---

*Eerie image, isn't it—a Jungle full of carousels, I mean? Still, I understand there *is* at least one; in good repair and still operating, in Swaziland. Present to some past king or other from a passing carnival that had some notion of getting home alive.

in the usual way—as an evaluator—when he was deputy director of manufacturing at a big aerospace firm. Jason was aggressive, knowledgable, effective and progressive ... and riding a Circle Machine.

One big problem he was facing at the time we met was that, while he was only in his early forties, none of the men in key positions under him was less than fifty-five. (And I'm being kind there; using chronological age. In terms of ideas and flexibility, most of these people were eight-five at the very least!)

The result was that Jason, while an innovator by nature— and actually brought into the company *because* of that very quality—was unable to get anything new tried, anywhere along the line, despite the fact that he was supposed to be head of the company's "new" product development program!*

Well, that kind of thing does happen to any executive once or twice in the course of an active career, doesn't it?

Sure it does.

But for Jason, it was a way of life!

This poor guy had started at a relatively small firm, had a considerable success there—yes, he was in charge of an innovative program, and it *did* succeed—and then moved into one of the long-established giants of the industry.

That was his first experience with trying to innovate with a company not really accustomed to innovation (and pretty well structured against it; the general feeling is, if we've become big and successful doing it one way, why mess around with something new?) and his success was extremely limited.

---

*Maybe they just hired him because it looked good to the directors or something. Things like that depress me. What a waste!

Frustrated, he had moved to another big company, again with a pretty good salary and a fairly high corporate rank, and again supposedly in charge of a department devoted to innovation. Again, his success was limited. And again, it was for the same reason.

The pattern repeated itself, again and again, at a whole dreary succession of new jobs . . . until at length he moved from the firm where I met him Full Circle back to the outfit where he had scored his first big success.

But *that* company (ironically, very much as the result of Jason's own early innovations!) had over the years become the same sort of Monster which had been frustrating him ever since he had left. Jason found himself alone, depressed, frustrated, almost frightened among people now steeped in the very history he had helped to make. A Stranger and Afraid, in a World he Damn Well made . . . !

The pattern was obvious, of course.*

Circle Machine—operating at full tilt. And the cure was just as obvious. Jason had first succeeded—and probably could *only* succeed— in a small-company environment. Going back to his original firm was really just a case of mistaken identity; he was equating a place with a situation, which is almost always a mistake. The place was the same, but the situation had changed.

He was the kind of man who, while very well placed in his particular specialty and highly competent at it, could only attain maximum effectiveness in an environment where his creative and innovative talents could be given free rein. If a larger company were able to offer this, the size wouldn't matter and Jason would have been just as successful as he had been in the first job. But the sad fact is that many really large

---

*To anyone but Jason. More's the pity.

organizations—particularly in industry—simply cannot offer such opportunity.

The result, for Jason, was frustration.

Even if he had, somehow, become top man in the larger milieu (and therefore, presumably, able to enforce his own will and personality upon the giant) it seems doubtful if he could have succeeded in the end. The larger a company becomes, the older it becomes, the more rigidly structured and history-oriented it becomes. Such firms *can* be changed. They can be, in effect, turned around and directed in different directions. But the likelihood of any single individual— even a man sitting at the very top of the pyramid—effecting such a change in direction and orientation is really pretty slim.

And until a man like Jason recognizes this fact, evaluates it with relation to his own personality and ambitions, and then acts upon his knowledge—until then—he will continue to ride the Circle Machine, around and around and around. No chance to get off.

And no brass ring. . . .

Of course there are more Circle Machines than one.

Let's have a look at some of them:

Jason's story portrays one side of the *small company-big company machine*; a man of his type simply is misplaced in a big or rigid organization. But the ride—on that same machine —is going to be just as dizzying for the executive whose nature demands security, the assurance of his own position in an established order, a more thoroughly planned and ordered life. He can no more be satisfied or fulfilled in a small company than a Jason can be in a big one. Both are riding that Circle Machine . . . but on opposite sides.

Another executive carousel can be the staff position-line position machine.

I know of one man whose whole career (until then) had been spent in line jobs. And, from one viewpoint, he might even have been considered successful. He had actually become president of an organization on two occasions . . . both of which incidents, I might add, ended disastrously.

An evaluation of this man disclosed the startling* fact that, not only had he been entirely miscast as chief executive —top manager—of an organization, he was really out of his element in any managerial spot of any kind (unless, perhaps, it would have been management of some small, esoteric, group).

His frustration was due to the fact that he was, by his very nature, more adapted to a staff position (planning, probing, advising, studying, analyzing) *close to* the presidency of a firm, but not exposed to the day-by-day catch-as-catch-can of immediate command and management.

(And of course there are plenty of men of the opposite type; staff positions are as deadly to them as line jobs are for a person of the type described above. They *need* the feeling of direct authority/responsibility, the daily decision-making of the manager's role. Put a man like this in a staff job where he can exert his influence only by indirection, and you'll have him figuratively climbing the walls!)

Another Circle Machine is the "wrong level" machine.

Dr. Laurence Peter said, in his now-famous treatise "explaining" why "nothing really works" that people tend to rise to their "level of incompetence," and stagnate there. Result: everyone is assigned to a job he can't do. That's the Peter Principle.

The principle thus described is, Lord help us, valid in

---

*To the evaluee. Not to me, brother. His job history alone made me hear the distant music of the carousel.

all-too-many cases. But the hell of it is that the "level of incompetency" *may* be reached *before* the individual hits the level where he *is* competent!

Remember back in World War II there used to be a joke around the defense plants that the only way to become a lead-man was to be a lousy machinist? If you couldn't run the machine, you got promoted to a supervisorial position.

Funny, huh? But funnier still is the fact that a lot of the people who actually *were* promoted under those conditions turned out to be crackerjack supervisors! While, as Dr. Peter correctly demonstrated, the fact that you're a competent subordinate does not necessarily indicate you'll be worth a darn as a supervisor: the fact that you're *not* much good as a subordinate also does *not* necessarily indicate you'll be a failure as the Boss.

I've come across plenty of cases where a man who is either unsuccessful or performing below par on his present level could, if given the opportunity, function brilliantly in a position of greater responsibility. The fact that you have a hard time carrying out another man's program does by no means argue that you couldn't carry out one of your own. The fact that you are strongly motivated for success, that you can see the big picture, coordinate things, interrelate them, establish priorities and manage others are abilities which would be of little use to you in a subordinate role . . . and vital in the top spot.

Another Circle Machine literally stands still.

This is the indispensible man machine; the one ridden by the executive who is performing in such an outstanding manner in his present spot that management hesitates to move him up. Some companies, recognizing this situation and its implications for frustration of their best personnel, have procedures whereby a man may transfer from one division to another—or one department to another—*without* his own boss's okay. Almost the sole reason for the existence of such a procedure is to prevent a supervisor from stifling the growth and progress of an underling because it would be "inconvenient" for him to have to replace him. But in a company which does *not* have such a procedure available, the alternative to the man thus stymied—while more difficult— still does exist. He *can quit* the moment he's sure his particular Circle Machine is standing still. Can, and *must* . . . or face a future filled with nothing but frustration.

And then there are the Circle Machines which can best be described as a set. They apply to poor souls who are, for one reason or another, misplaced in the lone-wolf, small-group or large-group categories.

Let's consider the lone wolves first.

Perhaps an individual has a little trouble communicating with others. His inner conversation may be brilliant, but he can't seem to make others understand—or maybe he really isn't motivated to do so. Maybe this guy is so self-sufficient that he really doesn't *need* the plaudits of others; maybe he's a guy who competes against the stopwatch rather than other runners. Well . . . how successful can a guy like this be in any kind of "team" effort? More likely than not, he'll sit there, swearing inwardly, while an approach he has already considered and discarded is attempted on a problem he knows he could solve if everyone would just go away and stop bugging him. His progress and his effectiveness, if any, is apt to be extremely slow in such an environment. But leave him alone —just him and the problem—and the results are apt to be amazing.

On that same team, though, there may be a man who would be absolutely lost if you leave him confronting the problem on a one-to-one basis. He *needs* group interaction; needs the stimulation of group effort, the competition

against other members of the group. He'll be all right, so long
as he's placed in such a milieu; happy and successful. But
leave him alone—in that same situation where his lone-wolf
peer can function so well—and you wind up with a frustrated, bitter and probably quite ineffective individual.

And this same man may find himself out of his element if
the group in which he functions is too big, or too small. The
bigger the group, remember, the more difficult consensus—
and immediate, effective action on decision—are apt to be.*
One man functions well in a big group; he finds a certain
assurance in being able to bounce his ideas around a large
number of minds; a sense of comfort in knowing, perhaps,
that a big organization is adding to or criticizing his ideas. He
likes taking a large number of inputs and subjecting them to
his own criticism. He would be less effective in a small group;
less prone to express himself, less able to function. But a man
with a slightly different approach—more oriented to decision
and immediate action—would be out of his element with the
larger group. The Circle Machine will surely take him for a
ride!

There are sedentary Circle Machines and action Circle
Machines.

A man oriented toward action—the "do it *now*" type—can
function, depending on other personality factors, in either a
line or a staff position (though a high level of activity is more
apt to exist among line people) whereas the sedentary type,
who paces himself and moves at that pace come rain or shine,
is more likely to function at his best in a staff position
(though there are plenty of cases of successful line managers
who operate that way.)

---

*Unless, of course, a strong leader arises within the group. This,
however, poses certain little problems of its own—as the citizens of Nazi
Germany discovered to their dismay.

The question is not one of line versus staff; it's a question of function and placement. If a man finds himself stymied, going from job to job, always on about the same level of the pyramid and therefore not progressing in his own development, perhaps he is a sedentary individual trying to function in an action job, or vice versa.

In such a case, a switch from line to staff, or staff to line, will not necessarily be a successful approach to the problem.

He's got to figure out his true orientation.

And he's got to make sure his *next* job fits him.

There are pressure people and there are nonpressure people—and misplacement of a nonpressure executive in a pressure job can deposit him as surely on the Circle Machine as can the opposite misplacement.

If a man enjoys the rapid pace and has a high sense of urgency for accomplishment—if he enjoys gut-busting pressure to hit a deadline—you not only are going to frustrate him by putting him in a situation where no such pressure exists, you are also running the risk that he will deliberately *create* pressure. Such a man will, consciously or otherwise, set up a situation of strategy and tactical interplay which will allow him to satisfy that inner boiler-gauge which must read at least 10,000 p.s.i. before his wheels really begin to turn over at all.

On the other hand, the man who likes to set his own pace and objectives, to bring a certain tranquility of thought to bear on a given problem uninfluenced by outside proddings, is very apt to go completely off the rails when he finds himself in the boiler-room. His powers of concentration and his ability to solve problems—the basic weapons of the executive—evaporate and fly out the safety valve when the gauge reads more than a fraction or so over 14.7 p.s.i.*

---

*Right! That's normal air pressure.

Both men are basically effective. Both men have value to an organization. There is room in the Jungle for both. But *only* when they're properly placed. Otherwise . . . all aboard for another swing around the carousel!

The forms of pressure can be anything you can imagine: economic, time-deadline, cost-accounting, even (God defend us all!) a boss's dictum to "look busy!" The form isn't really so important; the man on whom the pressure falls *is*. . . .

Another pair of Circle Machines are the ones labeled "working with *thing*" and "working with *ideas*."

Some extremely able people can be creative only if you ask them to improve the effectiveness of a component, a bit of hardware, something they can see, feel and manipulate. They are well placed when working with *things*.

Ask them to fool around with ideas—ideas, that is, completely or only peripherally related to actual practice—and you get (a) a blank stare, and (b) a frustrated guy.

On the other hand, the man who has a flair for dealing with concepts is going to blow it when you tell him to "fix the fanbelt." The truth is he is as apt to immerse the darn thing in water to see if it'll shrink as he is to tighten the nut that holds the generator in place. He can expound for hours on various approaches to new power principles which may move automobiles in the future. But hand him an engine with a cracked sparkplug and his chance of getting it to run again is pretty close to zero.

Sometimes in testing a really creative and idea-oriented guy, I'll get a response to a situation which might be dismissed as irrelevant. That's a good time for me to be careful. Because the response *may not* be; it may simply be so far out in fourth, fifth or sixth order functions that you don't really grasp it until you've considered it intensely for a while.

The ability of an Albert Einstein to enunciate the formula $E=mc^2$ did, indeed, point the way to creation of the atomic pile and, further along, to the atom bomb and hydrogen bombs. But Einstein *could not* have demonstrated it no matter how much hardware and money and personnel you placed at his disposal.

Practical application of his idea was the work of experimental physicists (rather than theoretical physicists or abstract mathematicians) and engineers. They and they alone could do it. And any one of them would have been equally misplaced in the theoretical role.

Stymie Albert Einstein behind a drawing board; place a screwdriver in his hand, and you can hear the carousel music begin. He is riding a Circle Machine . . . to nowhere.

There are generalist Circle-Machines and specialist Circle-Machines.

Generalists—those with the ability to see the big picture and with at least a working knowledge of a large number of fields and functions—are not only well-placed, they are *essential* to a small company. The Boss there may have to be head bookkeeper, production chaser, salesman and administrator all in one. Nothing sadder than watching a highly-trained specialist—a really fine salesman or an especially competent engineer, for instance—try to function in the general capacity. It *does* happen, sometimes, that such an individual discovers unsuspected capacity for generalist functioning in such a situation.

But it is rare.* As rare, I might say, as a really effective generalist—accustomed to wearing twelve hats in the course of a day and dealing with an array of problems in several areas of a business—functioning successfully when suddenly confined to a very narrow field of expertise. Again, it *has*

---

*It occurs on an order of frequency roughly analogous to that of a square grape.

been known to happen (perhaps the generalist was actually a bit misplaced, a bit misevaluated in the general field) but such cases just don't come along every day.

Generalists, by the way, are not *always* best placed in the small company environment. Large companies have plenty of room for them... and that room is usually at the top, because of the width of his abilities.

And sometimes very small companies, especially those dealing in esoteric items, frequently have a crying need for the special abilities of the very narrowest of specialists.

Again, it's a matter of marrying the right man to the right job . . . a question of evaluation on a highly individual basis. And if the evaluation is wrong, there you go on the Circle Machine!

Now we come to another group of Circle Machines.

They are labeled low, moderate and high responsibility and they're especially tricky to identify because the amount of responsibility an individual can handle may vary considerably due to the existence or nonexistence of a number of factors.

Basic intelligence, creativity, frustration-tolerance, perseverance and competitive instinct are all among the factors which may effect the answer.

An action-oriented man held strictly accountable for the success of a particular project but given, at the same time, little opportunity to act within the charter thus given is doomed from the start. It amounts to responsibility without authority . . . and it is destructive both to his own self-image and to his basic effectiveness.

He *wants* the responsibility. But he must have the authority to see the job through.

Others can accept responsibility only for short-tenured operations—at best, probably things which can be done this week or this month. Otherwise, they just can't deal with the frustrations involved. A ten-year plan, for which they are responsible, is going to stop them before they ever get started. Reduce that same assignment to a series of short-term goals—a two month plan, a three month plan, a six month plan even—and they can handle it. They can see the goal. They can approach it. It's real to them.

Some people require total responsibility/authority to function. Some need the steadying influence of a superior with whom they can, when necessary, check their own ideas and approaches. Some need the feeling that someone is literally breathing down their necks all the time.

Their effectiveness—their ability to do their jobs—depends on a realistic and accurate appraisal of their needs. And they will ride the Circle Machine *until they get it*.

And finally we come to a real whopper: the science-engineering-technology-administration-selling-and-business Circle Machine.

Which needs definition. Try this:

The scientist produces the concept; the idea.

The engineer brings it to a practical level.

The technologist makes the product.

The administrator keeps them all functioning effectively.

The salesman sells the product.

The businessman sees to it that the whole thing returns enough profit to keep the operation running.

Now: can a man sitting on one of these pegs function effectively if he bounces to another?

Maybe.

And maybe not.

There *are* individuals who can bounce quite happily from one to another-sometimes even cover two or more at a time—and do each job with ability and interest. But *beware*!

Even if you can fulfill *five* of those roles with success, it is no sign you'll be able to handle the sixth!

A man is what he is. Human beings are capable of growth; capable, even, of change under certain conditions. But the factors that make a man an effective salesman do not necessarily make him a businessman as well; a capable engineer is not also a capable scientist as a matter of course; a fine administrator is not necessarily also a technologist.

The abilities are individual.

So are people.

And the basic job of any man who would survive in the Executive Jungle is to make sure he's in a job that exercises an ability he does, in fact, possess. That requires realism. That requires honesty. And that, more frequently than not, also requires professional guidance.

If you're riding the Circle Machine—and you know whether or not you're riding one; a glance at your job record over the past decade will tell you just in case you're not absolutely sure—the simplest, cheapest and most effective way to get off is to seek professional evaluation of your abilities, interests, training, experience, etc.

Know thyself!

It is the first order of business whether you are a man with twenty years experience in the Executive Jungle, or just beginning your career. It's especially important in the latter case.

Of course, there *are* other approaches. One effective— though rather time-consuming—way of discovering your own niche is to work for a company with an established system for job-rotation of new personnel. That way, you'll get at least a taste of every part of the operation (plus a working knowledge of the whole picture which is likely unattainable otherwise) and, if you're honest with yourself, a clear notion of which part tastes best *to you*.

This can also be accomplished early in your career, if you are aiming at the small-firm environment, by trying a number of different jobs in a number of different companies. However, there's a negative factor here of which you should be aware: the constant movement from job to job and from company to company just looks like hell on your job résumé.*

But it does give the diversified experience and insight you need if you tackle the problem from such an angle.

Naturally, I still think professional evaluation would handle the matter with less fuss . . . and certainly in a shorter length of time. After all, friend, how much time do you *have*, anyway?

Know thyself . . . and, while you're about it, take a few pains to know *companies*. And to know *jobs*.

Again, there are two ways you can acquire this knowledge. You can find out for yourself by trying a number of jobs in a number of companies (or a number of jobs within a single company if it's composed of semi-autonomous divisions and has a job-rotation program) or you can find out from professionals who specialize in discovering and dispensing this sort of knowledge.

Trouble is, very few people actually approach their careers from such an angle—and by the time they're ready to seek the answers, quite a lot of time may have gone by. They may even find that they've been riding a Circle Machine. And the only person who can get you off is you. Personally. Yourself.

---

*Unless, of course, you happen to be in the aerospace business. That's one place where having an average of one new job every year will hardly raise an eyebrow. *Whew!*

Remember Jerry, the man who got the right answer at the wrong time? Your problems need not be as debilitating as his*—but you'll never be able to accept the right answer until the time is right, too. Timing is a crucial factor in getting off a circle machine ... but it's seldom too early or too late to expose yourself to insight and self-knowledge.

You may think at the time that none of it's having much effect.

And find out a month later—or a year—that the seed planted then has suddenly bloomed. And your time has come.

That's why I like to give people who come or are sent to me for evaluation as detailed and integrated a set of recommendations and suggestions as possible; that's why, if there's any chance they're ready to hear it, I try to detail my reasons for such an evaluation.

There's another reaction you get sometimes from the playback of an evaluation session; one that's often quite important from the client company's point of view and from the viewpoint of the evaluee as well. It's the reaction of surprise; perhaps even of downright amazement:

"All these things you tell me about myself ... I'd never been aware of much of that before ... !"

Well, then—does it fit?

Or:

"Well, yeah. You know—I've kinda suspected that about myself for a while, now."

There's one that almost always produces direct action. The things I've said were not really new to him, but they reinforce his opinion, perhaps make it possible for him to take immediate steps to achieve some goal he might never have

---

*Few are.

sought (or at least might have postponed for years) because it seemed just a little improbable, a little far out in left field.

Cathy, the late bloomer, was one of these.

And the results in her case were one of the chief satisfactions to be found in my line of work.

But most satisfactory of all is the suggestion and/or recommendation that helps an evaluee off the Circle Machine he's been riding to the point of depression and frustration. That, as the kids say, is where it's *really* at!*

Maybe, too, I can assist in this regard in more ways than helping the man to a greater insight into his own potentialities. Maybe in feeding the evaluation back to the client who sent this man to me I can project my enthusiasm for what I've discovered hidden in his personality to a degree that will infect his boss; maybe I can motivate the boss to help this guy off the Circle Machine and into the kind of work which will lead him to the success of which he was always capable.

I don't do this, of course, *only* to so motivate the manager. I really feel that way, or I can't say it. But remember—I'm doing that manager a hell of a good turn, too.

He's getting a happy and effective employee out of the deal. . ...

Hopefully, of course, the man might have climbed down off that carousel himself one day. But, when? How many times have I heard a man in his forties or fifties say:

"*Damn* it! Here I had to wait all this time to find out the

---

*You know, the more I hear of the New Language the kids seem to have invented lately, the more I wonder if they're not on the right track after all. The idea is communication, right? And, syntax or no, dictionary definition or no, it's hard to deny that these word-symbols *do* communicate. Anyway, that's where my head's at right now, baby. . . .

things which could have made such a difference in my life . . . !"

Well, sure.

But better now, my friend, than never. Better, even if only for one day, for one hour, to know yourself and know where you want to go and where you can go and where you're going. Better one minute of that than to be born, live and die without that additional bit of self-understanding.

Think how *many* people *never* have such an experience.

Think how it would be for . . . well . . . let's say, for you.

Yes.

Think of that. . . .

2
Smog

Nobody likes smog.

It spoils the view and dulls the famous sunshine of Southern California, it brings trafic to a virtual standstill in London, contributes to the general miseries of New York, and actually asphyxiated a number of people in Pennsylvania.

Virtually every major city in the world is worried about it, and most are now belatedly attempting some kind of countermeasures.* But in doing so, a startling discovery has been made:

No two brands of smog are alike!

The smog in Los Angeles is chiefly composed of unburned elements in leaded gasoline—but these are colorless; they

---

*Actually, I think the proper term would be "counter half-measures." But let it pass. Let it pass. . . .

choke but do not obscure. The mustard-brownish visible part of smog is of different composition altogether.

The smog in London, on the other hand, is chiefly of the visible type; it is composed of unburned coal and wood particles cast into the air because of the English preference for fireplaces or stoves in every room as opposed to central heating systems.

The smog of New York City is another matter entirely. . . .

Which of course complicates the matter of clearing the air. The problem, while common to every metropolitan area, is also unique with each. No single solution is possible, except in the sense that the origin of the difficulty is always the "civilized" habit of using the air we breathe as a sewer to carry away our unwanted byproducts.

And somewhat the same thing may be said for the Executive Jungle, where pollution problems have existed, apparently, ever since the first commercial-minded tribe of cave dwellers got the notion of selling well-chipped flint spearheads to a neighboring tribe in return for a supply of grain. Sooner or later, someone had to be selected to supervise the flint chipping and handle negotiations with the customers. And sooner or later, the person responsible began to get a bit confused. . . .*

That is the common origin of smog in the Executive Jungle.

It begins with confusion over the basic requirements of the job and leads, with hardly a moment's pause, to a sense of

---

*Don't we all? Think of it, sitting there scratching your lice and wondering about the flints-for-grain exchange rate and whether the tribe up the river was really going to market that new stone axe with the lemonwood handle and whether the slaves (i.e. women) were really going to go on strike for a better hack at the next aurochs-roast. A thing like that could confuse *anyone*. . . .

inadequacy and a determination—whether conscious or unconscious—to hide such unpleasant facts from the rest of the world.

Battle fleets, maneuvering with the enemy in sight, throw up smoke screens to hide their movements. And executives, anxious to conceal an inability to identify or deal with real problems, fill the air with smog—a miasma of unnecessary and unwanted pseudo-activity—to conceal their own inadequacy.

For instance:

A man we will call Paul found himself in the position as number-two man on a corporate structure founded and headed by Francis, a technically sophisticated engineer who functioned only on a general policy level. This left administration and management of the firm to Paul . . . who was more than a bit bemused by the whole situation.

The truth was that Paul had not the foggiest idea of management function. Nonetheless, he was absolutely determined to hold his position and give at least the appearance of a busy and effective executive. So he began emitting a smoke screen.

He introduced all kinds of minutiae—reports, conferences, audits, inspections, and outside "goodwill" activities—that had nothing whatever to do with the main job of obtaining maximum effect from human effort and maintaining the profitability of the company.

The factory was located in a small town, so Paul forthwith joined a well-known service club and encouraged all his lieutenants to join as well. Most did . . . at which point Paul began to keep *attendance records.* *

He "took an interest" in the personal and social lives of his

---

*Right there, everyone had to be aware the guy had flipped his wig.

people, demanding that they take a "proper" role in the community—and that their wives do so, too.

He wanted a complete report, on his desk every morning, of how much soap, how many paper towels, and how much toilet paper had been used in washrooms the day before. And the report had to be broken down in terms of which washroom used how much of what, of course.

He took real delight in making unexpected tours through the plant several times a day, inspecting coffee urns, looking for dust behind chairs, and generally making a nuisance of himself.

He initiated a giant project aimed at keeping a close monitor-eye on consumption of office materials: pencils, paper, carbons, erasers, etc. Apparently he was concerned that a secretary might be sneaking pencils out of the place. . . .

But when a real problem arose, the tune changed.

Paul had a bachelor's degree in personnel administration (I won't name the school, libel laws being what they are) and had held his job for quite a while, but he seemed peculiarly inept at diagnosing administrative difficulties.

In fact, when the problem was reported, he usually couldn't put his finger on the real cause at all. But "they" weren't going to catch Paul *that* way! No, *sir*! In any such case, he could always fasten attention on some small, utterly insignificant point, demand a fuller explanation or launch into such an explanation himself—and, in the end, apparently divert everyone's attention from the real matter at hand.

Ordinarily, the job tenure of a guy like this would be short.*

---

*Like, about seventeen minutes, maybe. . . .

But two things mitigated in Paul's favor. First, the firm's product had been an immediate success because it was a wholly new approach to a specific problem and its sales later underwent an enormous increase because of a change in world conditions; the general profitability rose markedly despite all his foolishness. Second, his ineptitude and nit-picking had a rather peculiar effect upon his lieutenants, most of whom—though no fault of Paul's, I might note—were extremely capable at their own jobs.

Instead of throwing up their hands and/or plotting an outright mutiny in order to force the company to replace him, these able men developed a kind of "band of brothers" philosophy. The contempt in which they held him forged a silent bond between them, pulled them together into a team which was determined to put forth its best efforts. And their common determination actually motivated them to stretch and exercise their best abilities.

Paul had actually united these men by placing them in opposition to a mutual enemy!

Of course, all this only postponed the result which had been inevitable from the inception of the situation. Little by little, the Top Man became increasingly aware of Paul's incompetence. The smoke screen he was emitting developed enough cracks for even that worthy to notice that all his activities seemed to lead nowhere. The chief executive found himself giving orders which were not carried out and receiving excuses which made no sense even to him.

The day of reckoning finally arrived. Paul had his long-expected confrontation with Francis, his boss. And when it was over, Paul was out on his ear.

His departure was attended by a not-too-silent celebration on the part of the lieutenants, and far-from-restrained recriminations on the part of Paul who told all who would listen how shabbily he had been treated after "all he had done" for the company.

The lieutenants' joy was short-lived.

As soon as Paul's office became vacant, each not surprisingly began to preen his own feathers and prepare a little acceptance speech against the moment when he would be asked to step into the breech. And each began a quiet program of subverting and backbiting all his former brothers-in-arms to jockey himself into the best position for that expected promotion.

This, in turn, threw the company into chaos! The end of union between the lieutenants, an *effect* of Paul's departure rather than mere coincidence, also meant the end of competent management anywhere in the company for a time. And at length, they were all disappointed.

Francis brought in a thoroughly able and experienced man to fill Paul's spot, and the new manager lost no time in settling the lieutenants' hash. The word was, in effect, "sit down, shut up and get back to work." And he was man enough to make it stick.

Within a very few months under competent leadership, Francis' company had ceased entirely its contribution to the smog problem. . . .

A somewhat similar—and entirely different—example of executive smoke screen came to my attention a few years ago at a firm where I was a consultant. Again, it involved two men; the Boss and his chief subordinate. Call them Glenn and Bob.

They had been together a long time.

Glenn was a man who had foresight regarding a certain product and the ability to get it included in the specifications of a great many items which were playing a major part in a gigantic defense buildup a few years ago. He made millions, and so did most of the people who had been around him at the time. Also, because when you make a great deal of money in a very little time you are virtually forced to invest it in new projects or new businesses or turn it over to the Internal Revenue Service, Glenn wound up at the top of a remarkable array of individual companies and divisions now attached to his original firm.

And Bob was his vice-president for administration.

He had been with Glenn almost from the first and a number of the companies had been acquired on his advice. His approach to administration was of a very earthy sort;* he was anything but sophisticated in the field and, I am sorry to say, evidenced very little ability to grow with the job.

Still, his administrative organization was at least stable— albeit for the wrong reasons. It was run pretty much from what might be called a historian's point of view: here were the payables, here were the receivables; here were the journal entries, here the payroll credits . . . more general accounting than anything else.

Forecasting? Budgeting?

No. Little or none of that. Because he basically didn't understand the requirements of his increased responsibilities, Bob's basic dictum seemed to be: never do anything for the first time; never try to worry about the future. Deal with the past and—at most—the present. They aren't so much of a puzzle.

Naturally, a man like that can't let his decisions be ques-

---

*To give you an idea: he showed me a bookkeeping system he's devised. Get a spindle with two prongs, balanced at the center. Put payables on one; put receivables on the other. If the spindle is still balanced . . . you've got it made! (*Oi, veh!*)

tioned; he might wind up in the position of having to explain why he did something . . . and he knew damn well he couldn't explain.

So he made sure he kept everyone off balance.

He was negative, of course, and left no doubt in anyone's mind about what would happen as a result of questioning, or stepping out of line in any way. He kept everyone frightened —everyone he *could*, that is—and did his best to keep everyone guessing about what he was really up to.

An accountant, for instance, might suddenly be asked a question relating to production which was entirely out of his field. He wouldn't know the answer, of course. And the scorn heaped upon him for this "oversight" was such that the accountant might either withdraw into a shell, or trouble to inform himself on this totally useless (to him) subject. The next question he would be asked, needless to say, would relate to some totally different field—again outside his ken, and again totally irrelevant to his work. A thing like that can keep you pretty dizzy.

Or: here's a little clerk-typist going to the rest room. And here's Bob, checking his watch and noting the time on a slip of paper, to see just how long she stayed in there.

Or: here's a secretary dropping something in the waste basket. And here's Bob walking over, picking up the basket, exhuming all the waste paper, and questioning her about why she threw away each one.

Fear was the central ingredient of Bob's brand of smog.

And it was also its genesis: Bob's *own* fear that someone would in the end find out how little he understood or was able to cope with his own job.

Of course such tactics didn't work with *everyone* in the plant. The independent department heads and/or managers were tigers in their own right and, if they really were competent in their jobs, had no compunction about turning right around and biting Bob squarely in the tail.

Usually, you only had to do that once. Tell him off, suggest that he get back to his own department and keep the threats and intimidations to himself, and his manner would undergo a permanent change. He would become very purposeful and direct, easy to get along with, and careful about overstepping bounds. Bob didn't give anyone a harder time than they would allow him to do.*

The only ones who really suffered were those who for reasons of personality—or because of their own incompetence—didn't dare call his bluff.

Bob was basically a scared little guy.

And in the end, his fear tactics left him on the outside looking in. Fear *never* produces really effective results; people whose morale is high are always more highly motivated to productive effort than those who work under duress.

And, more and more, Glenn became aware that his administrative department—under the aegis of his old friend—was a shambles.

He hired a well-known consulting firm to have a look at his company (there was a dissident stockholder group to deal with) and they made a number of recommendations, one of the more important of which related to Bob and another executive in the firm whose title was vice-president for corporate administration. The consultants pointed out that most of these two men's efforts were duplicative.

For a while, it looked like Glenn might actually ask the

---

*Most bullies are that way. So—spit in his eye, tiger! (I'll hold your coat.)

other man (who, as it happened, actually was capable in his job) to resign because one or the other had to go and he had been Bob's friend for a long time.

But Bob made such a decision unnecessary.

Staying with Glenn all those years had paid off handsomely for him. He had plenty of money, and he had over the years made quite a few investments in local real estate and in other enterprises. He saw what was about to happen—and he was not entirely stupid. He knew that, in the end, he could not play the kind of game he was playing.

So—why not do the graceful thing, right now? He told Glenn goodbye. He explained that, since the company was going so well and had grown so big, he felt his "job was done" and there was no more real reason for him to stay around. He'd wanted to retire for years, he said, and this seemed like the right time. Of course, he'd be on call for his friend if anything really serious came up. . . .

I don't really know whether Glenn believed all that or not. I suspect he didn't. But, however that may be, he certainly didn't give his old buddy any arguments. "We'll miss you," was the way he put it. And that seemed to satisfy everyone. . . .

Still another example of the kind of smog to be found in the Executive Jungle concerns a man we'll call Harry.

Actually, I've never been able to think of this guy as anyone but "Heels-Up Harry" despite the fact that his heels weren't *really* up. In fact, they were planted so firmly in the ground that I often wondered whether he might have developed a root system.

In a lot of ways, he sort of reminded me of Mike, the chief protagonist in "Steady As She Goes" (Part II, Chapter 11). Only, Mike was at least a man.

Harry seemed to be one, too, at first glance. But the more

you saw of this guy—especially if you had a chance to observe him in interaction with his superiors as well as his subordinates—the more you realized he was really a coward at heart. And a bully. He was capable of seeming fatherly, imposing, understanding, decisive, action-oriented and confident when dealing with those subject to his authority. He was the Boss, and they were never permitted entirely to forget it—though he was anything but overbearing.

With the company's president, though, it was a different story.

In that man's presence, Harry was a submissive, supportive, almost cringing little yes-man—all, of course, without overtly assuming the characteristics of such a person.* It was just that Harry never, on any occasion, allowed himself to say *anything* the president might not want to hear; never contradicted a view expressed by the president, no matter how absurd it might be; never gave his superior the basic courtesy of an unedited or absolutely honest opinion on anything.

Which was peculiar, really.

The president, I discovered in short order, was a gentlemanly and flexible person, objective and able to consider points of view contrary to his own and really quite anxious to obtain legitimate and thoughtful appraisal of his ideas. There was no reason for Harry to be frightened of offending him by saying what he thought. But Harry was scared spitless of him.

Perhaps this attitude of subservience would, in time, have aroused doubts in the president's mind about the caliber of man he had hired. But things were going pretty well and—you don't argue with success.

---

*Which, in itself, indicates a certain kind of talent—albeit not for management. Harry would probably have made one hell of an actor.

So for a long time Harry was left to run the show his own way. And that way was to resist all change of whatever kind. His answer was always no (except in one kind of situation, which we'll come to in a moment). But the words accompanying "no" differed, depending on which level of the company's personnel strata he was addressing.

If he was rejecting an idea from several tiers below, he always put it this way:

"Your idea does have some merit. But there are a lot of complications and we'll just have to say no. Thanks for trying. I really appreciate it, fella. But . . . no."

And, in most cases, the author of the rejected idea would take it pretty much on faith. After all, Harry was 'way up there—in the thin air region—and supposedly had a better view of the big picture.

But if the idea to be squelched happened to come from a strata close to, or just below, his own, Harry's tactics had to change accordingly. In that case, the rejection came out this way:

"Well, yes. It's not a bad thought, really. But I'm a little closer to the president than you are, and so I've got a little better insight into what he wants and what he doesn't want—and this notion of yours just isn't in the mainstream of his plans."

Alternatively, if he'd used that specific line before, it would be something like:

"I have every reason to believe our president has something in mind that would conflict with this . . ."

Sorry, Charley.

Once in a while, of course, when someone came up with an idea of really great intrinsic worth (or when enough people in the organization supported a particular proposal to keep it from being a man-to-man situation) Harry had to be a little faster on his feet and a little more devious in his tactics.

That's when he unlimbered the "further study" routine.

He would appear to give the plan serious and detailed consideration—perhaps even encourage the originators in their planning—and then "decide" it was "such a hell of an idea" that it really ought to have really detailed consideration.

In fact, it was so good, he was going to bring it to the attention of some experts.

"We'll bring in some consultants," he would say, "some experts from outside—technical people, marketing people, quality control consultants. Let them have a look at it. Let them advise us as to how to proceed. . . ."

Again, it was hard to argue with him because he wasn't specifically *rejecting* the idea. No, indeed! He was *all for it*; but, naturally, you wouldn't want him to proceed helter-skelter, would you? You *do* think it will stand up under scrutiny by real experts, don't you . . . ?

After that, Harry's only worry was (a) whether the experts might really find some flaw in the proposal that he'd missed, thus killing the whole plan, or (b) whether he would have the minor problem of actually discussing it with someone again from time to time before it was entirely forgotten.

Time was always on Harry's side. . . .

In really extreme situations, where the experts all agreed that the plan was a good one—and said so in a way that couldn't be missed by others in the office—and the general discussion simply wouldn't die down in a reasonable length of time, Harry had yet another string to his bow: this time he would make the originator of the proposal beat his own idea to death!

He would assign the unwary author to research the plan in such detail and to such a degree that the whole thing would simply become an unproductive task when compared to its possible benefits. Besides . . by that time, if the poor guy didn't realize he had no chance at all of getting the plan approved, he was too stupid to be allowed out without a keeper, anyway.

For somewhat lesser situations, where other tactics began to pall a bit, Harry had a ploy which almost never failed to remove the problem with no effort on his part at all. He simply disappeared.

He would go off on a trip—especially if a crucial moment for decision-making could be glimpsed in the offing—and *stay away* until someone else made the decision. That was doubly effective, so far as Harry was concerned; it shifted blame for any mistake to the shoulders of whomever finally had to make the decision while he was unavailable, and it got him a nice quiet vacation, besides. (For minor problems, Harry didn't even bother to remove himself for any length of time. It would simply become necessary to break his appointment with you because something "more immediate" popped up unexpectedly. And, by God, if you were fool enough to reschedule the appointment, you would find something else "popping up" over and over again until you finally got the message and gave up.)*

Amazingly, Harry actually managed to do all this while continuing to give the overt impression of a sincere, conscien-

---

*Still another game-plan of Harry's was to tell the Idea-Pusher the whole thing had been tried—with disastrous results—by someone else. Never mind if the two cases were as dissimilar as Red Riding Hood's grandmother and the Wolf. The best you were going to get by pointing out a fact like that was a pitying stare and a sad shake of the head. The guy was really *something else*. (What, I am not prepared to say.)

tious executive doing his best to keep the firm moving forward.

It took people a long time to get onto him. . . .

As I said earlier, however, there *was* one kind of situation which was an exception to Harry's rule of negativism:

If the president said do it, it got done!

Never, in all his career, did Harry voice a single objection to any project suggested by the president.* His acceptance of ideas from *that* source was noncritical; his demand for performance with respect to them bordered on the fanatical.

Not all the ideas were good ones, however.

Most were (after all, the company *did* manage to stay in the black) but some were not. And the ones that were not were usually obviously so. One of the specific duties of the Number Two Man in such a situation, therefore, would be to tell the Boss when he thought he was going off the rails.

But Harry wasn't up to that. He just wasn't up to that at all. And, come to think of it, he probably didn't know which were which anyway. . . .

Heaven knows how much longer it might have gone on—or where it all might have ended—had the president not decided to retire. And a new president was brought in from outside the firm. It took that gentleman about a week to figure Harry out, and to become firmly convinced there was no way on earth he could work with him. Harry was asked to resign.

And he did that. . . .

Recognize anybody you know? Recognize a situation—one that's been puzzling you a bit, maybe?

---

*"More surely shall a camel pass through the eye of the needle . . ." etc., etc.

Well, if you do, chances are you'd have figured it out sooner or later anyway . . . though perhaps not in precisely the same terms. At any rate, you'd have known you were inhaling an awful lot of executive smog.

Remember: it's never there by accident.

It has its origin in insecurity; the insecurity felt by a man who does not believe himself to be adequate to the job he holds. It is his smokescreen, intended to hide the truth, not only from his boss and his peers and his associates . . . but from himself as well.

If you spot such a miasma in your vicinity, the time to do something about it is *right then*. Conditions like that are never improved by waiting.

A man who finds a subordinate of his throwing up a cloud of executive smog, in particular, cannot afford much patience; he's already let matters get out of hand. Perhaps you owe him a chance to change or improve the situation— and again, perhaps you don't; it's a question only you can answer—but if you feel you do, you'll have to take a much firmer position with him than you have in the past.

In no uncertain terms, the smogmaster must be made to understand that there's no place for such tactics in your organization . . . and the best way to get something more than surface acceptance of the demand for change is to have him set up a program of specific objectives, real problems to be solved on a step-by-step basis leading toward a specific goal, and then see to it that he follows this program—or gets out of the company.

There *must* have been *some* reason you hired a guy like this; there must have been some promise he showed at some time. Or he wouldn't be where he is now. Maybe, given a real program and a specific directive, he can fulfill the promise. Maybe he's just, somehow, lost sight of the true purpose of management. And maybe he can find the trail again.

You won't know unless you try.

But even if he does succeed in reversing course—in knocking off the smog and getting down to the real business for which he was hired—it's not a thing you can ever afford to forget. Old habits are insidious. They creep back. From time to time (maybe you'd better even mark the calendar!) it might be a good idea to monitor the smogmaster again. Just to be on the safe side. . . .

If, on the other hand, it's your boss who's the source of the smog, what you do about it probably depends on your own ambitions, orientation, creativity . . . and the thickness of your hide.

If you want to stay very badly, and if you've the temperament to do so, perhaps it will be possible for you to "work around" this guy; bypass him when you can't get a decision, or when you know he's so negativistic that no suggestion would have a chance. If he's a procrastinator, accept it: you'll have to make the decision yourself in the end. And stand good for it. This guy's never going to back you.

And if, as seems more likely, the situation is completely impossible—well—there's that old résumé. Sitting there in the drawer, where it's been ever since you got *this* job. Just a little updating, now. . . .

A man who finds one of his peers playing a game like this has only slightly different alternatives. The first thing he's got to decide is just how much effect the smogmaster's ineptitude is going to have on his own responsibilities. If it's none (or, anyway, very little) perhaps the best thing to do is ignore the damn fool . . . and let nature take its course. All parties come to an end sometime, and guys like this can't last forever.

If, on the other hand, the smogmaster's incompetence is apt to be reflected in the quality of your own output (or if, by some mischance, he's even a friend of yours) then you'll have to fight it out toe-to-toe with him . . . or see if you can't talk the matter over sensibly (and if not, carry the whole enchilada a step higher to your mutual boss.) At any rate, there's nothing much you can lose, whether he's just an associate or a friend. A friend like this you can't afford, friend . . . !

And, if nothing works and the man's actually threatening your job or your reputation for competence with his nonsense, the place to take your problem is right out the door. Just as soon as you can find a more inviting prospect elsewhere.

All that, of course, applies to others.

You're not a smogmaster, of course.

Of *course*!

But . . . if on clear and sober and realistic appraisal of your own work-style on the job, you find one or two little points which *do* seem to match, don't you owe *yourself* the boon of your own coldly objective appraisal?

Are you *really* that insecure?

Do you *really* need all this misdirection, intimidation, evasion or whatever to hold onto your position? You know—there's damn few people who really do. And the awful part is that in the end, it won't work. The smog itself will give you away. Only a man planning evasive action needs a smoke-screen. . . .

Fear is a poor motivation—whether your own, or that which you inspire in others. So is confusion, evasion, misdirection. The job is to solve problems; your own and those of the company where you work. There is risk in any decision, uncertainty in any action—but these are legitimate risks, the kind you're hired to accept. At least they have some *chance* of success; and raising a miasma of smog does not.

How about setting up that step-by-step program we talked about earlier?

Set one up for the company and for the discharge of your own responsibilities. And set another one up—privately, of course—for reducing your own smog-output.

Do you have able lieutenants? Trust them, then; listen to what they say and if, in *your opinion*, they know what they're talking about (your opinion, you know, is your sole stock-in-trade, Mr. Executive!) try saying "yes—do it!" instead of "no" or "maybe" or "wait."

The job is to get it done.

The job is to plan for tomorrow . . . and next year, and beyond.

The job is to help—and even demand—everyone do his job and do it with a minimum of tangential effort. Smog isn't going to help anything, or anyone. Including *you*.

Yessir . . . everyone talks about smog.

Nobody likes it.

Everyone wants to get rid of it.

But the smog's not the real problem; its causes and even it's future effects have been studied, identified and projected long since. The problem is the same—whether it's within the purview of the Los Angeles Air Pollution Control District, or the sometimes misty precincts of the Executive Jungle.

The problem is getting ourselves to apply the solutions we know are necessary.

Before it is too late. . . .

3
So You Want To Be President

This chapter is intended as a kind of innoculation.

You wouldn't venture into the African veldt or go paddling up the Amazon without the proper course of immunization shots. Fevers abound in any jungle or wilderness area, and you take precautions against them.

Well, the Executive Jungle is no exception to the rule.

Stock-optionitis and big-officitis have been known to lay many a man low; the chills accompanying a siege of office politicsitis can be worse than dengue.* But of all the fevers, probably the most prevalent—and sometimes most debilitating—is presidentitis.

Sooner or later, almost every executive comes down with

---

*Sometimes called "Breakbone Fever." Leaves you weak as a kitten . . . just like office politicsitis.

it. The symptoms are bated breath, sweaty palms, insomnia and tremor of the psyche. The attack can be of short duration or long; the onset intense or mild.

Most victims recover without serious effect, but there are instances in which the malady is fatal to the career. A lingering, even lifelong susceptibility is not uncommon.

And, for a very few, it is a *natural* state.

Like the occasional individual whose temperature is always a degree or so above 98.6 throughout the course of his life, it is a condition probably necessary to existence. They'd be lost without it. And for these few, the effects are probably not harmful. They can use them to their own advantage. . . .

The real job is one of diagnosis.

Just about every young executive embarking on his career probably has a secret mental picture of that corner office with his name on the door above the word "President." Parents tend to impress their children with the notion that everyone ought to be ambitious; the presidency of the company where the grown child works, then, becomes the obvious object of this uncritically accepted dictum. Hence, the fever.

And the treatment is specific: a stiff shot of reality, injected intracranially. It's quite safe:

The shot can't hurt you a bit if you're *really* the kind of man who should sit behind that corner office desk.

And if you're not, a little reality can control the chills. . . .

  So you want to be president.
Really?
Why . . . ?
No—don't just snort and dismiss that question from your mind. It's important. The reasons people want to be pres-

ident of a company are as many and as diverse as the people themselves. And not all the reasons are good ones.

I knew one man—who had succeeded in moving into that corner office—who told me his real reason for wanting to become president had been "to have all the *free time* I wanted, to do the things I'd always wanted to do."

Honest to God!

By the time he admitted that to me, however, reality had finally set in:

"Now that I *am* president," he sighed, "of course I have far *less* time to do those things than I ever had before. And the way the company is growing, I'll have less and less as time goes on. . . ."

This man was lucky; he finally managed to move up to Chairman of the Board, a position which can in some cases yield a little more leisure, because it leaves someone else stuck with the day-by-day operational responsibilities of the presidency. But his case is the exception, not the rule. You can't count on anything like that. The man who accepts the presidency of a company accepts everything that goes with it. From that moment on, if anything's going to get done, he's likely going to have to set it in motion himself—and keep an eye on it, to make sure it keeps running.

Some men aim for the presidency because it is—for them— a kind of ultimate test in the arena of life; these are highly competitive types and that office represents ultimate victory. Some even turn out to be good at the job when they get it. Others are chagrined to discover that, far from being ultimate victory, achieving the presidency is only the beginning of the race.

For another kind of man, the presidency represents an opportunity to achieve "ultimate" power over others. These men frequently have an emotional need for such power, whether because of secret fears of their own adequacy and strength or in response to motives even darker.*

Now and then, too, you come across some poor soul who wants to be president (or, at any rate, a high-ranking executive) as a *compensation* for the fact that he has no leadership or command ability at all! These unfortunates seek the title not because they possess the intrinsic capability of influencing others or for inspiring confidence on the basis of leadership ability, but because they don't. They really believe the man who holds such a title needs no such ability because the rank somehow confers omnipotence—poeple will obey him just because he's the Boss.

Let's examine that notion for a moment:

In all the military services, it's a kind of article of faith that you salute the *uniform*, rather than the man who wears it.

Technically, if Brig. Gen. Benedict Arnold (they never really got around to court-martialing him, remember) appeared in uniform, he'd rate a salute until the provost could lay hands on him . . . and continue to rate one so long as he was entitled to wear that uniform.

The uniform is a symbol.

So is the salute.

But a map is *not* the country it describes, and a symbol is not the capability or position it represents. A salute does *not* mean you're a leader. It only means you are required to *try* to be one. It is a *demand*, not a guarantee of performance.

Anyone who has ever exercised independent command knows this.

Ship captains, in particular, make the discovery—if they

---

*If you don't know what I'm talking about here . . . congratulations.

weren't aware of it before—in the first couple of minutes after they assume command. It's a lonely feeling, and the feeling is entirely realistic.

There's *no one* a captain can really talk to in a completely unedited and open manner.* He is the *dispenser* of confidence, not the consumer. He is the author of decisions, not their executor. And he bears the responsibility not only for any mistake he makes, but for any he allows a subordinate to make.

The rule is clear: Only the man in command may be blamed.

Why *else* do you think captains sometimes elect to go down with their ships . . . ?

I'm amazed, sometimes, at how few people understand that.

And equally confounded by the number of people who simply don't understand what the role of command—of the company presidency—really requires.

I know a company comptroller who desperately wants to be president. Yet this man's experience is so narrow, so esoteric, that he would have trouble making any meaningful decision outside the area of his own expertise. God knows, the presidency can be tough enough even if a man has covered several of the bases—obtained a very wide area of experience —before he lands in that Big Hot Seat In The Sky.

Other people aspire to such a job through sheer naiveté.

I'm reminded of a low-level contracts workers I met who'd been with one particular company for a long time. The guy actually believed he was going to be president one day

---

*Unless it's someone outside the company, whose discretion can be trusted: an old friend who's a lawyer, or a priest, or even a doctor, maybe. Everyone has to talk to someone.

because he was such a "conscientious and responsible" fellow.

God help him . . . he was perfectly sincere!

(Oh, brother . . .*)

Demands upon the president can be considerable. And diverse:

—He is, first and foremost, the man who sets the tenor and personality of his company. It wears his face. If his personality is a healthy one, the company will be healthy; it will have a potential for growth and provide opportunity and recognition which will keep competent personnel producing, and attract able men to join the team. If not. . . .

—Sometimes he has to be the senior marketing executive; the subordinate in charge of that will be coming to him for advice when trouble appears. And sometimes, nothing will do the job except the actual, personal intervention of the president. If he's able to do that, well and good. If not. . . .

—He'll usually have to be the man who talks to the bankers (accompanied, usually by his treasurer or financial VP) because they look to him as the real manager of the firm; the key man in operations.

—Sometimes he has to be the public relations expert; the one who meets with security analysts in creating a market for the company's stock, or with outsiders who for one reason or another are interested in the firm. It's a role he will, most especially, have to be prepared to play—and play well—in times of real trouble. If not. . . .

—And a lot of his effort will be expended in handling stockholders; meeting with them, explaining the company's programs to them, seeking their advice and direction on a

---

*Oh BROTHER!

policy level, pushing through his own policies and programs. If he can do this, fine. If not. . . .

—Finally, there are the firm's employees. He will have to be labor negotiator, recruiter, advisor, father-confessor all in one . . . and he will have to keep the roles separate, lest he find himself trying to wear the White Hat every day of the year. If not. . . .

In short, he bears the cumulative responsibility for all the sub-responsibilities, the delegated responsibilities, for the welfare of his company.

That's the job; that's why he rates that corner office.

But it's only *part* of the price.

The other part is a bit of cost-accountancy which involves people outside the firm, outside the realm of his business affairs entirely. He's got to assess the cost in terms of his family relationships, along with everything else.

Nine-to-five men seldom become company presidents.

The man who holds the title of Boss is gone from the house before the kids are up; they'll very likely be asleep by the time he gets home. And he's still on call for emergencies (or any situation someone *thinks* is an emergency) twenty-four hours a day, seven days a week.

Look back again at that chapter *"But I'm Doing It All For You."*

It is not impossible to give your children a decent and loving background, a supportive and reassuring childhood, under the lifestyle conditions that lead to the presidency. But it is not easy; it will take some very careful consideration of priorities by you (that's one of a real executive's duties, isn't it?) and a good bit of sacrifice on the part of his family.

Maybe you can survive being president.

But what about them . . . ?

(You know—it's amazing how few sons of top executives really want to follow in the Old Man's footsteps. Even when their relationship with Papa has been a good one, it's the rule rather than the exception to hear such a Jungle Baby say, "Me—be *President*? No way, man! Do you think I'm *crazy*?" These are people who have had a close, inside look at the whole thing. They have better reason than most to know exactly what's involved, and their reactions, therefore, are well worth considering.)

Also, what about your wife? She's a member of the family, too, isn't she? Even if your kids are willing to see less of you, or if you can maneuver your time and attention in such a way as to make minimal imposition upon them—what about her?

"I don't get to see him" says one president's wife.

"I don't even feel I'm an important part of his life anymore," says another.

These women's complaints are legitimate.

They are from the heart.

They come from wives who truly love and respect their husbands; who have a real interest in sharing their lives with them. It's not that they don't want their husbands to succeed, or that they would selfishly deny him the satisfaction of moving toward a goal he has set for himself. But people do not marry to be alone, or to be lonely even when their mates are physically present.

How valuable is your marriage to you?

What's the priority . . . ?

Can your wife handle the long absences and the preoccupation and the day-by-day frustrations she'll have to endure as Mrs. Boss? Many women can; they are self-sufficient gals who complement their husbands, are independent of them, have their own interests, want a virtually untrammeled hand in managing their homes. But *not all* wives are built that way.

So the question, again, is one of individuals.

You want to be president?
Really?
Really?
You have the ability? You have the dedication? You have the background and the education and the personality and the willingness to sacrifice; the kind of family life that can take the impact of such a responsibility; the drive and guts to carry it through?

All right.

All right, then—it's your decision. The first, and by all odds the toughest, you'll have to make in a life that will be almost nothing *but* tough decisions from now on. You asked for it, brother. But don't forget, this is the real world. Not a dream. Not a fantasy. Not a "well, maybe. . . ."

The price is fixed. You'll pay it—or lose, in the end.

Old Harry S. Truman put it, I think, as well as anyone:

"If you can't stand the heat—stay outa the kitchen."

Part
4
The
Trail Ahead

The Trail Ahead

It is one thing to survive in the Executive Jungle.

But it is quite another to achieve real success. And one of the chief reasons is that so few of us can even define the word in the only way that matters—in terms of ourselves.

Webster says success is "attaining an end in accordance with one's desires" and that seems adequate enough. As far as it goes.

Unhappily, that isn't very far.

Before a man can measure his own or another man's degree of success or failure, using a definition, like that, he must first examine those desires; the goal at which the effort was aimed. And in that sense no universally-acceptable definition is possible.

For we are not dwellers in an anthill; we are not a mass and not a category.

We are individuals.

And we have individual needs and goals and abilities. Success for one man may be failure for another; satisfaction for one may be frustration for another. We are unique. Each of us. And we are not apt to change; not at another man's orders . . . not even at our own.

The Man in the White Hat is not going to turn into a hardnosed, tough-minded type.

The Miracle Man is not going to stop expecting—and demanding—miracles.

The Likely Candidate is not going to awaken some morning to find he really *can* do the job he couldn't do yesterday.

The Strangler isn't going to stop strangling.

Not, at any rate, because someone asked him to. Do you tell a legless man to grow new legs? Tell an ostrich egg to hatch a hen? We are what we are: no one of us is perfect. If we know enough about ourselves, however, a workable adjustment *is possible*.

The Man in the White Hat can be careful to assemble able lieutenants who don't mind wearing a Black Hat now and then; he can outline his objectives to them, break the objectives down into a number of short-term goals . . . and let the subordinates hit them, one by one.

The Miracle Man can first make sure that the key men in his organization are competent, and then get someone else—someone not under his authority, whose ability he can trust—to evaluate the goals he has set, to see if they are miraculous or realistic.

The Likely Candidate can resist the promotion to a position where he knows in his heart he can't function. And, if he's at all undecided about whether or not he can.hack it, he can obtain competent outside counsel.

Styles of management are as diverse as the individuals who apply them.

Lectures at management meetings frequently have titles like "Management By Exception," "Participative Management," "Inspirational Management," "Management By Peers," and "Management By Objectives."

We say: "We used to do this. Then we did that. Now we do it *this* way. . . ."

We say, "There seems to be an historical trend here; probably our current fad in management is not the end. . . ."

End?

There is no end.

Management is a growing and developing thing; an evolving thing where new techniques and approaches will always be tried and the results evaluated, and the next step taken, so long as men of imagination and ability seek improvement. The end is *not* in sight . . . and never will be.

But a direction *is* visible today.

A *course*, a *trail ahead* can be glimpsed among the trees and denizens of the Executive Jungle. And that trend is toward each manager performing his role—so long as it proves effective—in the style which is most comfortable *for him*.

It is management in the style that fits the individual manager.

There is no "best" style. Not for everyone. Best for one man may not even be possible for another. . . .

But selection of the style which is most comfortable and most effective is no snap, but it requires a preliminary step on the part of the individual manager. A difficult—even painful—step:

He must first know himself.

One of the truly amazing things about many of us human

beings is that we can have a sensitivity to and an understanding of those around us—our friends, business peers, bosses and subordinates—while blithely avoiding the same kind of close and objective insight into ourselves.

Logically, self-insight would be a starting point.

But human beings rarely live their lives on a strictly logical basis. Emotions enter into the equation, too, and that is a good thing because we are men, not machines. However, since one of the strongest human tendencies—a defense mechanism, if you will—is rationalization, most of us can rationalize or completely disregard those portions of our personality which we know in our hearts might prove embarrassing.

Sometimes this rationalization is almost acceptable.

If, by chance, a man's lifestyle and his approach to management are making him happy and effective, perhaps he can get along without looking too deeply into himself to see just who and what he is. I don't know. You seldom meet a man who has really achieved such a condition in all departments. But I suppose it's possible.

Usually, however, the careful and open-eyed "look inside" *is necessary* if you are to make truly meaningful decisions in terms of how you conduct your personal life, whom you hire, whom you promote, whom you transfer and whom you dismiss.

And usually it is necessary in deciding which style of management is best and more workable for you.

Such insight can be obtained in many ways. For a few—a *very* few—it comes in the form of an almost religious experience; a seeker delving deep into the mysteries of himself and the world in which he lives, and returning with answers that can be applied to daily life. But that is quite rare.

Another workable method, for those who can do it, is a

kind of objective self-analysis. A man with outstanding self-discipline and mental command of himself *can*, in fact, evaluate his own past actions in terms of reality and identify the processes at work inside him. He *can* decide the kind of person he is, label his true needs and wants, identify his abilities and inabilities, and arrive at a workable style. But again, such objectivity with regard to oneself is infrequent. And it is all too easy to kid yourself about who and what you are—while continuing to evade the truth.

For many of us, then, the best and most effective method of achieving insight is to obtain professional help in this self-evaluation.

The depth and type are up to you.

Perhaps the professional experienced in the field of your immediate interest, or a person serving as a vocational counselor can do the job. In a majority of cases, I think, it would fill the need. Your object is to arrive at a comfortable and usable work-style and life-style, not to achieve nirvana.

But in some cases, a deeper probing may be in order.

Clinical psychologists, psychiatrists, etc., are available, then. Their approach may take a bit more time, and the road may prove a bit bumpy—but the goal is well worth the trip. It's *your* life, brother. . . .

Insight, however, is not an end in itself so far as your performance in a management role is concerned.

Once you have a firm grasp on who you are, once you have decided what your legitimate goals and aspirations are, once you have settled upon the individual style of management best suited to your own personality, there is still the job of selecting the people with whom—or for whom—you will work.

There's a serious pitfall yawning here:

It is all too easy for a manger to hire an individual,

promote him, give him additional responsibility, and back him to the limit just because you like him and because his modus operandi happens to coincide with the management style you've selected.

And it's also awfully easy to say, "Gee . . . you know, I realize this is a capable guy, a guy who could do the job all right. But I just don't like him so I'm not going to hire him (or promote him, or whatever)."

Even the best of managers, with the most satisfactory management styles, can't afford to surround themselves with a totally homogeneous group of lieutenants. Even if personal likes and dislikes can be kept out of the matter, it's normal for a manger to hire subordinates—especially in key positions —whose M.O. matches his own.

(That, by the way, is why I want to see and talk to the president of any organization before I start doing evaluations for his company. That company will wear his face; the men who work there are pretty much "stuck with" his way of doing business. If there's going to be a personality clash or a clash of principles that would be destructive to the overall effort, the quickest way to know about it in advance is to know the man at the top. . . .)

But it's axiomatic with geneticists that cross-breeding frequently produces an improved product.

The Boston Terrier, for instance, has a weakness for upper respiratory diseases because of his nasal bone structure; the English Bull has a hard time giving birth because of the restricted pelvic girdle (they frequently need cesarians). But a cross breed can sometimes produce an animal with neither problem . . . plus all the best points of both types.

And so with management.

A heterogeneous management team frequently produces the best overall result, since it avoids by its diversity the inbreeding of highly similar minds and philosophies. The only thing to worry about, really, is getting a set of styles which are so extreme in their differences that a set of mutually-exclusive situations develop.

The important objective is to obtain agreement from all concerned on your management goals. How you get there is another matter entirely, and diversity of style is not only permissible . . . but, in most cases, even to be encouraged—so long as the goal is achieved.

The important thing is to get there.

That takes a bit of special self-discipline and objectivity on the part of the boss, of course. He's got to stay flexible. He's got to handle himself. But . . . what else did you *think* the boss's job was?

Now, then. One more point:

We were talking about success, weren't we? And the fact that success for one man is not necessarily success for another. That it's a question of self-knowledge, identification of goals which are satisfactory to the individual.

Remember, back in Part II, we examined the case of the Likely Candidate?

Well . . . what if a candidate for promotion, far from being unqualified, actually has the ability to do the job but, for one reason or another, doesn't want it?

Maybe he feels such a job would lead him in a direction he doesn't want to go; into some management milieu which would be somehow distasteful for him. Maybe it's a matter of the promotion involving a cross-country move to a part of the world he doesn't like and where he wouldn't be happy; maybe the promotion would be to a job he feels would require him to spend too much time away from him family. In any case . . he says no.

And what is the reaction of management?

In many companies, it's pretty darn negative. In fact, in many it's the "kiss of death."

How very foolish!

Here's a man who *must* have been performing his present duties pretty well, or you wouldn't have offered him the promotion. Maybe his reason was a temporary thing, something that will change with time; maybe it's a single-case sort of thing, and he'd be willing to take almost any other kind of move up the ladder.

And maybe it's just a matter of him wanting to stay right where he is; maybe *this* is success for *him*, here and now.

If his refusal is the "kiss of death" in your mind, *you* stand to be the real loser. You stand to lose an effective and useful employee. And more. Because you've also lost sight of yourself; the inner motivation for your reaction to his refusal.

You say you're "disappointed" in this guy?

Really? Or is it that you're disappointed in the way a gift-giver is disappointed when he gets a less than enthusiastic response from the recipient. Is it that you are disappointed in your *own* judgment . . . that you have the sneaking suspicion you may have made a little mistake in thinking he'd want the new job? That your own judgment of people is not perfect? And that you're taking it out on him in order to conceal this fact from yourself?

Think it over, brother. Think. . . .

And you . . . Mr. Promotion-Refuser. Don't give up the ship the moment you get a cold stare in response to your refusal. It is *not* the end of the world, even if you work for an outfit which has that "kiss of death" attitude toward cases like yours. Stick it out a while. Hang tough. Attitudes *do* change with time. New insights *are* achieved, even by your superiors. Today's fish-eye may become next year's (or even next month's) invitation to lunch.

And even if it doesn't—it's still not an earthquake; not Armageddon. This may be the only game in town. But there are other towns, and you've got to keep the whole thing in perspective. Remember, no industrial marriage lasts forever; even a relationship which has proved productive for a number of years may in the end turn sour. If it does . . . well . . . then it's time it was terminated.

Don't accept an unwanted and/or personally destructive promotion just to avoid the cold stare.

Don't fall victim to the Peter Principle boost that at last lands you in a "level of incompetence."

If you have to leave, *leave*.

But seek the same level—the one where you've been happy and effective—in the position to which you move. And watch your *timing.* . . .

Survival.

Insight.

Success.

Big words; important words; useful concepts. But all directed at a single objective, a single goal—the solution of those problems relating to security vs. insecurity; adequacy vs. inadequacy.

A man is not secure because he has a million dollars and power to hire and fire 10,000 people and a $200,000 home and a Rolls-Royce. These are externals; the man who possessed all of them may be the most insecure person on earth.

A man is not adequate because he can occupy an office with the word "President" on the door, because he can give orders to other men lower than he on the corporate pyramid, or because he is head of a household.

He is adequate if he can actually perform the functions demanded of him in the positions he occupies.

He is secure if he has a clear understanding of himself and an appreciation of his own intrinsic worth.

In that sense, it matters very little whether he is the

superior or the subordinate, jobseeker or executive recruiter, evaluator or evaluee.

A man is a man.

And reality is reality. . . .

Those are the principles.

One man's principles, certainly; the groundrules by which I, personally, score the game. But they are general. They take the overall view. And a road sign saying "New York: 2,700 mi." isn't really all that much help to a man motoring through the California desert.

What's needed besides this overall statement, I think, is a suggestion of shorter-range objectives; aphorisms, if you will; bromides, even, if you're feeling uncharitable—at any rate, a set of more specific road signs along the trail ahead.

Again, the routes to be traveled are individual.

Not universally applicable.

But as a starting point—why not try these on for size if you're:

The Boss

—*Know thyself.* (And if you don't understand what that means by now . . . oh, *brother!*)

—Know others, know your specialty, know your area, know your job, know companies. *Know!*

—Be realistic.

—Be fair.

—Be loyal

—Love your family (and love them *first!*)

—Pay any man what he's worth . . . no more, no less.

—Ask a recruiter to fulfill the specific job requirements you *need* . . . not just what you want.

—Establish priorities (do first things first).

—Go through the line of authority—or change the line.

—Seek and accept professional help when you need it.

—Dump: bad programs, products and people . . . and don't look back.

—Don't cover for any of these three.

—Don't say "I told you so."

—Don't confuse friendship with business.

—Don't confuse enmity with business.

—Staff an executive with an eye to compensating his weaknesses.

—Engineer a job to fit any really remarkable candidate or employee.

—Subtle techniques are sometimes superior to obvious ones.

—Decide. And back your decision.

—Remember you set the pace.

—Remember you are the innovator . . . and the approver of innovation.

—Don't expect people to change—but don't forget techniques can change, and do.

—It pays to bend . . . a little.

—Don't kick the ineffective upstairs or support them just because they're charming.

—Check even those you trust most.

—Be as nice as you can . . . within the limits of the job.

—Stay honest.

—Assign people to jobs that fit them.

—Learn how to say no . . . and *say it* when you must.

—State your intentions; make sure your people understand.

—Dump bad deals . . . even late in the game.

—Standardize procedures.

—Make sure what you ask of your people—and what you've promised your board—are equally realistic.

—Don't second-guess.

—If someone's performance is poor, find out *why* before you scream.

—If your personnel turnover is high, ask ex-employees why.

—Hire with care; fire with restraint.

—Keep an eye on your own Achilles heel.

—Keep your cool.

The Job-Applicant

—*Know Thyself* (and get professional help if you're not sure you do.)

—Know jobs, know your specialty, know companies, know others, know the area.

—Be loyal.

—Make it easy for the résumé reviewer: type it, include your name, address, phone number (and alternative phone).

—Cover all time-periods.

—Don't make the résumé too technical.

—Keep it to two pages or less.

—Tell why you left each of the previous jobs.

—Give him your salary history.

—Keep it honest.

—Remember to leave something for the interviewer; remember getting the job interview is the name of the game.

—Don't take just any job, even if the bank account is getting thin.

—See if you can get a look at or an interview with the Boss; remember, it's his personality that sets the tenor of conditions at work.

—Consider only jobs for which you feel qualified.

—Don't take jobs at companies with high employee turnover.

—State your objectives . . . for growth, for personal satisfaction, for performance.

—List your birthdate on the résumé, not your age.

—Write a specific, individually-typed cover letter for each
company and each position you apply for.

—If you can't actually have the résumé set in type, at least
don't send one that is handwritten, a carbon copy, a stencil
duplication or a spirit reproduction.

—Examine the whole package offered, not just the salary.

—Remember job campaigns often take time.

—Ask for an interview . . . and *never* be late for it.

—Also, don't be too early.

—Try to look natural, but neat.

—Don't be afraid to ask questions in an interview.

—*Always* tell the company where you apply if the application is confidential.

—Do your homework; learn as much about the company as
you can so your questions will be meaningful to you.

If You're the Recruiter/Evaluator:

—*Know Thyself* (And be wary of personal, as opposed to
objective, reactions to the applicants.)

—Check everything.

—Avoid combining men of similar weaknesses.

—Remember the candidate is a critical part of any employment contract, and act accordingly.

—Remember many people tend to inflate their titles,
salaries, previous responsibilities and accomplishments.

—Don't just hand the company a live body.

—Don't confuse likability or dislikability with ability.

—Pay people what they are worth.

—Make sure job specifications and criteria are realistic.

—Remember having a degree doesn't necessarily imply competence.

—Remember interest must be backed by abilities.

—Remember latent ability may substitute for experience in some cases.

—Experience may be a substitute for a degree.

—Give people evaluation-playback only on what they are willing and capable of hearing.

—Suggest possible alternative plans to people who have poor plans.

—If you're an outside evaluator, take the cases on a flat fee so both of you can forget the cost from there on.

—Get as uninhibited, unstructured a statement as you can.

—See if a man leans too heavily on "crutches," and whether the extent of his dependence is perilous to his performance.

—Recommend other sources of personal assistance when needed.

—Keep an eye peeled for Circle Machines.

—Test according to the situation rather than arbitrarily.

—Look for trade-offs in job specifications.

—Look only for differences that make a difference.

—Avoid excessive leniency.

—Avoid excess stringency.

—Avoid excess.

—Avoid halo-effect.

—And remember: *You* do not have to live with the poeple you recommend!

The Employee
—KNOW THYSELF.

—Avoid excess leniency/stringency with superiors and subordinates.

—Establish priorities; do first things first.

—Don't accept promotion if you don't want *that* job.

—Be loyal.

—Go through lines of authority . . . or be prepared to quit.

—Document.

—Don't confuse friendship—or enmity—with business.

—Personal satisfactions may substitute for a few of the conventional rewards—money, relative titles, etc.

—Flattery may get you some small advantages at times. (But don't imagine it's a panacea.)

—Bending a little can pay off handsomely.

—Consider your suitability for the job, the company, the group, the specialty, the type of position, the area. And consider the same things for any promotion or new job you're offered.

—Don't be afraid to say no when you have to.

—Take only jobs that fit you.

—Get and accept competent advice if you're not sure what *does* fit you.

—When you're right, don't accept a no—not even a nice no.

—Speak up; talk back.

—If you like it here, sweat it out.

—Toughminded managers are easiest to work for.

—But if you work for a demanding boss, you must be careful to establish *specific* criteria with him. Beware of generalizations.

—Always try to work things out first with a guy who gives you trouble before you take the matter up elsewhere.

—Set life goals, set career goals . . . and strive for them.

—Be positive.

Well . . . that'll do for a start, anyway.

You'll want to add a few of your own—and maybe strike a few of mine—as you go along.

Above all remember that no industrial marriage lasts forever; none need be for life. It is valid only so long as both your needs are being met. And when it is no longer valid, well, that's life—and a part of it is change. Just make sure the change is in the direction you're headed.

The groundrules under which you can operate to maximum capactiy are your first order of business. They are the requirements you, personally, set for obtaining the most out of a career . . . and a life. They are individual. They are yours.

The Executive Jungle is vast and it is dangerous.

But so is life itself.

The way is plain before you:

Know yourself . . . act meaningfully and live.